SOCIETY FOR NEW TES

MONOGRAPH SERIES

General Editor: G. N. Stanton

57

COMMUNITY AND GOSPEL
IN LUKE–ACTS

Community and gospel in Luke – Acts

The social and political motivations of Lucan theology

PHILIP FRANCIS ESLER

Barrister of the New South Wales Supreme Court and
Part-time Lecturer in Religious Studies and Divinity,
University of Sydney

CAMBRIDGE
UNIVERSITY PRESS

Published by the Press Syndicate of the University of Cambridge
The Pitt Building, Trumpington Street, Cambridge CB2 1RP
40 West 20th Street, New York, NY 10011–4211, USA
10 Stamford Road, Oakleigh, Melbourne 3166, Australia

© Cambridge University Press 1987

First published 1987
Reprinted 1989
First paperback edition 1989
Reprinted 1994, 1996

British Library cataloguing in publication data

Esler, Philip Francis
Community and Gospel in Luke–Acts: the
social and political motivations of Lucan
theology. – (Monograph series/Society for
New Testament studies)
1. Bible. N.T. Acts – Criticism, interpretation,
etc.   2. Bible. N.T. Luke – Criticism,
interpretation, etc.   3. Christian communities
in the Bible
I. Title   II. Series
260   BS2545.C4/

Library of Congress cataloguing in publication data

Esler, Philip Francis.
Community and gospel in Luke–Acts.
(Monograph series / Society for New Testament
Studies; 57)
Bibliography.
Includes index.
1. Bible. N.T. Luke – Criticism, interpretation, etc.
2. Bible. N.T. Acts – Criticism, interpretation, etc.
3. Sociology, Biblical.   I. Title.   II. Series: Monograph
series (Society for New Testament Studies); 57.
BS2589.E85   1987   226'.4067   86-28415

ISBN 0 521 32965 5 hardback
ISBN 0 521 38873 2 paperback

Transferred to digital printing 2001

WS

TO MY MOTHER AND FATHER

CONTENTS

vii

ACKNOWLEDGEMENTS

This book is an edited version of my Oxford doctoral thesis of the same title. The thesis was the result of three years' stay in Oxford, beginning in October 1981. Throughout this period the Reverend Robert Morgan, of Linacre College, Oxford, supervised my research. To him I owe an immense debt of gratitude, both for initially suggesting the possibilities of a social-scientific approach to New Testament criticism and then for guiding my research into this particular topic with an exemplary degree of dedication and interest. He suggested numerous fruitful lines of enquiry and saved me from many errors.

In preparing my thesis for publication I have greatly profited from improvements suggested by my examiners, Professor M. Hooker and Dr C. Rowland, and later by Professor G. N. Stanton and Canon J. L. Houlden. The flaws which remain, of course, are entirely my own responsibility.

I have incurred many other debts. My stay in Oxford was financed by a scholarship from the Commonwealth Scholarship Commission. The detailed administration of my scholarship was ably looked after by the British Council. In 1983 the Trustees of the Hall–Houghton Trust awarded me a studentship which enabled me to travel extensively through Turkey and the Middle East in furtherance of my research.

During the early stages of this project, I greatly profited from discussions with my friend Bernard Carey, a political scientist from Sydney, who was then in Oxford. My general approach to the relationship between Church and State owes much to my conversations with Bernard, and to our collaboration on various projects, during the last decade.

I am also most grateful to Margaret Yee, of St John's College, Oxford, for the encouragement she gave me throughout my time in Oxford.

Lastly, my wife Patricia has been exposed to this work at close range, first as a thesis and then as a book, since our marriage in April 1983. Although continually called upon to consider this or that idea, to assess the style of various passages and even to put up with discomfort and not a little excitement in the Middle East, her support and good humour have never faltered.

Sydney,
5 July 1985

ABBREVIATIONS

ANCL	*Ante-Nicene Christian Literature: Translations of the Writings of the Fathers down to A.D. 325*, edited by A. Roberts and J. Donaldson (Edinburgh: T.O.T. Clark, 1867–97)
AJ	*Antiquitates Judaicae* of Josephus
Beginnings	Jackson, F.J.F., Lake, K. and Cadbury, H.J., eds., *The Beginnings of Christianity*, Part I: *The Acts of the Apostles*, 5 volumes (London: Macmillan & Co., 1920–33).
BJ	*Bellum Judaicum* of Josephus
Bultmann, *HST*	Bultmann, R., *The History of the Synoptic Tradition*, ET by John Marsh (Oxford: Basil Blackwell, 1972)
Cadbury, *Making*	Cadbury, H.J., *The Making of Luke–Acts* (London: Macmillan & Co., 1927)
CBQ	*Catholic Biblical Quarterly*
Conzelmann, *Luke*	Conzelmann, H., *The Theology of St Luke*, ET by G. Buswell (London: SCM Press, 1982)
Charles	Charles, R.H., ed., *The Apocrypha and Pseudepigrapha of the Old Testament in English*, 2 volumes (Oxford: Clarendon Press, 1913)
Dibelius, *Studies*	Dibelius, M., *Studies in the Acts of the Apostles*, edited by H. Greeven (London: SCM Press, 1956)
EJ	*Encyclopedia Judaica* (Jerusalem: Keter Publishing House Jerusalem, 1978)
ET	English translation
ExpT	*Expository Times*
Fitzmyer, *Commentary*	Fitzmyer, J., *The Gospel According to Luke (I–IX)*, The Anchor Bible (Garden City, NY: Doubleday & Co., 1981)
Gasque, *History*	Gasque, W.W., *A History of the Criticism of the Acts of the Apostles* (Grand Rapids, Mich.: William B. Eerdmans Publishing Co., 1975)
Haenchen, *Commentary*	Haenchen, E., *The Acts of the Apostles: A Commentary*, ET by R. McL. Wilson (Oxford: Basil Blackwell, 1982)
HTR	*Harvard Theological Review*

Hatch and Redpath, *Concordance*	Hatch, E., and Redpath, H. A., *A Concordance to the Septuagint and the Other Greek Versions of the Old Testament*, 2 volumes (Graz: Akademische–N. Verlagsanstalt, 1954)
JAAR	*Journal of the American Academy of Religion*
JB	*Jerusalem Bible*
JBL	*Journal of Biblical Literature*
JRS	*Journal of Roman Studies*
JSJ	*Journal for the Study of Judaism*
JSNT	*Journal of the Study of the New Testament*
JTS	*Journal of Theological Studies*
Kümmel, *Introduction*	Kümmel, W. G., *Introduction to the New Testament*, revised edition (London: SCM Press, 1975)
Loeb of Josephus	The Loeb edition of Josephus in nine volumes, with Volumes I–IV edited by H. St. J. Thackeray (1926–30), Volume V by H. St. J. Thackeray and R. Marcus (1934), Volumes VI–VII by R. Marcus (1937–43), Volume VIII by R. Marcus and A. Wikgren (1963) and Volume IX by L. H. Feldman (1965)
LXX	The Septuagint
Maddox, *Purpose*	Maddox, R., *The Purpose of Luke–Acts* (Edinburgh: T. & T. Clark, 1982)
NEB	*New English Bible*
NovT	*Novum Testamentum*
NTA	*New Testament Abstracts*
NTS	*New Testament Studies*
NZSTh	*Neue Zeitschrift für systematische Theologie und Religionsphilosophie*
OCD	*The Oxford Classical Dictionary*, 2nd edition, edited by N. G. L. Hammond and H. H. Scullard (Oxford: Clarendon Press, 1970)
RSV	*Revised Standard Version*
Safrai and Stern, *The Jewish People*	Safrai, S. and Stern, M., *The Jewish People in the First Century: Historical Geography, Political History, Social, Cultural and Religious Life and Institutions*, 2 volumes (Assen: Van Gorcum, 1974–6)
Stern	Stern, M., *Greek and Latin Authors on Jews and Judaism*, 2 volumes (Jerusalem: The Israel Academy of Sciences and Humanities, 1974–80)
Studies in Luke–Acts	Keck, L. E. and Martyn, L. J., ed., *Studies in Luke–Acts: Essays Presented in Honor of Paul Schubert* (London: SPCK, 1968)
Talbert, *Perspectives*	Talbert, C. H., ed., *Perspectives on Luke–Acts* (Danville, Va: Association of Baptist Professors of Religion, and Edinburgh: T. & T. Clark, 1978)
TAPA	*Transactions of the American Philological Association*

TDNT	Kittel, G., Friedrick, G. and Bromiley, G.W., eds., *Theological Dictionary of the New Testament*, ET by G.W. Bromiley (Grand Rapids, Mich.: W.B. Eerdmans, Publishing Company, 1964–76)
ThZ	*Theologische Zeitschrift*
TS	*Theological Studies*
VT	*Vetus Testamentum*
ZNW	*Zeitschrift für die neutestamentliche Wissenschaft*

1

THE SOCIO-REDACTION CRITICISM
OF LUKE-ACTS

1. Social and political influences on Lucan theology

At one point in *The Theology of St Luke,* during a discussion of the relationship between the church and the world, Hans Conzelmann asserts that Luke 'lays as the foundation of his defence of the Church a comprehensive consideration of its general position in the world; he fixes its position in respect of redemptive history and deduces from this the rules for its attitude to the world'.[1] To hold this opinion Conzelmann must assume both that Luke's theological position (his attitude to redemptive history) and his views on how the church must adapt to its social and political context are quite distinct and that the first has generated the second. Upon just a little reflection, both of these assumptions begin to appear highly arbitrary and unlikely. Consider what model they imply for the manner of Luke's composition of his Gospel and Acts. Is it not that of a glorified armchair theorist, who ponders over purely religious questions before issuing forth from his scriptorium to enlighten his fellow-Christians as to the correct attitude which they and their community should adopt to their social and political environment? Not that Conzelmann is alone in subscribing to this model of theological activity. It has an ancestry at least as old as the pre-exilic traditions of Moses' Torah-laden descent from Mount Sinai, and flourishes still in much European theology, as Latin American theologians tirelessly observe.

But now set Conzelmann's two assumptions on their head. What if Luke did not sharply differentiate the theological realm from the social and political, but saw them, in fact, as closely inter-related? What if social and political exigencies played a vital role in the formation of Luke's theology, rather than merely constituting the areas in which it was applied? With these assumptions we are forced to envisage quite a different role for the theological activity of the evangelist. He appears now as a figure embedded in the life of his community at all its levels, religious, social, political and economic. He emerges as someone stirred to take up his pen not from an interest in theologizing for its own sake, but because he fervently believes that the Gospel, properly interpreted and presented, is a message of salvation for his fellow-Christians across the whole range of their troubled existence.[2]

The dominant theme in this work is that these alternative assumptions and this alternative model are correct. Accordingly, the general thesis argued in what follows is that social and political factors have been highly significant in motivating Lucan theology; in other words, that Luke has shaped the gospel traditions at his disposal in response to social and political pressures experienced by his community. It is not claimed here that such factors constitute a total explanation of why Luke–Acts was written. Proper account must always be taken of specifically religious aspects of the evangelist's motivation. Nevertheless, it has become increasingly clear to the present writer in the course of this work that it is entirely unrealistic to expect to be able to appreciate the purely religious dimension of Luke–Acts apart from an understanding of the social and political realities of the community for which it was composed. It is submitted that the results obtained from the argument below are a rich confirmation of Peter Berger's view that the relation between religion and society is always dialectical.[3]

To demonstrate that the social and political circumstances of Luke's community have shaped his theological understanding obviously has wide ramifications in other areas of theology. By restoring the connection between a particular New Testament theology and the historical experience of the community for which it was formulated, it is to be expected that a range of possibilities and paradigms will emerge which could assist in the creation of contemporary theology similarly attuned to the struggles of other groups at this moment in human history.[4]

2. Towards a socio-redaction criticism of Luke–Acts

Somewhat surprisingly, amidst the battery of critical approaches to the New Testament there is none which is really suited to explicating the relationships between Luke's theology and his community. The necessary methodology must be characterized both by its capacity for isolating the evangelist's unique theological intentions and by its having some apparatus for probing deeply into his social and political setting. The first requirement can only be satisfied by some form of redaction criticism; in reaction to form criticism, this focuses upon the role of the evangelists as authors in their own right, who have each expressed a particular theological viewpoint, rather than treating them as collectors of traditional material. The continuing viability of redaction criticism has recently been confirmed by the work of scholars such as E. Güttgemanns[5] and, more notably, W.H. Kelber.[6] They have demonstrated that the transition from oral traditions to written texts, from orality to textuality, involves not a steady progression (as Bultmann and others imagined) but a sharp break in the entire mode of perceiving and presenting the Gospel.

Yet redaction criticism, as it has developed over the last thirty years, has not acquired the conceptual equipment needed to satisfy the second requirement – the analysis of social context. Some explanation is necessary for this curious phenomenon. The form critics, after all, were interested in the social setting of the individual units of tradition which they investigated. Thus Bultmann wrote:

> The proper understanding of form-criticism rests upon the judgement that the literature in which the life of a given community, even the primitive Christian community, has taken shape, springs out of quite definite conditions and wants of life from which grows up a quite definite style and quite specific forms and categories. Thus every literary category has its 'life situation' (*Sitz im Leben*: Gunkel), whether it be worship in its different forms, or work, or hunting, or war. The *Sitz im Leben* is not, however, an individual historical event, but a typical situation or occupation in the life of a community.[7]

Unfortunately, the form critics never arrived at any firm understanding of the life situations so integral to their approach. Perhaps this was not so surprising in the case of Martin Dibelius,[8] who moved synthetically from assumed life situations (especially the sermon) to the New Testament data, but it is certainly so in the case of Rudolf Bultmann, whose procedure was analytical, proceeding from a detailed analysis of the text to postulation of the situations in which the forms had arisen.[9] Perhaps the result would have been different if anyone at the time had heeded Oscar Cullmann's acute observation that form criticism could only be set upon a firm foundation by the development of a special branch of sociology capable of studying the norms governing the growth of popular traditions.[10]

When redaction criticism was initiated after the Second World War, the concern of its proponents with the significance of the unique and individual contribution of each evangelist did not entirely deflect their attention from the question of social context.[11] Consider what W. Marxsen, the author of the pioneering redactional study of Mark, had to say on this matter:

> Thus we inquire into the situation of the community in which the Gospels arose. The community ought not to be unqualifiedly viewed as located in a specific place, though we shall keep in mind the possibility of defining it exactly. Our concern is much more with what is typical in this community, its views, its time, perhaps even its composition. Hence a sociological element is present throughout. But over against form history this element is joined to an 'individualistic' trait oriented to the particular interest and point of view of the evangelist concerned.[12]

Like the form critics, however, the redaction critics also failed to utilize or generate a method for investigating social context. Marxsen's perceptive recognition of a 'sociological element' in his task must be set against the strange fact that nowhere in his work on Mark does he avail himself of a sociological method; his approach is entirely literary-historical. Historical method, as is becoming more widely appreciated, is directed to the particular, the unique and the unusual.[13] It is rather unsuitable for recovering the usual, typical and recurrent features of a past community, upon a comprehension of which, however, hangs the possibility of appreciating its social setting. If one asks what kind of approach does hold the promise of furthering research into these features, the answer can only be one which draws upon ideas and techniques from the social sciences. It is an exercise in futility to attempt social analysis and yet ignore those very disciplines which take this matter as their subject and which have a long history of grappling with it. These disciplines, especially sociology, make it their business to examine just those typical and recurrent aspects of social behaviour and institutions which we must investigate in the context of Luke's community.

This advocacy of the use of the social sciences is not breaking fresh turf in New Testament exegesis. Since the early 1970s exegetes have been turning increasingly to the social sciences in the hope of finding new ways to understand and interpret the New Testament.[14] The most original and impressive work in the field has come from Gerd

Theissen, now Professor of New Testament at Heidelberg University. His first contribution was an article published in 1973 on itinerant radicalism and the tradition of the sayings of Jesus, as seen from the perspective of the sociology of literature.[15] After this he produced a string of articles and books dealing with early Palestinian Christianity,[16] the social structure of the Hellenistic communities and the tensions to which they were subject,[17] and the theory of the application of sociology to the New Testament.[18] Most of these studies have now been translated into English.[19] The other major works in this area are the superb article by W.A. Meeks on the relationship between Son of Man theology and sectarian pressures in the Johannine community (1972)[20] and his recent book *The First Urban Christians* (1983),[21] the article by R. Scroggs on the sectarian nature of earliest Christianity (1975),[22] the book by J.G. Gager which applies such sociological concepts as millennarianism, cognitive dissonance and conflict to the New Testament (1975),[23] the book by B. Holmberg on Paul and power[24] and that of J. Elliott on I Peter.[25] B. Malina has made a particularly interesting contribution from the viewpoint of cultural anthropology.[26]

Parallel with the growth of interest in this sociological approach to New Testament exegesis has come an ever-growing concern with the social background of early Christianity.[27] Many of the scholars engaged in the latter pursuit eschew the use of ideas and techniques from the social sciences and content themselves with the traditional methods of historical analysis. For reasons explained below, however, more useful results will be obtained if these researchers do engage in some degree of sociological analysis, at least to the extent of examining their own preconceptions.

The methodology adopted in this book distinguishes it from the existing literature in the field to the extent that it takes up the broad approach of redaction criticism and fuses to it a conscious application of ideas and techniques drawn from the social sciences. This approach also differentiates our methodology from that utilized in the few other attempts which have been made to explain the theology of a New Testament work in terms of the social and political pressures upon the author's community – such as the article by W.A. Meeks on John's Gospel, the last chapter of his *First Urban Christians*, and the study of 1 Peter by J. Elliott. These works are devoted to exposing the relationships between theology and its social context and functions but are unable to adopt redaction criticism, as one can in the investigation of Luke's theology. Accordingly, throughout what follows the prevailing methodology is called 'socio-redaction criticism'. This is a more exact designation than 'sociological exegesis', which is used by J. Elliott of his style of analysis of 1 Peter, because of the importance of the redactional element in our investigations.

In the remainder of this chapter, we shall outline the methodology of the social sciences in order to indicate how they may be applied to New Testament exegesis, respond to objections which have been made to such an enterprise and, finally, describe the sociological model which will be employed throughout this book.

3. The methodology of the social sciences

To see what the social sciences, especially sociology, can offer to New Testament study, it is essential to understand how they operate, to observe the methods used and the kinds of results obtained by scholars working in these disciplines. The question of the extent to which sociology and anthropology, for example, are sciences as much as the physical sciences such as physics and chemistry must be left unexplored. This raises very difficult issues, such as the role of human free will and human unpredictability in the social context.[28] There is a long history of attempts by sociologists to argue that their discipline is a science, but many sociologists strongly resist this classification.[29] Nevertheless, much sociological research does attempt to use scientific method, or a fairly close approximation to it, and without some appreciation of that method, therefore, it is no easy matter to penetrate the language employed by social scientists to describe their various forms of research, or to evaluate the status of the results they produce.

The ultimate aim of science is the formulation of laws which describe constant relations between phenomena.[30] But this is not its only aim, and, in practice, the discovery of laws is possible only in the most advanced sectors of scientific research. The difficulties which are involved in demonstrating that sociology and anthropology are as genuinely scientific as, for example, physics and chemistry, are nowhere more apparent than in the fact that there are no social laws yet known which apply trans-historically to all societies.[31] Nevertheless, other more modest aspects of scientific method are within the reach of sociology and anthropology. The three levels of research evident in the physical sciences – description, classification and explanation[32] – are all present in the social sciences, with the exception of the highest form of explanation, laws.

The vital role of description (the first level of research) results from the fact that only after the scrutiny and comparison of a wide range of material is it possible to develop appropriate explanations of it. Much sociological research still locates itself largely on the descriptive level (although scarcely to the total exclusion of classification and explanation), as sociologists attempt to come to terms with the astonishing variety of social phenomena. Classification, the second level of research, is an intermediate stage between description and explanation and involves the grouping together of similar phenomena. This reduces the almost infinite variety of particular facts to a number of categories. Until categories have been determined one cannot define relations between them.

An example of the often decisive impetus a convincing classification can give to scientific progress is the effect on biology of the classificatory system elaborated by Linnaeus in the eighteenth century. It is readily apparent, however, that the social sciences do not lend themselves to systems of classification as rigid and as clearly delineated as those, for example, current among biologists. The classifications in the biological sciences are often justly called 'natural' classifications; at present, no such claim can be made for any classificatory system used by sociologists. For the present and the immediate future we must proceed on the basis that any classificatory system generated by sociologists is not 'natural', that is, it does not correspond with the inherent ordering of reality but is an abstraction, an intellectual construct devised to assist researchers in grappling with the vast diversity of social phenomena. Max Weber referred to each category in such a system as an 'ideal type':

> An ideal type is formed by the one-sided *accentuation* of one or more points of view and by the synthesis of a great many diffuse, discrete, more or less present and occasionally absent *concrete individual* phenomena, which are arranged according to those one-sidedly emphasized viewpoints into a unified *analytical* construct (*Gedankenbild*). In its conceptual purity, this mental construct (*Gedankenbild*) cannot be found empirically anywhere in reality. It is a *utopia*. Historical research faces the task of determining in each individual case, the extent to which this ideal construct approximates to or diverges from reality ...[33]

Howard Becker and John McKinney, two American sociologists, have devoted considerable attention to the theory and application of such types. They prefer to call them 'constructed' rather than 'ideal' types, to emphasize their artificial nature and to steer clear of any suggestion that they are ideal in the Platonic sense. McKinney defines the constructed type as 'a purposive, planned selection, abstraction, combination, and (sometimes) accentuation of a set of criteria with empirical referents that serves as a basis for comparison of empirical cases'.[34] In the present book, the word 'type' is used for the ideal type of Weber and the constructed type of Becker and McKinney, these being essentially identical. Put simply, a 'type' is a tool 'intended to institute precise comparisons'.[35] Furthermore, where 'type' is the term used to describe one unit in a classificatory system, 'typology' denotes the complete system, the assemblage of such types. One well-known example is Max Weber's typology of authority, in which he differentiated three relevant types: rational, traditional and charismatic authority.

To construct a typology which will have relevance in a wide range of empirical situations – that is, one which is relatively free from time and space markings – it is necessary to base it upon as many empirical cases as possible.[36]

Finally, it must always be remembered that a typology is an instrument, a tool of research. McKinney observes that the most widespread misuse of the typological method involves the unjustifiable reification of types.[37] Once a set of characteristics has been abstracted out and formulated into a type, the temptation is to forget that it is merely a tool for ordering concrete phenomena and to begin treating it as a social law.

The third level of scientific research is that of explanation, which consists of demonstrating the dependence of two phenomena. Explanation is inextricably linked with prediction, since if A and B are dependent, then one can predict that A will be present if B is present.[38] This level of research is only possible when enough phenomena have been described and the basic classifications in the field have been sufficiently defined. The process of explanation normally begins with a theory, which is an integrated set of relationships that has already received some degree of empirical confirmation. David Willer correctly insists upon the desirability of restricting the term 'theory' to an at least partially validated set of relationships.[39] Prior to such validation it is not a theory but a set of hypotheses. We may define hypotheses as relations deduced to exist among unobserved facts.[40] Once we have a theory and an hypothesis based upon it, the next stage is to test the hypothesis empirically. This is the verification stage of explanation.[41] The hypothesis will either be confirmed, which will strengthen the claim of the theory to be a law, or it will be only partially confirmed or simply disconfirmed, in which case it may be necessary to modify or even discard the theory.[42]

Before we outline the dominant forms of verification in the social sciences, some attention must be given to the meaning of models (especially *vis-à-vis* typologies, with which they are often erroneously identified) and their role in the process of explanation in the social sciences. A model is a conceptualization of a group of phenomena, a simplified and schematized picture of reality, which is capable of generating a set of hypotheses which, once verified, may either found or substantiate a theory. One example of a model is Herbert Spencer's presentation of society as an organism evolving steadily and irreversibly.[43] Models are distinguished from systems of classification such as typologies by their having what may be regarded as an inner dynamic: since they are fashioned from a set of terms in a state of inter-relatedness, the variation of one of those terms will produce a predictable response in the entire set. This dynamic built into models enables them to be used to generate a wide range of hypotheses. David Willer uses the term 'mechanism' for this dynamic.[44] Typologies, on the other hand, lack a 'mechanism', they merely classify phenomena into certain accentuated categories and do not specify what may be expected of mixed cases falling in between the types.[45] Models are explanatory and predictive, typologies, *pace* McKinney,[46] are not. The use of types can lead to the development of hypotheses about particular situations, but only *after* the typology has been applied to the situation, careful comparisons have been made and the search has commenced for an explanation of the divergences noted between fact and typology. Models, on the other hand, arm researchers in advance with hypotheses to test upon the relevant empirical data.[47] The account of the legitimation of a new social order presented by Peter Berger and Thomas Luckmann in their work *The Social Construction of Reality*,[48] which is the central sociological concept used below, is best understood as a model. The implications of this for the conduct of this study are dealt with later.

The comparative method

We now conclude this treatment of the methodology of the social sciences with a brief discussion of the uses of the comparative method: first, to assist in the verification of hypotheses (the third level of scientific method) and, secondly, as a means of generating insights and fostering the sociological imagination.[49] As to the first issue – how can social scientists verify their hypotheses? In the natural sciences experiment is the main method of verifying hypotheses; but only occasionally is experiment possible in the social sciences, for it is very difficult to isolate phenomena in order to establish reciprocal relations between them as demanded by the experimental method. In any event, experiment is only possible with contemporary social structures and institutions and can be of no help in the use of sociological approaches to historical materials. In the absence of experimental verification social scientists fall back on the comparative method.[50] The process of comparison assumes similarities and differences; one does not compare things which are totally like or totally unlike. But to verify hypotheses it is necessary to make what Duverger calls 'close comparisons'.[51] The aim here is to compare two items which have as many features as possible in common and then to explain the differences. This method is analogous to an experiment where all conditions are kept constant, except for the variable whose behaviour is to be observed. For such a comparison of social data to be effective it is obviously necessary that the comparison be between two or more structures or institutions from contexts which are both similar culturally and not too distant chronologically. Otherwise the comparison will be too artificial to contribute to the verification of hypotheses.

The second use of the comparative method is quite different. It involves what Duverger calls 'distant comparisons', by which social structures or institutions from widely different cultures are compared. These commonly consist of comparisons across distinct historical periods. Here one is looking for resemblances rather than the differences investigated by the use of close comparisons. Since the things compared are so far removed from one another, it is natural that they are different. The main focus of interest is the extent to which they are similar and the significance of those resemblances. With this form of comparison the researcher is not seeking to verify hypotheses but to generate them, because the insights which are produced by the comparisons will prompt a whole range of questions to put to the historical data under consideration. In other words, this is a way of fostering the sociological imagination. Duverger appropriately describes distant comparisons as one means of 'provoking the shock which produces discovery'; they are more 'an attitude of mind consisting of keeping eyes open for relationships, analogies and resemblances' when faced with phenomena than a rigorous method.[52]

One approach available under either method of comparison is the application of an existing typology to a case under consideration. It is not necessary that the comparison be made between different sets of data, as was the case, for example, with de Tocqueville's early comparisons of the social and political institutions and structures of France, Britain and the United States.[53] As we have seen, a good typology is based upon as wide as possible a range of empirical data, and its resulting high level of generality will improve its usefulness when used in a comparative exercise upon a particular set of data. With close comparisons, of course, it will be necessary that the types have been developed from data culturally similar to the case under study or at least be stripped of temporal and spatial markings. This is not necessary with distant comparisons, since as long as there is some point of analogy to enable the comparison to be made in the first place, it does not matter if there are wide divergences between typology and data.

One other form which distant comparisons may take, apart from those involving two sets of data or a typology and one set of data, must be mentioned here to lay the foundations for the argument of this book. This is the comparison of the conceptualized phenomena in a model with actual cases. One must tread carefully here. As already explained, the function of a model is to generate hypotheses which, if verified, may be used to substantiate a social theory. And there is nothing in principle to prevent a particular historical case being used to test the hypotheses deriving from a model, as long as all necessary precautions have been taken to ensure that there is no cultural inconsistency between model and data which would have the effect of precluding the meaningful testing of hypotheses from the model in that particular case. In spite of this, however, the propositions of a model can plainly be utilized in a quite different way – not to generate hypotheses, but to supply material for a distant comparison with a particular historical situation. This process is very similar to the distant comparisons between fact and typology, only here the material brought to the actual case is a set of dynamically related propositions, not a mere classification. The use of Berger and Luckmann's *The Social Construction of Reality* in what follows will illustrate this process.

One fundamentally important caveat, implied throughout the preceding methodological discussion, must now be emphasized and applied to the entire task of using sociological ideas in New Testament exegesis. No social laws have been found which apply across different historical periods. When we bring to a New Testament text comparative material in the form of contemporary data, typology or model we have no justification whatever for assuming that what was the case outside New Testament society was the same within it. That is to say, comparative materials of whatever character can never be relied upon to plug holes in our knowledge of the social world of the New Testament. For it may be in just those places where we do lack information that the greatest divergences occur from our own experience. Comparison can suggest an entirely fresh way to approach this or that feature of the New Testament, may suggest an entirely new range of questions to put to it, but the comparative method cannot prove the viability of that approach or answer those questions. Such results can only flow from a painstaking examination of the text itself, and in that task the traditional types of criticism retain a great deal of their relevance.

4. Objections to the application of the social sciences to the New Testament

Resistance to the use of the social sciences in New Testament exegesis takes two broad forms. The first is an objection to the very idea of the enterprise: namely, that the social sciences are reductionist, that they purport to provide a total explanation of the biblical data and leave no scope for purely religious factors or the activity of individuals to figure in the explanatory task. The second is an objection at the practical level; its proponents do not rule out the use of the social sciences as a matter of principle, but they maintain that they are no use in exegesis because, for example, they are too dependent upon contemporary cultural patterns to assist in understanding first-century texts. These two objections must now be considered in turn.

There is little to be said for the reductionist criticism. Certainly some of the founders of sociology, such as Emile Durkheim,[54] believed that social factors could totally explain religion. And K. Kautsky did write a reductionist account of Christianity from a Marxist viewpoint.[55] Today, however, sociologists are far more humble about the possibilities of their discipline. They realize that, although the investigation of a given phenomenon using sociological concepts and techniques will result in an explanation of that phenomenon, such an explanation will be inevitably partial, in that the phenomenon will almost certainly be susceptible to other forms of explanation, such as economic or political or even purely religious ones. Bruce Malina has described this process as follows:

... to explain sets of data – and not models – from the perspectives of biology, sociology, political science, economics,
and the like is not reductionistic. Rather, such varied explanations pushed to their limit simply reveal how much can be
known and explained by using a given model. The data set,
the range of information, remains intact.[56]

Moreover, by pointing out the recurrent and typical features of a social
phenomenon, sociology establishes the necessary context within which,
and only within which, its unique features can be appreciated.[57]
Throughout the course of this book, for example, the sociological
approach adopted will continually serve to throw the creative activity
of the Third Evangelist into sharp relief.

Perhaps the most noteworthy example of the second line of
objection to the use of the social sciences in the study of early
Christianity – that it is impractical – is to be found in an article by
E. A. Judge,[58] an ancient historian who appears to have pioneered
the prosopographical approach to the New Testament which has been
fruitfully employed by W. A. Meeks in *The First Urban Christians*.[59]
In one section of his article, Judge begins by referring to B. Holmberg's claim in *Paul and Power* that much New Testament scholarship
is affected by the 'idealistic fallacy', which consists of interpreting
historical phenomena as being directly formed by underlying theological structures and of ignoring the continuous dialectic between
ideas and social structures. He then goes on to question whether
Holmberg has balanced his dialectic between ideas and facts, theology
and social structure:

> His methodological stance does not bestride ideas and facts
> in an equally secure manner. In particular he does not have
> his foot on firm ground on the factual side. The extensive
> reading list conceals a dangerous gap. It couples with New
> Testament studies a strong admixture of modern sociology,
> as though social theories can be safely transposed across the
> centuries without verification. The basic question remains
> unasked: What are the social facts of life characteristic of
> the world to which the New Testament belongs? Until the
> painstaking field work is better done, the importation of
> social models that have been defined in terms of other cul-
> tures is methodologically no improvement on the 'idealistic
> fallacy'. We may fairly call it the 'sociological fallacy'.[60]

A little later in this section, in commenting on the approach of Gerd Theissen, Judge writes:

> I should have thought there was no hope of securing histori-
> cally valid conclusions from sociological exercises except by
> first thoroughly testing the models themselves for historical
> validity.[61]

From these statements it is possible to summarize the chief features of Judge's understanding of sociological models and their role in historical research:

1. Sociological models must be historically tested or 'verified' before they can be applied. Presumably, this means that they must closely fit the historical data to which they are to be applied, otherwise they will be discarded.
2. Sociological models are 'defined' with respect to particular cultures. This hinders their being applied to first-century society.
3. It is possible to carry out historical 'field work' prior to the use of models. In other words, Judge is espousing an empiri-cal hunt for 'the social facts of life characteristic' of the New Testament world, free from theoretical presuppositions.

None of these propositions, however, is consistent with the methodology of the social sciences, as just described. The first of them, the notion that typologies and models must first be subjected to historical verification or validation before they can be applied involves the error of viewing them not as mental constructs, as research tools, but as something akin to social laws. As long as the comparative material has some analogy to the situation it is quite unnecessary that it correspond exactly. Reading between the lines of Judge's article, one senses that his real worry with sociological exegesis is that its exponents will attempt to plug holes in first-century data by drawing upon relevant features of the comparative materials they apply to the New Testament text. As we have seen, this would be a serious misuse of the comparative method, one which must be avoided. The answer to the second feature of Judge's attitude is that soci-ologists are well aware of the desirability of producing models and typologies which, as far as possible, have been stripped of temporal and spatial markings. In developing his well-known typology of sects, Bryan Wilson has consciously aimed at achieving this result.[62] But, in any event, distant comparisons can be made even where the model does show signs of its cultural context.

The case for using the social sciences in biblical exegesis is most thoroughly established by demonstrating not merely that this is a useful additional approach to the text, but also that the traditional historical mode of analysis is defective precisely in as much as it fails to utilize concepts and perspective from sociology and anthropology. Consider the third aspect of Judge's attitude, his espousal of historical 'field work', of a hunt for 'characteristic' social facts *prior* to the use of models. Here Judge is advocating what amounts to a fairly pure form of empiricism, and this exposes his position to the same objection which can be made to such empiricism in any field: namely, that it is quite impossible for a researcher to collect facts without his or her already subscribing to a whole range of theoretical presuppositions. To define a field of enquiry and to make decisions as to which are the significant facts within that field, an historian must have already made a number of decisions at the theoretical level. In such a case, those decisions usually take the form of intuitive hunches. By not consciously and deliberately acknowledging and reflecting upon his or her preconceptions, the historian runs the risk of imposing modern notions of categorization and significance upon data from a period where they may be quite inappropriate. When Judge speaks of 'characteristic' social facts, for example, he is employing a term of comparison – to say a fact is characteristic, distinctive, of one society only makes sense in the context of other societies where it is not. Yet until Judge acknowledges, conceptualizes and justifies the implicit comparison he is making with other societies we can have no confidence in any claim that a particular fact is characteristic of the society in question. This is where a theoretical input from the social sciences, especially in the use of models and types, is needed. As T. F. Carney has accurately put it: 'Models bring values – in the subject matter and in its analyst – out into the open'.[63]

This failure to sort out the conceptual basis of their craft is quite common among historians and New Testament exegetes applying historical–critical methods. It is reflected not just in pretensions to purely empiricist methodologies but also in the non-reflective use of models and typologies. Historians and theologians who express antipathy to these heuristic devices unwittingly employ them whenever they speak, for example, of city-states, patronage, class and status, feudalism and capitalism, sect and denomination. A greater awareness of the logical status of such terms would improve the clarity of their application and would also serve to remind historians and historical theologians of the inevitability of a sociological perspective in their work. There is an elegant expression of a view similar to this in the first chapter of Peter Brown's *Religion and Society in the Age of Saint Augustine*.[64] Here Brown suggests that historians have much to learn from psychoanalysis, from 'the disciplined and erudite study of living societies by the social anthropologist' and from 'the sense of perspective and of unexpected combinations in much sociological literature'. For Brown, what the social sciences have to offer is assistance in understanding the present and then the past; they remove 'the patina of the obvious that encrusts human actions', they allow us to pierce the stereotypes and conventional formulae of human action in the present, so that we can obtain a far more clear-sighted view of the past.

5. Legitimation and Luke–Acts

The primary contention of this book is that much of what is unique in the theology of Luke–Acts should be attributed to Luke's desire to explain and justify, to 'legitimate', Christianity to his Christian contemporaries; in other words, that his main objective is one of 'legitimation' (a concept considered immediately below). I argue that Luke wrote in a context where the members of his community, who were mainly Jews and Gentiles (including some Romans) who had been associated with synagogues before becoming Christians, some of whom were rich and some poor, needed strong assurance that their decision to convert and to adopt a different life-style had been the correct one. To substantiate this approach extensive use will be made of sociological perspectives, and it is now necessary to introduce the most significant of these – 'legitimation' – to pave the way for the argument which follows.

My approach to legitimation is derived, with some modifications, from *The Social Construction of Reality*, by P.L. Berger and T. Luckmann, which was published in 1966.[65] Subtitled *A Treatise in the Sociology of Knowledge*, this work has acquired something of a classic status among sociologists and other scholars working in the social sciences, although it has not escaped criticism.[66] Its authors describe the book as an 'enquiry' (p. 30) into the manner in which social reality is constructed, but it may perhaps most usefully be regarded as a model of the genesis and maintenance of society and social institutions.

According to Berger and Luckmann, legitimation is a process which is carried out after a social institution has originated in the first place. In essence, legitimation is the collection of ways in which an institution is explained and justified to its members. Berger and Luckmann focus almost exclusively upon the form of legitimation which is necessary in the second and subsequent generations of the existence of such an institution.

But legitimation should not be thought of as applicable solely to those who are raised in the second generation. Even in the first generation adult members of the new order will need to have it explained and justified to them, especially where they have some residual allegiance to the old order, or where their new position exposes them to pressures which might make their loyalty waver. The creators and subsequent leaders of new movements might be unshakeable in their convictions, but many of the rank and file will profit by, or even require, careful legitimation of their new beliefs and practices. Berger himself recognizes the importance of legitimating a new social order to its adult members in a later work, *The Social Reality of Religion*.[67]

Although Berger and Luckmann do not burden *The Social Construction of Reality* with examples of specific historical data from which they have developed their model, it is a simple task to cite numerous cases where the leaders of new movements have thought it necessary or desirable to legitimate those movements to their members. Assistance in where to look for such legitimatory processes is available in an article by A.F.C. Wallace, in which the author attempts a broad taxonomy of what he calls 'revitalization movements'.[68] He uses the term 'revitalization' to describe the whole range of attempted, and sometimes successful, innovation of entire cultural systems, or at least substantial portions of those systems. The main phenomena he includes within this classification are revolutions, religious revivals, charismatic movements, sects and cargo cults, and reform, mass and social movements generally. It is clear that legitimation plays a vital role in nearly all of these movements, and in many cases there exists documentation, produced by their instigators and leaders, which fulfils a plainly legitimatory function. With respect to revolutions, for example, J. Baechler has accurately written that 'there is no revolutionary phenomenon without at least the germ of an ideology, to give it meaning and to serve as its justification'.[69] Very often such ideologies have been distilled in the form of revolutionary manifestos, which tend to become legitimatory documents for the new order if the revolution succeeds. In recent times this flourishing genre was inaugurated by the American Declaration of Independence (4 July 1776) and the French *Declaration of the Rights of Man and the Citizen* (26 August 1789). A document close to the time of Luke–Acts, yet performing much the same task, is the *Res Gestae Divi Augusti*, in which Octavian left a permanent record of his achievements in such a way as to legitimate the new political order he had bestowed on Rome. Religious sects (as described in Chapter 2 below) have also been a source of legitimating documents. Some of the writings emanating from the medieval millennarian sects discussed by Norman Cohn in *The Pursuit of the Millennium*, for example, have a legitimatory function.[70]

Having shown that the function of legitimation is, as Berger and Luckmann put it, to make 'objectively available and subjectively plausible' (p. 110) the meaning of a social institution, we may now examine some of the particular aspects of the process. One purpose which frequently motivates a legitimating process is that of integration. The institution will only make sense as a totality to the participants in diverse institutional processes if it is integrated, if it is characterized by its parts intermeshing into a whole. This may be referred to as the 'horizontal' level of integration and plausibility. But there is also a vertical dimension to the need for integration and plausibility: namely, that each individual in the institutional order must feel that his life, in its various stages, is meaningful, that his biography makes sense in this institution. Through this aspect of legitimation, therefore, the history of the institution and the biography of its individual members are united (pp. 110–11).

The integrative purpose and function of legitimation is most clearly seen in what Berger and Luckmann called the 'symbolic universe' fashioned for a new social order by its legitimators. A symbolic universe is a body of theoretical tradition which integrates different provinces of meaning and encompasses the institutional order in a symbolic totality (p. 114). By 'symbolic' is denoted reference to realities other than those of everyday experience (p. 113). Within such a universe, the members of the institution have an experience of everything being in its right place and also of the various phases of their biography as ordered; as they look back into their past or forward into the future, they conceive of their life unfolding within a universe whose ultimate coordinates are known. Over the institutional level as well, symbolic universes operate as sheltering canopies. The symbolic universe also orders history; it locates all collective acts in a cohesive unity that includes past, present and future. Thus individuals are linked with their predecessors and successors in a meaningful totality, so that they can conceive of themselves as belonging to a universe which was there before they were born and will be there after they die.

A little reflection quickly discloses the *prima facie* applicability of this model to Luke—Acts. For the elaborate historical framework of Luke—Acts provides many resemblances to the model and offers a rich selection of data for detailed comparison. First of all, more than any other New Testament writer, Luke takes great pains to present Christianity as a faith with a past. His Gospel begins with a number of incidents involving pious Jewish men and women who are firmly located in the ancestral beliefs and practices of Judaism while all the time looking forward in hope to the redemption of Israel. Throughout Luke—Acts the author continually emphasizes the loyalty of Jesus and his followers, especially Paul, to Jewish tradition and the way in which the Christian event is the fulfilment of that tradition. Secondly, there are many places in the work where one senses the present for Luke's audience, but perhaps the most prominent of these is Acts 20.28—32, where Paul addresses the elders of Ephesus and warns them to be on their guard against 'fierce wolves' who will invade the flock of God. It is impossible not to feel that Luke is writing for his Christian contemporaries, for whom this prophecy has become a harsh reality. Finally, Luke establishes a future for the Christian faith, both by providing in Acts a sequel to his Gospel — a fact which, as C. K. Barrett has observed,[71] itself has definite implications for an understanding of Lucan eschatology and by presenting the *parousia* as delayed and not imminent, as demonstrated by H. Conzelmann.[72] Thus, along the lines of the model of legitimation outlined immediately above, Luke creates a symbolic universe which orders history in such a way as to provide a past, present and future for his Christian contemporaries. He links them with their predecessors and successors in a meaningful totality.

At this point we must introduce a particularly common characteristic of the symbolic universe erected to legitimate a new social order — the claim that it is not novel, but is actually old and traditional. Berger has nicely explained this process in *The Social Reality of Religion*. Imagine yourself, he says, a fully aware creator of a society, 'a kind of combination of Moses and Machiavelli', faced with the problem of best ensuring the continuation of your institutional order which has just been established *ex nihilo*. Even when the means of power have been employed, for example, in checking one's opponents and ensuring the succession of power to one's designated successors, there still remains the problem of legitimation — which is all the more urgent because of 'the novelty and thus highly conscious precariousness of the new order'. The problem, Berger suggests, is best solved by applying the following recipe:

> Let the institutional order be so interpreted as to hide, as much as possible, its *constructed* character. Let that which has been stamped out of the ground *ex nihilo* appear as the manifestation of something that has been existent from the beginning of time, or at least from the beginning of this group ...[73]

Movements which include in their legitimatory apparatus the claim to be old and traditional are extremely common, especially in societies at a pre-industrial stage of development. Rebellions and revolutions often espouse 'the revival or reintroduction of an idealized society that allegedly existed in the society's own past'.[74] Examples include the counter-revolution in the Vendée in 1793, the ideology of the Confederate rebels in the American Civil War and the ideology of the Franco forces in the Spanish Civil War.[75] A fine example from the first century CE is the *Res Gestae Divi Augusti*.

Many new religious movements also legitimate themselves as re-assertions of pristine beliefs and practices long dormant. The writings of Luther and many of the other Reformers are obvious cases in point. With respect to the New Testament itself, W. A. Meeks has recently argued that in his letter to the Galatians Paul defines and defends the radically new Christian order in terms drawn from the old, Jewish order which gave it birth.[76] That much of the theology of Luke–Acts is also informed by this particular legitimatory strategy will be argued in subsequent chapters.

So far our analysis of legitimation has not taken into account the effect of any forces which may impede the creation of a symbolic universe. But a social world is rarely constructed *in vacuo*; the experience of a Prospero or a Robinson Crusoe is not common. Often a new world can only be created in the teeth of opposition from the upholders and defenders of one already in existence. In *The Social Construction of Reality* Berger and Luckmann note that the maintainers of a society often fail in their attempts to socialize and keep socialized all the inhabitants of that society. The problem becomes particularly acute when one group comes to share a version of the symbolic universe different from that adhered to by society at large. In such a case, 'the deviant version congeals into a reality in its own right, which, by its existence within the society, challenges the reality status of the symbolic universe as originally constituted' (p. 124).

This poses a threat to the dominant institution, which then commences repressive measures against the new group. The new group must counter these and confrontation results. Each group will develop a theory to justify itself *vis-à-vis* the other, or, as Berger and Luckmann put it: 'Two societies confronting each other with conflicting universes will both develop conceptual machineries designed to maintain their respective universes' (p. 126).

Once again, Berger and Luckmann do not supply examples of this phenomenon. On the political level, however, it can be illustrated from the propaganda battles which occur in revolutions, with the revolutionaries and the threatened establishment each attempting to have its view of reality prevail with the populace. When the model is applied to religion, on the other hand, it is obvious that the archetypal example of the process is the confrontation between an existing church and a sect which has broken, or is attempting to break, away from it. In such a case the conceptual machinery which the sect develops to maintain and justify itself as against the church from which it split will be reflected in the theology of the sect. A detailed explanation of the differences between 'church' and 'sect' from a sociological point of view is deferred until Chapter 3.

It is very important to remember that the opposition which a sect encounters from the church from which it arose is not based solely upon doctrinal differences, for a sect threatens the position and status of the persons responsible for maintaining and servicing the church. Inasmuch as the sect raises the possibility of drawing further members out of the church and even, eventually, threatening its continued separate existence altogether, it poses a risk to the privileged position which the leaders of the church enjoy. This aspect of the antagonism a church will feel towards a breakaway group is far too often forgotten. Peter Richardson, for example, when he is discussing the persecution of Christians by Jews in the first few decades of the existence of Christianity, remarks that in 'this situation it would beg the question to apportion "blame": Christian teaching (rightly) gave offence to orthodox Jews, and the inevitable result was opposition aimed at stamping out Christianity'.[77] Once a sociological imagination is exercised on the New Testament texts, it becomes impossible to impute such a simple motive to Jewish opposition. The clash between the old faith and the new was to a large degree a struggle for power, although this is not to deny that strong feelings over doctrinal matters also played a part. We must, accordingly, be continually open to the political implications of the New Testament texts.

But in addition to its leaders feeling their positions threatened by a sect, there is another essentially non-doctrinal issue which may provoke in a church massive hostility towards the sectarians: namely, an identity of membership and even of interest as between a church and a particular ethnic group, so that the sectarian threat to the church is also perceived as endangering the ethnic group. Such a threat might arise, for example, where the sect begins recruiting outside its own ethnic group and even establishes liturgical practices, involving the outsiders, which imperil the boundaries erected to maintain the integrity of that ethnic group against foreign invasion. We shall see in Chapter 4 below how significant this fact was in the development of that form of Christianity subscribed to by Luke's community.

One final matter remains in a consideration of the confrontation of church and sect. The differences between the two are rarely settled by a process of rational discussion leading to a peaceful resolution. Even at the level of doctrine – and we have seen that they are likely to be at loggerheads on political and sometimes also ethnic issues – the nature of the disputes between church and sect is not likely to allow their easy resolution. As Berger and Luckmann put it: 'From the point of view of intrinsic plausibility the two forms of conceptualization may seem to the outside observer to offer little choice' (p. 126). In such a situation, rather than relying merely upon the theoretical ingenuity of their respective legitimators, church or sect or both may attempt to apply force directly to reach a solution. The one with the bigger stick, normally the church, has the better chance of imposing its view of reality. Naked power will supplant discussion. Often the power which the church uses in its attempt to restrain or even eliminate a sect will be provided by the police or judicial powers of the state. The state will tend to be amenable to such a course of action because of a coincidence of interest between itself and the church in suppressing the sect. This coincidence will occur where the church enjoys something of a religious monopoly in that society; this has been explained by Berger and Luckmann as follows:

> Traditional definitions of reality inhibit social change. Conversely, breakdown in the taken-for-granted acceptance of the monopoly accelerates social change. It should not surprise us, then, that a profound affinity exists between those with an interest in maintaining established power positions and the personnel administering monopolistic traditions of universe-maintenance. In other words, conservative political forces

tend to support the monopolistic claims of the universal experts, whose monopolistic organizations in turn tend to be politically conservative. Historically, of course, most of these monopolies have been religious. It is thus possible to say that Churches, understood as monopolistic combinations of full-time experts in a religious definition of reality, are inherently conservative once they have succeeded in establishing their monopoly in a given society. Conversely, ruling groups with a stake in the maintenance of the political *status quo* are inherently churchly in their religious orientation and, by the same token, suspicious of all innovations in the religious tradition. (p. 140)

One could cite many examples of this process, but two will suffice for the present. First, Luther's *Letter to the Princes of Saxony*, written in July 1524, and pointing out to them the dangers inherent in Thomas Müntzer's millennial agitation, and his subsequent pamphlet *Against the Thievish, Murderous Gangs of the Peasants* (1525), which did much to rouse the princes of central Germany against the rising Müntzer had so helped to foment,[78] exemplify the tendency for a church leader to enlist the state against what is perceived to be a common threat. Secondly, a very large number of the African religious leaders who broke away from European mission churches in Africa in the last three centuries to found independent sects were imprisoned, banished or even executed by colonial administrations, often at the behest of the missionaries.[79]

The suitability of this aspect of the model to Luke–Acts is quite apparent. Although there were many religions competing for attention in the eastern parts of the Roman empire in the first century CE, Judaism did enjoy something very close to a monopoly within the separate Jewish enclaves, some of which were recognized and sanctioned by the Romans as *politeumata*,[80] in the Greek cities of the East. Throughout Luke–Acts there are many occasions in which the Jews attempt to enlist the support of the Roman authorities against Jesus and his followers in a fashion richly consonant with the model. Luke's response to this forms a vital part of the symbolic universe he constructs in the work, as will appear in later chapters.

We have now completed our outline of the model of legitimation -- specifically, the legitimation of a sect with a history of staunch opposition from the church from which it arose; this will be applied in a comparative way to particular aspects of Lucan theology throughout this book.

2

THE COMMUNITY

1. Luke's audience – a Christian community

Although the aim of this book is to analyse the interrelationships between Luke's theology and the social and political pressures upon his community, certain preliminary issues must be dealt with first. These issues, three in number, are considered in this chapter. They are: first, the justification for claiming that Luke was writing for a Christian community; secondly, the approximate time and geographical setting in which he composed his two volumes; and, thirdly, the ethnic and religious background of the members of his community.

Many commentators on Luke have felt that the preface, dedicating his Gospel to one Theophilus (1.1–4), was a natural place to begin a search for the audience he hoped to reach.[1] They have tended to presume that Theophilus was a leading figure in whichever group Luke had in mind as his first readers. But this is an erroneous presumption. As a result of a careful survey of the Hellenistic literary conventions of preface composition, H.J. Cadbury was able to demonstrate that the relation of author and addressee was usually formal and rarely affected the contents of the work.[2] Theophilus may or may not have been typical of the reading public for whom the work was intended; its real readers may well have been different. The possibly formal nature of the prologue weighs against too great an eagerness to treat it (after the manner of G. Klein, for example) as containing a theological programme for Luke–Acts.[3] The ambiguous nature of many of the terms employed in Lk 1.1–4 is a further reason for caution in viewing it programmatically.[4] Nevertheless, the preface does contain language broadly indicative of Luke's purpose in writing the work, especially in Lk 1.4.[5] Accordingly, the most desirable course of action appears to be to defer consideration of the preface for the present and concentrate upon analysing the text of

Luke–Acts for what it might tell us of the wider public for whom Luke wrote. It would be unsatisfactory, of course, if this analysis produced results which conflicted with the general Lucan purpose enunciated in the preface. We shall briefly return to Lk 1.1–4 in the Epilogue to confirm that no such conflict exists.

A matter of great importance in interpreting many aspects of Luke–Acts is whether its author meant his work for non-Christian, as well as Christian, readers. The assertion that he did is frequently made by those who attribute to him an apologetic desire to convince the pagan authorities of Rome that Christianity was politically harmless. A number of considerations militate against any part of Luke's audience's having been outright pagans. The chief of these is that Luke plunges his readers into the atmosphere of Judaism and the Old Testament at the very beginning of his Gospel and leaves them there until the end of Acts. He often alludes to the Greek Old Testament in a way which would have been opaque, even unintelligible, to someone unfamiliar with its language and contents.[6] Nor could pagans easily have obtained such familiarity. A. D. Nock has written that 'there is no indication of substantial knowledge of the Septuagint except as heard by those who frequented synagogues or were concerned to write polemical treatises against Christianity: as a book it was bulky, expensive, and inaccessible'.[7] Similarly, Luke assumes that his reader is acquainted with a large amount of knowledge to do with Jesus' proclamation of the gospel, otherwise he would need to explain such expressions as 'the Son of Man' and 'the Kingdom of God', and to provide at least some background information on some of the parables, the beatitudes, the apocalyptic discourses and the Lord's Supper.[8] Finally, we know how Luke would have thought it appropriate to address pagans with no knowledge of Jewish or Christian teaching merely by looking at the approach he has Paul adopt before the Athenians on the Areopagus; namely, by appealing to an aspect of their own religious tradition but also using philosophical language and literary allusions which his audience would understand. The same strategy was later adopted by the second-century apologists Aristides, Justin Martyr and Athenagoras.

But there is more to be said for Luke's audience than simply that it was Christian. First of all, we must ask whether he was writing for a particular Christian community, most probably his local congregation. There has been a tendency for many years to relate each of the larger New Testament works to a specific community for which it was written. Thus, for example, we speak of the Marcan, Matthean and Johannine communities. Some scholars have resisted this tendency with respect to Luke, although they rarely say why. E. A. LaVerdiere and W. G. Thompson opine that Luke, as opposed to Matthew, had in view many communities rather than one single community,[9] and this view is shared, equally without any evident justification, by R. F. O'Toole.[10] The preferable position, however, is that Luke, just like the other evangelists, did have a specific Christian community in mind. One of the places in Luke–Acts where one feels most immediately that Luke is using apostolic history to speak to the present of his own audience is in Paul's prophetic address to the elders of the Ephesian ἐκκλησία (Acts 20.17–35). Paul refers to the Ephesian ἐκκλησία as a 'flock', of which the elders are shepherds, and warns them that after his departure 'fierce wolves' will invade the flock and men will rise up from within it speaking a perversion of the truth to mislead the disciples. There is more here than a generalized message to Luke's readers that Paul had foreseen the troubles in store for Christians in the years ahead. For the context Luke establishes for these troubles is the local Christian community, the 'flock', with clear boundaries between itself and the outside world, which is threatened by enemies crossing those boundaries from without, while others rise up within. This image of the separateness and fragility of the Christian congregation is also reflected in the remarkable exhortation of Jesus, unique to the Third Gospel: 'Do not fear, little flock, for the Father has been pleased to give you the Kingdom' (Lk 12.32). This repeated use of the flock image suggests that Luke found it appropriate to the circumstances of his own readers, in other words, that they too were members of a small Christian community beset by difficulties from within and without.

But even if Luke had written for more than one community, that fact would not invalidate the methodology adopted in this book or the results produced by it. For what will emerge during the course of our investigation is an understanding of particular relationships between Luke's theology and his social, political and religious setting; these relationships if not restricted to one community, would only have obtained in an ensemble of Christian congregations of a certain type, all of them being characterized by a quite circumscribed set of tensions within their memberships and with the world outside.

2. When and where

Suggested dates of composition of Luke–Acts range from the sixties of the first century CE, before Paul's putative trial and death in Rome,[11] to some time in the first half of the second century. The early date still commands some support and has been vigorously championed recently by J. A. T. Robinson,[12] while the later date is defended by J. O'Neill[13] and others. An impressive pedigree can be documented for both extremes.[14] The most commonly accepted view today, however, is that the work was composed after the destruction of Jerusalem in 70 CE and before the end of the first century. These latter chronological limits are supported by the evidence, not just a spirit of compromise.

For over a century many commentators have argued that Luke–Acts was written before Paul's trial and death, essentially because the work ends before these events, and if Luke had known any more details of the apostle's history he would have included them. This extremely subjective view not only reads down or ignores the hints of Paul's impending doom scattered around the latter chapters of Acts;[15] it is also incompatible with the impressive case which can be made, on the basis of the two passages in his Gospel in which Jesus predicts the fate in store for Jerusalem (19.43–4; 21.20–4), for Luke's having written after the destruction of Jerusalem in 70 CE. It is widely accepted that Luke has inserted the details in the first passage, which is unique to his Gospel, and significantly altered Mk 13.14 in the second, to present a picture of the destruction of Jerusalem which accords with what happened when the four legions under Titus sacked the city. Our principal source for these events is Josephus, but it is unlikely that Luke used Josephus, in spite of M. Krenkel's arguments to the contrary.[16]

C. H. Dodd, however, has challenged the notion that these two passages are Lucan *vaticinia ex eventu*.[17] He has argued that the military operations outlined by Luke were no more than the regular commonplaces of ancient warfare and that the language used by Luke in the two passages is thoroughly Septuagintal and originates in particular in accounts of the sack of Solomon's temple by Nebuchadnezzar in 587 BCE. Nevertheless, even these arguments cannot overturn the view that Luke wrote after 70 CE. In the first place, it is erroneous to suggest that the Lucan description of the sack of Jerusalem merely rehearses features common to any such operation in the ancient world. Not every attack on an ancient city involved the construction of some form of circumvallation (Lk 19.43). Josephus, in fact, records that the Romans initially attempted to take the city by frontal assault without surrounding it with a wall and only decided to erect one when the campaign had been proceeding for some time without success.[18] Nor was it inevitable that the city would be so effectively destroyed that not one stone was left on another (Lk 19.44). Many cities captured after siege were not razed, and that this fate befell Jerusalem (except for three towers and some of the wall, which the Romans left as reminders of the scale of their victory)[19] was largely due to the particular circumstances of the campaign. Finally, not all sieges ended with the inhabitants of the captured city being led off as captives among all nations (Lk 21.24), as occurred after the sack of Jerusalem, with some being sent to labour in Egypt, while larger numbers were despatched to the provinces, there to be killed in the amphitheatres by sword or wild beast.[20] Secondly, little significance can be attached to Luke's use of Septuagintal language in the two passages. Luke indulges in Septualgintalisms throughout his two volumes, and his sense of style would almost inevitably have sent him back to the language used in the Old Testament for phrases appropriate to Jesus' prophecies. But there is a third consideration which weighs very heavily against Dodd's arguments and in favour of a post – 70 CE date of composition. That Luke diverges from Mark's apocalypse by introducing the feature that 'ages of Gentiles' (καιροὶ ἐθνῶν) (Lk 21.24) must occur after the sack of Jerusalem but before the return of the Son of Man means that he does not regard the destruction of Jerusalem as itself an apocalyptic event. It is difficult to credit a Christian living before 70 CE with such an attitude. On the basis of these considerations, accordingly, it is accepted in what follows that the *terminus a quo* for the composition of Luke–Acts is 70 CE.

There is one generally recognized criterion for establishing its *terminus ante quem*: the fact that Luke nowhere displays the slightest acquaintance with Paul's letters, some of which appear to have been available in a collected form by *c.* 95 CE.[21] This date is to some extent supported by the attitude to Roman authorities in Luke–Acts, a subject canvassed at length in Chapter 8 below. To anticipate a conclusion reached in that chapter, it is highly probable that Luke wishes his audience to believe that a Christian hauled before a Roman court could expect a fair hearing from it, including a chance to reply on the facts to any accusation (Acts 25.16). By the time Pliny wrote his famous letter to Trajan[22] on the Christians of Bithynia some time between 109 and 111 CE,[23] this was no longer a tenable position. Pliny had been in the habit of asking Christians brought before him to recant and of executing those who did not. He appears to have known of no imperial rescript which made merely being a Christian a punishable offence, but, by virtue of the immense *imperium*[24] vested in him as a provincial governor, he was able to order Christians to recant and to punish them for *contumacia*, direct disobedience, if they failed to do so. Pliny must have been induced to follow this severe line because he was already of the view that they were a suspect group whose members had been tried elsewhere and of whom criminal behaviour might be expected. Now one must not immediately conclude that the attitude of the governor in Bithynia was only one example of a more widespread phenomenon. But this does, indeed, appear to have been the case. Pliny himself speaks of *cognitiones* ('trials') of Christians at which he was never present,[25] and which must have occurred somewhere other than Bithynia. And one must also bear in mind the evidence in early Christian authors for some kind of persecution or harassment of Christians in the time of Domitian.[26] On the other hand, little assistance is afforded by the fact that Ignatius of Antioch was sentenced to death around the time of Pliny's letter,[27] since there is no evidence that any others in the Antiochene church shared their bishop's fate.[28] Nevertheless, there is evidence that an attitude of antipathy to Christians had appeared among the Roman authorities some time before 110 CE, possibly as early as the time of Domitian, and this would have rendered Luke's pro-Roman policy an exercise in futility.[29] What use would it have been to assure his Christian contemporaries that a fair trial awaited them in a Roman court if the presiding magistrate was likely to short-circuit the whole process by simply ordering them to recant their faith?

Unfortunately, it is difficult to place Luke–Acts more precisely between 70 and 95 CE. However, some time may have elapsed since the destruction of Jerusalem and allowed the non-apocalyptic attitude to that event displayed in the Third Gospel to have developed. Moreover, there are signs, discussed in Chapter 3 below, that Luke's community had encountered severe opposition from Jewish authorities. This suggests a time, perhaps as early as the eighties of the first century, after the rabbis had organized themselves at Jamnia and had begun tightening up on Christians in the synagogues and even excluding them altogether.[30] We conclude, therefore, that the most likely date for Luke–Acts appears to lie in the mid- to late eighties or the early nineties of the first century CE.

The most probable conclusion which can be drawn as to the place of composition of Luke-Acts is that it was a city. H.J. Cadbury has most fully shown why Luke must have written the work in an urban context.[31] To justify this view he cites phenomena in the text such as editorial additions of the word 'city' to proper place-names, the focusing of the teaching of Jesus and of early Christian missionaries almost exclusively in cities,[32] the introduction of named cities into unlikely places in the source-materials,[33] the frequent mention of a city as the scene of an episode even when he does not name the place[34] and an interest in the secular standing of particular cities.[35] In addition, Luke's immersion in the Hellenistic culture of his day, which is apparent not just in the inclusion of the dedications to Theophilus at the start of his Gospel and of Acts, but also in other, less frequently noted, features, such as the fine literary Greek of the sea-voyage and shipwreck description in Acts 27, most probably indicates an urban setting.

Even though an attempt to determine the specific city in which Luke-Acts was written is beyond the scope of this book,[36] the conclusion that Luke wrote in a city of the Roman empire where Hellenistic culture was strong or even dominant is of great assistance in reaching an understanding of the social and political world in which his community found itself. For there is a large volume of historical research available which tracks the structural patterns common to such cities, as well as detailing their particular histories. Moreover, a body of sociological literature has begun to appear devoted to the characteristics of cities at a pre-industrial stage of development.[37] These historical and sociological ideas and approaches will be applied later, especially in Chapter 7, which deals with Luke's position on riches and poverty.

3. Jews and Gentiles in Luke's Community

Introduction: the case for a Gentile audience
The rest of this chapter is devoted to the balance of Jews and Gentiles in Luke's community. Not all the data in Luke-Acts relevant to this issue can be fully discussed here, however, since some of this material arises more naturally in connection with later topics, such as table-fellowship. Our present aim, therefore, is to reach conclusions based upon a significant proportion of the data and to indicate how those conclusions will be confirmed in subsequent sections of this book.

There are three possibilities for the Jewish–Gentile mix in the Lucan community:

1. Totally or predominantly Gentile, with Jews absent or an insignificant minority; or
2. A mixture of Jew and Gentile, in which each group is significant; or
3. Totally or predominantly Jewish, with Gentiles absent or an insignificant minority.

The vast majority of scholars favour the first option, one or two the second,[38] and virtually none the third, although there have always been those who have thought that Luke wrote for a Jewish audience, even if the Gentiles were the largest component in his own congregation. The view taken in this work is that the second option is nearest to the truth, with the qualification that most of the Gentiles in Luke's community had not converted to Christianity from idolatry, but had previously been associated with Jewish synagogues.

It is, admittedly, no light matter to reject the virtually unanimous belief among New Testament scholars that the Christians for whom Luke wrote were predominantly Gentile. Yet might not the very universality of this belief have deadened generations of scholars to the need for probing its lineage and credentials? It is a remarkable fact that the Gentile character of Luke's audience is so confidently regarded as one of the assured results in the field that there is no recent article or monograph devoted to justifying the prevailing view. Even J. Jervell, who has done more than anyone to illuminate the intimate links which Luke strove to forge between Judaism and Christianity, refused to accept that there were a significant number of Jews in Luke's community.[39]

The current orthodoxy on the Gentile character of Luke's audience stems largely from the influential view of F. C. Overbeck, as originally expressed in his classic commentary on Acts, which was published in 1870.[40] According to Overbeck: 'Nothing could be clearer than that Acts has abandoned Jewish Christianity as such and is written from the point of view which recognizes Gentile Christianity as the absolutely dominant element in the Church.'[41]

That such wide credence should be given to Overbeck's belief in the Gentile make-up of Luke's audience is rather remarkable when one considers that Overbeck dated Acts to the second or third decade of the second century CE.[42] Re-locating Acts to the far more probable eighties or early nineties of the first century has the effect of rendering his viewpoint much less plausible.

Accordingly, the position on Luke's audience expounded by the highly influential Overbeck cannot be relied upon today, given the date for Luke–Acts accepted in this book. But we must now consider specific arguments advanced by contemporary Lucan commentators to support a Gentile audience for the work. Although no detailed and extended defence of this orthodoxy exists,[43] the subject is dealt with *en passant* in works on other topics, and from these one can summarize the arguments generally offered as justification. They fall into a number of groups.

The first group is a miscellany of minor arguments conveniently collected by J. Fitzmyer.[44] He claims that the Greco-Roman literary tradition evident in the prologues to the Third Gospel and Acts, those aspects of the two volumes indicating a provenance outside Palestine, Luke's use of the Septuagint and the fact that he and his contemporaries spoke Greek, all argue for a Gentile community behind the work. But none of these features leads to this conclusion, since one would expect to encounter all of them even in a work written by an educated Jew for other Jews of that milieu. They all apply to the writings of Philo of Alexandria, for example.

The second group of arguments centres upon Luke's apparent abbreviation or omission of characteristically Jewish emphases and issues from his sources. The most commonly cited examples are the antitheses found in Mt 5.21–48 (unless these are from Matthew's special material), the controversy over clean and unclean in Mk 7.1–23, and various struggles of Jesus against the rabbis. All of these issues may be subsumed under the related headings of purity and the law. A proper understanding of these subjects, which is of crucial importance in appreciating Luke's strategies and intentions, requires a lengthy investigation of the relevant data in the text; this is provided in Chapters 4 and 5 below. Suffice it to say for the present, however, that far from indicating a predominantly Gentile community behind Luke, his presentation of table-fellowship and the law provides some of the most convincing evidence available of his local congregation having been composed of a mixture of Jews and of one-time Gentile synagogue-attenders.

The third argument is a highly significant and influential one. It consists of inferring a Gentile audience from Luke's manifest desire to relate the salvation offered in the Gospel to non-Jews. Underlying this argument is the assumption that one may draw conclusions on the composition of Luke's community by observing any significant pattern of emphasis among those people whom he singles out in his

Gospel and in Acts as sharing in the message of salvation. This is a sound assumption, given that this and subsequent chapters will reveal the extent to which his aims are etiological, by which we mean that he attempts to justify the current practices and beliefs of his community by tracing their origins in the ministry of Jesus and the events of the church's first generation. The difficulty for the currently dominant view of Luke's audience is that an examination of the work on the basis of this assumption reveals that the recipients of the good news are depicted not as former pagan idolaters, but rather as Gentiles who had previously attended synagogues and Jews, with both groups bound together in the table-fellowship of the Christian congregation. The extent to which Luke has worked this pattern into his overall design is exposed at many points by comparison with Paul's letters, which function as an invaluable historical control for the actual course of events in the church's first generation. In the rest of this chapter we will consider the general indications of a universalist tendency in Luke–Acts and then demonstrate how its author has shaped the traditions at his disposal to portray the original Christian mission in the Diaspora as involving the conversion of Jews and pious Gentiles and the establishment of table-fellowship between them. That his aim in so doing was to legitimate the very same balance and unity in his own local community will be argued here and abundantly corroborated in later chapters.

The universalist theme in Luke–Acts

There are a number of features in Luke–Acts, not attributable to Mark or Q (the sayings source generally believed to have been used by Matthew and Luke), which, in spite of scepticism from some scholars, such as G. D. Kilpatrick,[45] are rightly regarded as disclosing a universalist theme, that is, an undoubted interest of its author in the non-Jewish world as a locus for the salvation effective in Christ. This theme commences with the words of Simeon, who recognizes in Jesus the salvation which God has prepared before all peoples, 'a light for the illumination of the Gentiles and the glory of your people Israel' (Lk 2.31–2).[46] It should be noted, however, that Simeon also includes Israel in the divine plan. Soon after this, Luke alters Mark by extending the quotation from Is 40 to include the words of Is 40.5 (LXX): '... and all humanity will see the salvation of God' (Lk 3.5–6). Thirdly, Luke traces the genealogy of Jesus back to Adam (Lk 3.23–38), although this may reflect a desire to establish the credentials of Jesus as Messiah rather than an interest in universal mission.[47] On the other hand, the reference by Jesus to the actions of Elijah and Elisha among Gentiles (Lk 4.25–7) is undoubtedly meant to foreshadow a mission among non-Jews in the Christian period; the detailed implications of this crucial passage will be considered a little below. Fifthly, Luke describes those who will feast in the Kingdom of Heaven as coming from north, south, east and west (Lk 13.29), whereas the Matthean parallel only mentions east and west (Mt 8.11). It is unclear whether Luke or Matthew is following Q more closely here, but certainly Luke's version is in keeping with his universalist tendency. The sixth feature is the Lucan version of the Parable of the Great Banquet (Lk 14.15–24; Mt 22.1–14). Unlike Matthew, Luke describes how the host sent out his servants to collect two groups of new guests after the original guests had declined. The first group collected are the poor, crippled, blind and lame from the host's own city. The second are people from the open roads and hedgerows. T. W. Manson plausibly argues that the original guests are meant to represent righteous Jews, the first of the new guests to represent the religious lower classes, such as publicans and sinners, while the second group of new guests, who came from beyond the city boundaries, stands for Gentiles.[48] This is correct, except that there is no reason not also to give a literal significance to the poor and the crippled, etc., who are invited to the banquet. Lastly, there is the message which Jesus left with his disciples prior to his ascension – that repentance for the forgiveness of sins would be preached to all nations (Lk 24.47).

This evidence suggests an openness to non-Jews within the scheme of salvation, although not, it should be noted, to the exclusion of the Jews (Lk 2.31–2; 14.15–24). We must now consider more exactly what type of non-Jews Luke has in mind, and for this we will start with what Jesus says to the Jews in Nazareth at the start of his public ministry (Lk 4.16–30).

The incident at Nazareth (Lk 4.16–30) and pious Gentiles
There is little doubt that the pericope concerning the reception of Jesus at Nazareth (Lk 4.16–30) fulfils a programmatic function within Luke–Acts as a whole. Not only has Luke used this incident as the context for the inaugural preaching of Jesus in his Gospel, but he has transferred it from its location in Mark, well into the public ministry of Jesus (Mk 6.1–6), to the beginnings of that ministry. That Luke's form of the story is twice as long as Mark's and contains many additional features has led some scholars to postulate an additional

source or sources behind it.[49] But the preferable view, expressed by U. Busse and J. Fitzmyer, for example, is that Luke has freely re-worked Mark (and, to a lesser extent, Q) without help from other sources.[50] This consideration inevitably undermines the value of Luke's version as a source for the attitudes and actions of the historical Jesus. Many features of this pericope will be discussed in the course of this book, but for the present the relevant section is 4.25−7.

It is something of a commonplace of Lucan scholarship to see in these three verses a prediction and authorization of a mission to the Gentiles which was not to occur until after the time of Jesus. Little, if any, attention had been paid to the detailed implications of these verses, however, until the publication in 1969 of an important article by L. C. Crockett.[51] Crockett makes two illuminating suggestions. First, he regards the reference to the story of Elijah being sent to the widow in Zarephath as anticipating the eating together by Jew and Gentile in Christian table-fellowship. This is an attractive proposal, in spite of the fact that Luke does not expressly mention in 4.25 that Elijah did eat with this Gentile widow (as in 1 Kgs 17.15). Luke may well have been able to rely upon his readers already being familiar with this feature of the story. Secondly, Crockett very plausibly proposes that the reference to the purification of Naaman the Syrian with the prophet Elisha's help in 4.27 anticipates the baptism of the Gentiles which leaves them cleansed and ready for fellowship with Jews in the Christian community.

In spite of the merit of these suggestions, there are two further areas of interest in these verses which Crockett has failed to notice. First, there is the fact that the primary stress in Lk 4.25−6 falls on the 'good news for the poor' theme announced in 4.18−19; this issue is taken up in Chapter 7 below, which deals with Luke's attitude to poverty and riches. The second area is the religious disposition of Naaman following his being cured of leprosy through the intercession of Elisha. From that point on he acknowledged no God in all the earth except Yahweh (2 Kgs 5.15). Yet he was not circumcised; he did not become a Jew. He remained a Gentile and the military commander of a Gentile king. In Naaman do we not see an early type of the Gentiles, especially Roman military and administrative officials, whom Luke depicts as often already sympathetic to Judaism and as having a very favourable attitude to Jesus and the Christian movement, even to the extent of becoming Christians themselves? We must now examine the role which Gentiles such as these play in Luke−Acts.

God-fearers in Luke–Acts

During the first century CE (and for a long period thereafter) large numbers of Gentiles living in the cities of the Roman empire were attracted to Judaism. Some of these merely aped Jewish customs, while others went all the way to becoming Jews through circumcision. It is widely accepted that there was an intermediate group, usually referred to today as 'God-fearers', whose devotion to Judaism, especially its powerful monotheism, led them to attend Jewish synagogues, but without becoming circumcised.[52] A.T. Kraabel, however, has recently challenged the existence of these God-fearers on the strength of their alleged absence from Diaspora synagogues from the period which have now been excavated.[53] His argument, which is largely an argument from silence, fails for two reasons. First, there is literary evidence for the strong influence of Judaism on Greeks and Romans[54] and the existence of God-fearers in large numbers (in Antioch, for example) is attested in Josephus.[55] Secondly, there is at least one definite example, known from the Diaspora synagogues, of a Gentile sympathizer with Judaism. An inscription from the synagogue in Akmonia describes how it had been restored by certain Jewish officials, although originally constructed by one Julia Severa.[56] Now we know that this lady was not a Jewess, since another inscription from Akmonia describes her as a priestess of a pagan god.[57] Since she paid for the construction of the synagogue she must certainly have been a sympathizer with Judaism and perhaps may even have attended synagogue services.

Josephus employs the phrase σεβόμενοι τὸν Θεόν of Judaism on at least one occasion with respect to Gentile sympathizers.[58] The phrase σεβόμενοι τὸν Θεόν occurs seven times in the Septuagint: five times of the attitude of Jews to Yahweh (Jos 4.24; 22.25; Is 29.13; 66.14; and Jon 1.9), once to describe the reverence of Jews for other gods (Jos 24.33b), and once to describe the attitude of that eminent non-Jew, Job, to God (Job 1.9). The word Θεοσεβής only occurs four times in the Septuagint, once of a Jew (Ex 18.21), but three times of Job (Job 1.1, 8; 2,3).

Having defended the existence of God-fearers during the first century and beyond against Kraabel's attack, we must now examine the role they play in Luke–Acts.

Two passages in the Third Gospel deserve a brief mention. First, there is the centurion of Capernaum, whose servant Jesus heals from a distance (Lk 7.1–10). This is a Q incident (cf. Mt 8.5–13), but only Luke has the centurion send off a group of Jewish elders, who inform

Jesus that 'he loves our people and built the synagogue for us' (7.5). Some uncertainty surrounds the question of whether Luke or Matthew is closer to Q on this point,[59] but in any event the centurion figures in Luke–Acts as a prototype of the government officials who will later show such interest in the Christian message. Secondly, Luke says of the centurion standing at the foot of the cross that when he saw Jesus die 'he glorified God ...' (Lk 23.47). In other words, the centurion enters into a personal relationship with God. Neither Mark nor Matthew mentions such a reaction (Mk 15.39; Mt 27.54).

Few passages in Luke–Acts are of greater moment in reaching an understanding of the author's intentions than that describing the conversion of Cornelius and its subsequent ratification by the Church in Jerusalem (Acts 10.1–11.18). Here Luke brings the theme of the receptivity of devout Gentiles to the message of salvation, evident in his references to Naaman and the two centurions just mentioned, to a grand climax by depicting the first Gentile convert in Acts as just such a person. Luke has placed this narrative at this point in Acts to invest it with paradigmatic significance and meaning, not because it is an accurate historical account of how the mission among the Gentiles actually began.[60]

Luke brings to the surface two major issues in the Cornelius incident and keeps them before our eyes throughout the rest of Acts: first, the religious disposition of Cornelius prior to his becoming Christian, and, secondly, the fact that Peter, a Jew, enters into table-fellowship with Gentiles.[61]

In Acts 10.2 Cornelius is described as 'pious and God-fearing' (εὐσεβὴς καὶ φοβούμενος τὸν Θεόν) with all his household, doing many works of charity for the people and praying to God continually. A little later he is described as 'a just and God-fearing man [ἀνὴρ δίκαιος καὶ φοβούμενος τὸν Θεόν], highly regarded by the entire Jewish people' (10.22). The phrase φοβούμενος τὸν Θεόν does not appear to have the force of a technical expression here, especially since in 10.2 φοβούμενος is one of three present participles used in succession to extol the virtues of Cornelius. Of course, the only Gentiles likely to revere the Jewish God are those who have come in contact with Jews, as had Cornelius. We are not told if Cornelius attended synagogue, but from what we have learned of God-fearers in our previous discussion it would be rather surprising if he did not. It has been plausibly suggested by K. Romaniuk that there is a measure of similarity between the description of Cornelius in Acts 10.1–2 and that of Job in the Septuagint (Job 1.1);[62] this is interesting for the fact, already noted, that Job is the only non-Jew in the Septuagint to whom the epithet Θεοσεβής is applied.

A most striking feature of the Cornelius story is that the qualities which the centurion manifests, especially the fact that he worships God, are not merely descriptive of his character or useful in locating him among a particular group of pious Gentiles. They are also presented as essential prerequisites for the conversion of Gentiles to Christianity. This little-noticed but highly important fact is revealed when Peter says to Cornelius and those gathered in his house: 'Truly I understand that God does not have favourites, but that anyone in any race who fears him [ὁ φοβούμενος αὐτόν] and acts justly is acceptable to him' (10.34–5). This means that it is not just any Gentile who is worthy to receive the Gospel, but only someone like Cornelius, who fears God and acts justly. As this conversion paves the way for and legitimates all later Gentile conversions, we must assume that Luke is endorsing Peter's conditions as being applicable in all those later cases. This interpretation is confirmed in Acts 15.17, where it appears that the Gentiles singled out for inclusion in God's people are those already consecrated to his name. It comes as no surprise that the usual source of Gentile converts in Acts is among those associated with synagogues, for only in that context were there normally to be found Gentiles who did fear God.

The last issue arising out of the Cornelius episode to be dealt with at present is the implication that Peter's missionary *sine qua non* carries for our understanding of Luke's community. While a full discussion of this matter must await the treatment of the other conversion accounts in Acts, undertaken later in this chapter, we may note at this point how unlikely it is that Luke would have taken such pains to prescribe these credentials for a convert to Christianity if they had not characterized all or at least a considerable proportion of the Gentiles in his community at the time of their conversion.

There are approximately twenty conversion accounts in Acts subsequent to that dealing with Cornelius. Their prominent feature is that Luke portrays Christian evangelism as having been successful almost entirely among Jews and God-fearers attending synagogues where the Gospel was first preached. We begin their examination with Paul's evangelism in Pisidian Antioch (13.16–52), since this is the first time in Acts that his actual words in a missionary context are reported at length. Paul initially addresses his audience in the synagogue in that city as 'Israelites and those who fear God' (οἱ φοβούμενοι τὸν Θεόν) (13.16) and later as 'Brothers, sons of the race of Abraham, and those among you who fear God' (καὶ οἱ ἐν ὑμῖν φοβούμενοι τὸν Θεόν) (13.26). There is little doubt that the φοβούμενοι τὸν Θεόν are Gentile God-fearers, like Cornelius. In subsequent chapters of Acts, however, the word σεβόμενος (with or without τὸν Θεόν), which, as we have seen, is attested in Josephus for God-fearers, is used with respect to Gentiles of this type. In spite of Paul's havirrg these two groups before him, however, he pitched his message of salvation at first only at the Jews. Otherwise, there would be no point in his announcing to the Jews, after they have blasphemously contradicted his preaching: 'It was necessary that the word of God be proclaimed to you first. But since you have rejected it and do not consider yourselves worthy of eternal life, look, we are turning to the Gentiles' (13.46). Here Paul implies that, before the Jews rejected God's word and eternal life, the message of salvation was meant for them alone. The social and religious reality of this can only be that Paul, at least as Luke presents him, envisaged admitting Jews but not Gentiles to the Christian community, an admission presumably effected by baptism and maintained through eucharistic fellowship. In announcing that he is turning to the Gentiles, Paul means that he will thenceforth admit them to the Christian community, clearly not to the exclusion of the Jews, but in addition to them, for even after this incident he continually preaches in Diaspora synagogues and wins Jewish as well as Gentile converts. In other words, the crucial development in the spread of the mission throughout the Diaspora is to be the establishment of Christian communities containing both Jews and Gentile God-fearers. That the two groups entered into table-fellowship with one another profoundly shocked orthodox Jewish sensibilities for the reasons and with the consequences discussed in Chapter 4 below.

   Luke's version of events in Pisidian Antioch helps us to tease out the implications of his rather cryptic narrative of early evangelism in Syrian Antioch (11.19–21). Luke does not specify where this evangelism was initiated, but it is possible to deduce that it was the synagogue. In Acts 11.19–20 reference is made to two waves of missionary activity in Antioch, the first to Jews only and the second to Gentiles *as well*.[63] But we have already mentioned the evidence in Josephus for the large numbers of Gentiles who attended Jewish synagogues in Antioch, so it is difficult to imagine how the gospel could have been preached only to Jews. This difficulty dissolves in the light of the analogy with events in Pisidian Antioch. We may presume that although Jews and God-fearers heard the message in the synagogue, at first only the former were allowed to join the Christian community. With the arrival of the second wave of evangelists, however, the pious Gentiles were also admitted.

Although the results of Paul's preaching in the synagogues in Salamis (13.5), Athens (17.7) and Ephesus (19.8) are not specified, Luke's narratives of the evangelism in three other cities bring out very clearly the success of the Christian missionaries among both Jew and Gentile synagogue-attenders. These are the accounts concerning the cities of Iconium (14.1), Thessalonika (17.1–4) and Beroea (17.10–12). The Gentiles who converted in Thessalonika are described as 'a great crowd of the pious Greeks [τῶν τε σεβομένων Ἑλλήνων πλῆθος πολύ] and not a few of the prominent women' (17.4). The use of the word σεβόμενος reminds us of its occurrence in Josephus with this meaning. Luke mentions that in Iconium and Thessalonika many Jews did not convert and became hostile to the missionaries (14.2; 17.5–9, 13).

There are three conversion accounts where table-fellowship is given considerable prominence, in addition to the Cornelius narrative. We begin with events in Corinth. Luke records that after Paul arrived in that city he lodged with a Jew called Aquila and Priscilla, his wife. Since he and Aquila shared the same trade of tent-making, they worked together (18.1–3). But each sabbath Paul went to the synagogue and attempted to convert 'Jews and Greeks' (18.4). He subsequently encountered heavy Jewish opposition there and departed from the synagogue with the portentous words: 'Your blood be upon your own heads; from now on I can go to the Gentiles unpolluted [καθαρός]' (18.6).[64] His decision did not herald in a mission to the pagans in the market-places and workshops of Corinth, however, for, in what is an unintentionally comic feature, Luke describes him as moving into the house of the God-fearer (σεβόμενος τὸν Θεόν) Titius Justus, who lived right next door to the synagogue (18.7). Although little or nothing is made of it in existing Lucan scholarship, the fact that Luke has Paul take this step further illuminates the patterning of the Gentile mission which is observable throughout Luke–Acts. In moving in with Titius Justus, Paul must leave the house of Aquila and his wife, although there is nothing in the text, or in references to this couple in the Pauline corpus (Rom 16.3; 1 Cor 16.19), to suggest that they had failed him in any way. What 'going to the Gentiles' means to Paul, therefore, is the deliberately public establishment of table-fellowship between Jews and Gentiles, or at least those Gentiles who, like Titius Justus, already revered Yahweh and thereby came within the class defined by Peter at Acts 10.35. Moreover, Paul's residing with Titius did not mean the end of the mission to the Jews. Luke probably means his readers to understand that by selecting his location next to the synagogue Paul was well placed to keep in contact with the Jews and the God-fearers who went there. This is surely confirmed by Luke's relating that after Paul had taken this step, Crispus, the *archisynagogus*, and all his family came to believe (18.8). In addition, Paul later shows that he has nothing in principle against evangelizing in a synagogue context, for this is precisely what he does at Ephesus (19.8).

The second conversion where table-fellowship is a significant issue is that of Lydia, a God-fearer (σεβομένη τὸν Θεόν), whom Paul met one sabbath in Philippi (16.11−15). This woman clearly satisfied Peter's conditions for conversion, and the story ends like that of Cornelius, with Paul staying in her house and, presumably, eating from the same table with her. Thirdly, there is the conversion of the gaoler of Philippi, not previously a God-fearer it seems, but reduced to a receptive frame of mind by the miraculous events in his gaol (16.25−30). After baptizing him and his household, Paul and Silas go to his house and share a meal with them (16.31−4).

Apart from this incident involving the gaoler at Philippi, there are only three occasions in Acts on which Luke describes Paul as preaching in a non-Jewish context or to people without a Jewish connection − at Lystra, Athens and Ephesus. Yet even these narratives fail to displace the Lucan presentation of Christian evangelism as so far explained. At Lystra Paul addresses an audience of pagans idolatrous to the extent of wanting to sacrifice to him as Hermes and to Barnabas as Zeus. Yet his impassioned plea is quite unsuccessful. In fact, it is barely enough to stop the crowd offering them sacrifice, let alone to make them become Christians (14.8−18). At Athens, too, Paul preaches in the agora and on the Areopagus (17.17−34). But even here he does not appear to have had much success and the few people who do convert (17.34) may actually have been among the God-fearers (οἱ σεβόμενοι) whom he has also addressed in the Athenian synagogue (17.17). Thirdly, Paul preaches in the lecture-room of Tyrannus in Ephesus (19.9−10), following his departure from the local synagogue because of Jewish opposition. The result of this evangelism is that 'all the inhabitants of Asia, Jews as well as Greeks, heard the word of the Lord' (19.10). This seems the one favourable report in Acts of missionary preaching to an audience which may have included pagan idolaters. Even here, however, Luke does not say this explicitly. There were, after all, Jews among the audience and many of the Greeks may have been understood as being God-fearers.

The foregoing analysis of conversion accounts in Acts has brought to light a definite pattern in Luke's presentation of his material. This pattern has two aspects. First, the Gentiles whom he does describe as becoming Christian are almost exclusively drawn from among the ranks of the God-fearers. There is not a single example in Acts of the conversion of a Gentile who has definitely been an idolater previously. Secondly, the meaning of the mission to the Gentiles is not primarily that they have become an object of evangelistic endeavour instead of the Jews, but that table-fellowship in Christ's name may now be established between them and the Jews. Before drawing conclusions for the composition of Luke's community from these remarkable results, it is necessary to be sure that this pattern does not merely reflect the historical experience of early Christianity. Hard evidence as to the actual composition of the first generation of Christian communities is only to be found in Paul's letters and even here it is in rather short supply. Nevertheless, comparison with the Pauline data does confirm what historical probability would in any event lead us to suspect: namely, that Luke's so strangely uniform and idealistic portrayal of the first Christian congregations is not an accurate reflection of the historical reality of their origins.

The very different picture of early Christian evangelism observable in Paul's letters has recently been discussed by W. A. Meeks in *The First Urban Christians*. Meeks makes some interesting observations on how Christian evangelists would have begun preaching the gospel in a new city. Their first task was to establish contacts, and this was normally done by meeting fellow-expatriates or fellow-practitioners of whatever trade they might pursue.[65] Once this was done, the evangelists could rely on the rumour-mill of crowded Hellenistic cities to attract the curious to listen to their preaching. It is apparent that Gentiles drawn to the gospel in this fashion would be very little different from their neighbours; in particular, we would expect them to have a typically pagan attachment to idolatry. For converts such as these the expression 'to turn to God from idols', used by Paul of his addressees in 1 Thess 1.9, would be an apt description of the conversion process. Yet, as we have just seen, the outstanding feature of the Gentiles whose conversion is related in Acts resides precisely in the fact that virtually none of them turns from idolatry to Christianity or first encounters the gospel in the shops of the artisans or in the market-place.

Meeks also notes that the pattern in Acts of beginning the mission in the synagogue accords ill with Paul's own declarations that he saw his mission as primarily or even exclusively to the Gentiles (Gal 1.16; 2.7–9; Rom 1.5, 13–15; 11.13ff.; 15.15–21). Meeks concedes, of course, that such statements are not to be taken absolutely; Paul's becoming 'as a Jew to the Jews, to win Jews' (1 Cor 9.20) is not merely rhetorical, because if he had never been in contact with synagogues he would not have 'five times ... received at the hands of the Jews the forty lashes less one' (2 Cor 11.24). Nevertheless, Paul's policy as he himself describes it is very different from the way it is portrayed in Acts. Apart from the floggings just mentioned, there is not a word about synagogues.[66] It appears from 1 Thess 2.9 that Paul also evangelized where he worked, but this is not the way the mission was fostered in Acts. In Corinth, for example, Paul practised tent-making with Aquila, but evangelized in the synagogue (Acts 18.1–4). Put briefly, the historical Paul occasionally used the Jewish connection in his evangelizing, but preferred to rely on other networks, whereas the Paul of Acts almost invariably utilized the synagogue as his springboard for the mission in each of the Eastern cities.

This confirms that Luke has shaped his version of the early days of Christianity, either by modifying a source where one was available, or by creating his own account where one was not. A revealing example of this process is his depiction of the mission at Thessalonika (17.1–4), against which we may set, as an historical control, the facts as they appear in 1 Thess. According to Luke, the first community in this city was composed solely of Jews and Gentile God-fearers; there is no mention of ex-idolaters being members. Furthermore, Luke relates how the other Jews were resentful at Paul's success and stirred up the city against the Christians (17.5–9). On the other hand, the addressees of Paul's letter to the Thessalonians were idolaters prior to their conversion (1 Thess 1.9). Moreover, the opposition to the Thessalonian Christians addressed by Paul had come from their own fellow-countrymen, not from the Jews, as is clear from 1 Thess 2.14.

Comparison of the Lucan picture of the spread of Christianity around the cities of the Roman East with that provided in the Pauline epistles inevitably casts the gravest doubt on the current orthodoxy regarding Luke's community. Given the working hypothesis, widely accepted among New Testament scholars and repeatedly confirmed in this book, that Luke shapes the history of first-generation Christianity to speak to the concerns of his own contemporaries, we must ask why he would present the authorization and origins of the extension of the gospel to the Gentiles in such a way as to cast a shadow of illegitimacy over any Gentiles who had been idolaters, if people such as these constituted the predominant group in his own community. Any ex-idolaters in Luke's audience would hardly have derived an integrating sense of connection with the Christian *Urzeit* from his version of its history. No, Luke's programmatic bias in favour of Gentile God-fearers and almost total omission of ex-idolaters from the early congregations are most plausibly explained as a modification of the historical facts, designed to accord with the composition of his own community, in particular with the fact that its Gentile members, or a significant proportion of them, had been adherents of Yahweh and synagogue-attenders prior to their becoming Christians.

Yet it was not only devout Gentiles that Luke's congregation had received from the Diaspora synagogue; there were also Jews. The argument just outlined for the existence of the first group within his community works equally well for Jews. Throughout the course of Acts, the Christian evangelists who preached in the synagogues are described as winning converts among Jews as well as God-fearers. It does appear that there were fewer Jewish converts than Gentile and that some Jews rejected the gospel, often with great violence. Nevertheless, in virtually every locus of evangelism a number of Jews did come over to Christianity. Had not God told Ananias, after all, that he was sending him to baptize the blind Paul, who was to carry his name 'before Gentiles, kings and Israelites' (Acts 9.15)? Accordingly, the argument for assuming God-fearers to have been a significant component in Luke's community applies also to the Jews. We recall our earlier interpretation of the Parable of the Great Banquet in Lk 14.16–24, to the effect that the first group of new guests were poor or sinful Jews and the second were Gentiles. We may take this as an accurate picture of the membership of Luke's local congregation.

When one remembers that Luke–Acts was probably written between 85 and 95 CE, it is difficult to imagine how New Testament scholars could ever have come to discount the possibility of a significant Jewish presence among Luke's audience. Some of the Jews who became members of Christian congregations in the forties of the first century CE may have been about sixty years old when Luke–Acts was written. Moreover, they may have had children, including circumcised sons, at the time of their conversion who would only have been middle-aged when Luke was writing. After all, the children of the first converts are explicitly included within the new dispensation by Peter in his first speech (Acts 2.39). In commenting upon 1 Peter, J. H. Elliott adopts a position similar to this; given that 1 Peter was written somewhere between 69 and 96 CE, he finds it impossible to accept that Jews would have disappeared from the Christian congregations of Asia Minor, leaving an all Gentile audience.[67]

In view of this it is quite beside the point for S. G. Wilson to assert: 'It was almost certainly a predominantly Gentile church. The influx of Jews had ceased long before ...'[68] For while a split between the Christian congregations and institutionalized Judaism had very probably taken place by the time Luke−Acts was published (see Chapter 3 below) and evangelism in the synagogue had ceased, Luke's community must still have contained a significant number of Jews. They may well have been ostracized by their fellow-Jews for endangering Jewish ethnic identity by sharing table-fellowship with Gentiles (see Chapter 4 below) and they may even have been the target of a Jewish campaign to have them abandon the Christian community. Faced with such pressures, they must have required considerable reassurance that their decision to convert, even if it had been taken long before, had been the correct one. One of the aims Luke had was to provide such reassurance − or, to use the language of the model outlined in Chapter 1 above, 'legitimation' − to the Jewish members of his community.

Interesting confirmation of a synagogue background for Luke and his audience is provided by the pronounced use of Septuagintal expressions throughout his two books.[69] Although this is too complex a topic to be investigated here, it is worth noting that F. L. Horton has recently argued that Luke's Septuagintal style may well reflect a special form of Greek employed during synagogue services but not in everyday discourse among Jews of the time.[70] Thus, Luke's use of such language and his apparent expectation that it would be appreciated by his audience may reflect the fact that both he and his readers were familiar with Septuagintal Greek from their previous association with the synagogue.

3

SECTARIAN STRATEGIES

1. Introduction

There is a growing awareness today of the benefits which flow to New Testament studies from viewing early Christianity as a sectarian movement in some way comparable to other such movements, both from our own time and from previous historical periods, whose beliefs and practices have been investigated by historians, anthropologists and sociologists. This is, however, a fairly recent development in New Testament scholarship. In fact, the palm for the first methodologically conscious and detailed attempt to apply contemporary sociological studies of sectarianism to early Christianity goes to Robin Scroggs for an essay published as late as 1975.[1] Since then some New Testament scholars have begun using sectarian perspectives with growing sophistication and effect.[2] Several other writers have picked up the sectarian theme, even if their appropriation of the relevant sociological insights is far more tentative.[3]

Given this continuing hesitation as to the need, and uncertainty as to the means, for studying early Christianity as a sect, it is necessary to begin this treatment of the sectarian strategies in Luke–Acts with an outline of the sociological ideas which will be employed. The broad line argued in this book is that Luke's unique presentation of his material constitutes a symbolic universe designed to legitimate for the Christians of his community the new movement of which they were members. The investigation carried out in this chapter, and repeatedly picked up later, is of central importance to this broad argument because of our belief that many of the most prominent features of his theology ultimately stem from and reflect the powerful tensions, social and political as much as religious, which accompanied the emergence from Judaism of that form of Christianity adhered to by the members of his community. The phrase 'sectarian strategies' has, accordingly, been adopted as the title for this chapter because, as will

emerge below, socio-redactional analysis reveals that so many characteristic features of the text have been carefully formulated by Luke
to help his community cope with the pressures upon them as a result
of their sectarian status in relation to Judaism and the Hellenistic
world at large.

2. The sociology of sectarianism: typology and model

In Chapter 1 we foreshadowed that the distinction between 'church'
and 'sect', as understood by modern sociologists, would play an
important role in our understanding of the position of Luke's community, and it is now time to elaborate upon this distinction and
related aspects of sectarianism. Our discussion begins with some views
expressed by Max Weber in an essay published in 1915, in which he
argued that the fact that some individuals were differently qualified
in a religious way stood at the beginning of the history of religion.[4]
Some individuals, such as shamans, sorcerers, ascetics, pneumatics
and sectarians were characterized by 'heroic' or 'virtuoso' religiosity,
the rest by 'mass' religiosity — the latter term covering those whom
he described as religiously 'unmusical'. He thought that heroic
religiosity was frequently to be found in 'sects', that is, 'associations
that accept only religiously qualified persons in their midst'. On the
other hand, mass religiosity was usually located within a 'church',
that is, 'a community organized by officials into an institution which
bestows gifts of grace'.[5] The terms 'church' and 'sect' are, of course,
not descriptions of empirical data but ideal or constructed types in
the sense discussed in Chapter 1 above. Weber thought that between
church and sect there was an inevitable conflict:

> For the church, being the holder of institutionalized grace,
> seeks to organize the religiosity of the masses and to put its
> own officially monopolized and mediated sacred values in
> the place of the autonomous and religious status qualifica-
> tions of the religious virtuosos.[6]

Some of the examples he gives of this tension are the opposition of
early Christian bishops to pneumatics, of the Russian state church
to sects, and of the official management of the Confucian cult to
Buddhist, Taoist and sectarian pursuits of salvation of all sorts. Thus
Weber's treatment of the church—sect distinction was not restricted
to Christian cultures, and it is argued below that another case which
fits into this scheme is the reaction of first-century Judaism to

Christianity in Palestine and even within the Diaspora cities where the Jewish communities often had separate legal status as *politeumata*.[7]

It was Ernst Troeltsch, however, rather than Weber, who generated what has become the classic formulation of the church—sect distinction. It is worthwhile to summarize briefly how he contrasted these two types of religious movement.[8] As for their attitudes to the world, a church largely accepts the secular order in which it is located and is a conservative force in society, while the attitude of a sect to society and the state may be indifferent, tolerant or hostile. As for the question of recruitment, a church draws members from all strata in society, but is often particularly allied to, and dependent upon, the upper classes, whereas a sect recruits predominantly among the lower classes. Initiation into a church occurs simply by virtue of an individual being born into it, but one is initiated into a sect on the basis of a conscious conversion. On the issue of the scope of salvation, a church seeks to embrace the whole world within its apparatus of redemption, while a sect offers salvation to the small group of the elect who comprise its membership. A church teaches that there is an objective treasury of grace in its hierarchy, priesthood and sacraments, whereas sects tend to be anti-sacramental, anti-clerical and anti-hierarchical. As for methods of organization, finally, a church is a large, hierarchically organized institution, but a sect is composed of small, largely autonomous groups. Implicit in these typological contrasts, but perhaps not sufficiently emphasized by Troeltsch, is the fact that sects, at least in a Western and Christian context, normally require exclusivity of commitment, that is, they do not admit of dual allegiance.[9]

A significant problem with Troeltsch's typology, raised by B. R. Wilson, is that in modern pluralist societies the usefulness of contrasting church with sect has greatly diminished, even in countries in which a particular church is established. The reason for this is that sects do not normally arise today in schism form, or in protest against, existing churches. In general, contemporary sects spring up among those who are outside the churches or have little involvement with them.[10] This inevitably means that the element of protest which continues to characterize sects is directed not so much against the church, as commonly in the medieval Europe upon which Troeltsch focused his attention, but 'against the secular society, and, in some measure, possibly also against the state'.[11] While this is a valuable criticism, it does not preclude application of the typology to the beginnings of Christianity, which did originate from within Judaism and did constitute, at least in part, a protest against various features of that 'church'. Nevertheless, Wilson's observation alerts us to the need for giving more careful attention to the attitudes of Luke's community to society and the state than in Troeltsch's typology. Attention to such issues is also demanded, it will be recalled, by the model of legitimation presented in Chapter 1 above, especially in view of the likely alliance between a religious establishment and the political authorities to suppress a new religious movement.

Because the position of his community with respect to society and the state, as well as to Judaism, is such a critical question for Luke, we are profitably able to enrich the sectarian side of Troeltsch's church–sect distinction by bringing to bear on the data in the text Wilson's widely influential sectarian typology. 'The sectarian movement', he writes, 'always manifests some degree of tension with the world, and it is the type of tension and the ways in which it is contained or maintained that are of particular importance.'[12] From a consideration of a very wide sample of sectarianism, some of it beyond the influence of orthodox Christianity, Wilson has generated a typology which details seven modes of containing or maintaining this tension, or, as he calls them, seven sectarian 'responses to the world'. Four of these must be introduced here, to pave the way for what follows.[13] The *conversionist* response, which is highly relevant to Luke–Acts and to other New Testament texts, rests upon the belief that the world is corrupt because individuals are corrupt and if individuals can be changed the world will be changed. Salvation is seen as a profoundly felt, supernaturally wrought transformation of the self, although the transformation will normally only be possible on the promise of a change in external reality at some future time or the prospect of the individual's transfer to another sphere. The *revolutionist* response, secondly, is to declare that evil is so rampant that only the destruction of the existing natural and social order will suffice to save humanity. Often this destruction, which will be effected by a god or gods and will be followed by a new state of salvation for some, is perceived as being imminent. Such a response is typical of millennarian movements and sects. The third response, labelled *introversionist*, is to see the world as irredeemably evil and salvation as attainable only by the fullest possible withdrawal from it. This may be an individual response, but as a response of a social movement it leads to the establishment of a separated community preoccupied with its own holiness code and its means of inoculation from the wider society. The *thaumaturgical* response, fourthly, is characterized by the individual's concern with relief from present and specific ills by magic. Here, the demand for supernatural assistance is personal and local.

It is important to realize that Wilson explicitly disclaims the notion that his seven types of responses will always appear in any high degree of purity in the real world.[14] It is quite possible that one religious movement may contain features from more than one of the types. To cite an example from the New Testament period, the monks of Qumran were 'introversionist' in their desire for isolation from Judaism in general and 'revolutionist' in their belief that the existing social order was about to come to a calamitous end. In examining the Christianity of Luke's community we will have occasion to draw upon several of these features.

We are now equipped with a typological apparatus for instituting precise comparisons with the data in Luke–Acts: a combination of Troeltsch's typology for the broad church–sect question and Wilson's typology for a more detailed and precise examination of the variety of sectarian responses in the text. This appears to be the first occasion on which this procedure has been adopted with respect to Luke–Acts, although there are eminent precedents for the desirability of the exercise in the writings of J. H. Elliott and W. A. Meeks on 1 Peter and Pauline Christianity respectively.[15]

It is a point of the highest importance, however, that a typological apparatus is not in itself a sufficient sociological input to make the most of a socio-redactional analysis of Luke–Acts. Typologies merely classify phenomena into certain accentuated categories for the purpose of allowing comparisons with empirical data; they do not specify what may be expected of mixed cases falling between the types, nor can they explain or predict development from one type to another. Typologies have no diachronic function. As applied to an historical work, this means that although a typology may be used in comparison with the facts at this or that time in the relevant period, it has no role whatsoever in explicating how one factual situation led to another. Thus, as far as Luke–Acts is concerned, we shall soon see the usefulness of applying our typological apparatus, first, to the situation of Luke's community at the time he was writing and, later, to that of the first community in Jerusalem; but on the question of how the first community developed into the second, our typology can, of its very nature, have nothing to say. This is a task for a model, a related group of conceptualized phenomena with a 'mechanism', an inner dynamic, which has an explanatory and predictive function.

One of the early attempts to construct a model for sectarian development was made by H. Richard Neibuhr, who envisaged that, over time, sects would develop into churches.[16] One critical reaction to this model, raising an issue picked up below, has come from B. R. Wilson, who has pointed out that many contemporaneous sects remain sects and do not develop into churches, even with the passage of several generations.[17] Revolutionist groups like the Jehovah's Witnesses, for example, maintain their millennarian fervour over long periods and do not accommodate themselves to society in the way suggested by Niebuhr's model. Wilson's criticism does not, however, invalidate the model, it merely demonstrates that its area of application is narrower than Niebuhr may have thought.

It is a somewhat unfortunate feature of modern sociological investigation of sects and related phenomena that very little attention has been given to the process by which a reform or renewal group within a church manages to continue to exist within the church or attracts such opposition that it secedes or is expelled, thereby acquiring sectarian status. Much work has been done on the background social conditions which might precipitate sectarian development, but the actual mechanics of the process, except to the extent that they involve a charismatic leader in the Weberian mould,[18] are rarely considered and no model has been formulated to explain them. This would appear to be a serious theoretical obstacle to a sociological approach to Luke–Acts, which contains abundant data relating to the beginnings of Christianity as a movement or party within Judaism and its gradual estrangement from that faith, at least in its institutional form.

Fortunately, however, there is one work which offers invaluable material on the development of internal religious movements into sects which may be used for making 'distant comparisons' (explained in Chapter 1 above) with Luke–Acts: namely, David Barrett's *Schism and Renewal in Africa*.[19] This book deals with the phenomenon of 'independency' in Africa, the fact that during the last one hundred years schisms from mission churches on that continent have been taking place at an unprecedented rate, so that by 1967 there were some 5,000 distinct ecclesiastical bodies which had arisen in this way. But in addition to the groups which had split away from the missions, there were approximately 1,000 reform, renewal or revival movements still within the missionary churches. Moreover, most of the 5,000 independent groups began their existence as movements within the churches. Much of Barrett's book is concerned with generating a multi-causal theory to explain this phenomenon, and most of the causal factors he advocates relate to the tribal nature of African society and the impact and results of missionary activity upon it. Obviously, such factors are far removed from the social context of the origins of Christianity. Nevertheless, the recurrent features which characterize the passage of a reform movement within a church to an independent religious group, sectarian in nature, outside that church are comparable to the development of Christianity as it is presented in Luke–Acts.

The impulse towards independency presupposes a 'vast reservoir of dissatisfaction with the religious *status quo*' (Barrett, p. 34), a feeling of deprivation caused by intense socio-religious strains induced in African society by what are perceived to be attacks by the missionaries upon its traditional structures, such as the family. At this point there emerges a leadership with a major innovating idea capable of tapping this feeling of dissatisfaction and launching a movement of protest, renewal or reform. This is the function of a charismatic personality in the Weberian sense,[20] a visionary, seer or prophet (p. 218) who is able to understand the unhappiness of his co-religionists, articulate a convincing response to it and gather around him a group of loyal supporters.

It is virtually inevitable that such a movement will be a cause of tension in the missionary church in which it arose. This is so because it will always, at least to a certain extent, be characterized by new attitudes, new idioms and new ventures of faith which will be highly disturbing to other members of the church (p. 183), especially conservative African pastors, superintendents or bishops (p. 219), whose position and status are tied to the existing *status quo*.

Nevertheless, these reform movements do not always break with their parent churches; the Jamaa (Family) charismatic movement, for example, was begun in 1945 among the Luba of Katanga, but despite its many unorthodox features its 20,000 adherents have almost entirely remained within the Roman Catholic church because of sympathetic treatment by the missionaries. On the other hand, some movements split away almost immediately from their parent churches. The most usual course is for a movement to exist for what may be a considerable period of time, even twenty years, before splitting off from the church.

A reform movement may become independent of its own accord, by secession, or it may be expelled by its mother church. In either case, however, there is often a strong element of the fortuitous in the whole process. The dissidents tend, of course, to cause increasing discomfort and consequent hostility among the conservative and nominal ranks of the church (p. 222), but the flashpoint, when the movement departs, is frequently due to an unfortunate train of misunderstandings and circumstances, originally unintended and unforeseen by both sides (p. 182). Often the exodus of the reformers is precipitated by a changed attitude on the part of the church, the leaders of which have grown impatient with the unorthodoxy of the movement and attempt to control or institutionalize its work of renewal (pp. 214–15, 222).

On some occasions, part of a renewal movement actually remains within a church while the rest secedes. When the bulk of the Soatanana revival seceded from the Lutheran church in Madagascar in 1955, for example, 10% of those involved stayed behind within the church.

Following secession, the church often moves to cut off outside aid, including personnel and financial support, from the seceding group, to exert pressure upon the dissidents in order to force them back into the fold (p. 164). Furthermore, both parties tend to engage in a campaign of invective and this aggravates the situation and hardens the breach, eventually past the point of no return (p. 220). The churches even invoke the arm of the law and since 1700 a startlingly large and steadily mounting roll of charismatic leaders have been dealt with by the state.

3. Sectarian strategies in Luke – Acts

Church and sect

The threshold question for the usefulness of these sociological ideas in discovering Luke's intentions and strategies is whether his community can be regarded as sectarian along the lines set out in Troeltsch's church–sect typology. In answering this question one must always remember that to be able to designate a religious phenomenon 'sectarian' is not an end in itself, as one might gather, for example, from Robin Scroggs' 1975 essay 'The Earliest Christian Communities as Sectarian Movement'.[21] A typology is not a set of pigeon-holes into which empirical data are to be slotted.[22] Nevertheless, it is a necessary prerequisite to the fruitful application of sociological ideas to establish that the typologies and models sought to be employed are in fact relevant to the data under investigation. And even during this preliminary process questions may arise which can be dealt with subsequently.

Is there, accordingly, a close enough 'fit' between Troeltsch's typology and what can be determined as to the status of Luke's community to make the sociological exercise worthwhile? It should be noted at the outset that this is yet another area where one must attempt the difficult, but not impossible, task of differentiating between the dramatic time of the events in the narrative and the time in which Luke was writing. An appropriate place to begin is with Paul's prophetic address to the Ephesian elders in Acts 20.17–35. We have noted previously that this is one of the places where one feels most immediately that Luke is speaking to the present of his own community, especially with respect to the troubles that are besetting it from within and without. We have also mentioned the interesting fact that the community is referred to as a flock (20.28, 29), which recalls Jesus' exhortation 'Do not fear, little flock, for the Father has been pleased to give you the Kingdom' (Lk 12.32). From this image we understand that the Christians are gathered in small congregations with recognizable boundaries between themselves and non-Christians. In Acts 20.28 Luke actually equates the flock and that peculiarly Christian form of association, the *ekklesia*, and specifically distinguishes this from the synagogue by reading *ekklesia* instead of *synagoge*, which occurs in the Septuagintal passage alluded to in the verse.[23] The church at Ephesus was led by elders (*presbyteroi*), and this form of ecclesiastical organization was no doubt operative in Luke's own community.[24] The Christian communities of the eighties and nineties of the first century CE were, moreover, largely self-governing.[25] From these details one may conclude that Luke's community was small, essentially autonomous, lacking a rigid hierarchical organization[26] and that it had a separate identity *vis-à-vis* Judaism, as required by Troeltsch's typology.

Nevertheless, these correspondences are not sufficient to establish the applicability of the typology to Luke–Acts, for the reason that we have yet to establish that dual membership of a Christian community and the local synagogue had become very difficult, if not impossible, for a Christian. After all, the early community in Jerusalem was not very different from Luke's in size, autonomy and leadership and its members were distinguishable from ordinary Jews by virtue of their Messianic beliefs and by the experience of baptism and eucharistic table-fellowship; yet many of the early Christians still regarded themselves as fully a part of the Jewish people, as shown by their participation in the Temple cult. To this extent the early community in Jerusalem was like the reform movements which exist within African missionary churches before they become independent, in the manner already described.

The primary issue, therefore, is to demonstrate that the members of Luke's community were characterized by exclusivity of commitment to it, in other words, that a simultaneous allegiance to the synagogue, which has been accurately described by W. Schrage as the national and religious fellowship of the Jews,[27] was either difficult or even impossible.

There is evidence elsewhere in the New Testament for Christians being excluded from the synagogue. The Gospel of John, in particular, contains the clearest sign of a definite Jewish policy of expelling anyone from the synagogue who confessed Christ, in the repeated use of the word ἀποσυνάγωγος (Jn 9.22; 12.42; 16.2). On the other hand, it is unlikely that such a decisive separation was effected through the use of the *birkath ha-minim*, the curse against heretics which was inserted into the Thirteen Benedictions late in the first century CE, possibly as early as 80 CE.[28] This curse appears as the twelfth benediction in the Palestinian Recension and runs, as far as is relevant here: 'And may the Nazarenes and the heretics [*minim*] perish quickly; and may they be erased from the Book of Life.'[29] Many scholars, such as W. Schrage and J.L. Martyn,[30] argue that once this curse had been inserted in what was the daily prayer of every Jew, continued attendance at the local synagogue by Christians would have become impossible, since the non-Christian members of the congregation would have been very careful to ensure that this benediction was uttered properly and without abbreviation. In fact, as W. Horbury has pointed out in an excellent article on the subject, the incidental exclusion of heretical prayer-leaders by means of the *birkath ha-minim*, even if they were accompanied by other members of the congregation, falls far short of the Johannine grievance.[31] The view taken by Horbury, which is accepted here, is that although the *birkath ha-minim* was in use around the end of the first century,[32] it simply reinforced a more drastic exclusion of Christians which had been carried out prior to, or at the same time as, the introduction of the curse.

But can it be shown that Luke's community had also been separated from the synagogue? Several features in the text suggest that such a separation had occurred. Horbury cites a series of reports in Acts which describe local Jewish opposition resulting in the withdrawal of Paul from the synagogue (Acts 18.7; 19.9) or his forced departure from town (13.50; 17.10, 17) and notes that at Lk 6.22 ostracism is expected generally.[33] Although, as J.L. Martyn has noted,[34] features such as these do not go as far as the bitterly felt expulsion in John's Gospel, this does not mean that an irrevocable split had not occurred between Luke's community and Judaism. If this split had only taken place in the recent past of his community, Luke could surely have decided that it would have been far too glaring an anachronism to insert into his narrative an event known by his readers to have happened much later. There is other evidence in Luke–Acts, however, to indicate that there had been a decisive enough break with Judaism to make the possibility of his Christian contemporaries also having frequented the synagogue most unlikely.

One important piece of evidence for this separation occurs in Lk 4.28–30. These verses describe how the congregation in the synagogue of Nazareth attempt to kill Jesus by casting him down a cliff, but he escapes through their midst. What the Nazarenes intended for Jesus was plainly a lynching, although the manner of death may have reflected the procedure for a stoning carried out in accordance with Jewish law.[35] This incident forms the climax of the passage describing the inaugural preaching of Jesus' ministry and its reception by the Jews of Nazareth (Lk 4.16–30). We have already shown in Chapter 2 above that Lk 4.16–30 does have the programmatic function in Luke–Acts widely ascribed to it, but to a far greater degree than has hitherto been realized. The message of salvation which Jesus quotes from Isaiah (4.18–19) is regarded by Luke as being fulfilled in the 'today' of his own community, not just in that of the congregation of Nazareth. The whole passage refers forward to the time when the rejection of Jesus at Nazareth has been matched by his rejection by a large part of Israel and when the message of salvation has been extended to Gentiles, rich and poor alike – in other words, to the time of Luke's own community.

The significant question for the present is why the hostility of the Jews in Nazareth takes such an extreme form. Why does Luke describe them as having attempted to murder Jesus the very first time that he opens his mouth in public? It is very strange that so singular an event as this has stirred barely an eddy in Lucan scholarship. The possibility that Luke is merely reporting historical fact should probably be rejected; Lk 4.28–30 are so indelibly stamped with Lucan stylistic features as to suggest that Luke created this incident, rather than reported an earlier tradition based on historical fact.[36] If we assume that there is no historical background to this incident, the most plausible explanation for its inclusion in the text is that it reflects a problem which was of passionate and contemporary interest to the evangelist's audience. D.L. Tiede has also argued for Luke's presentation of the suffering and rejected prophet being a 'pointed commentary on his own time'.[37] The only particular problem troubling Luke's community which is likely to have induced him to rework the Marcan *Vorlage* of this incident, to include an attempt on Jesus' life, is extreme antagonism from the local synagogue.

But it is possible to suggest a context for the incident even more specific than this. Such assassination attempts were hardly a commonplace in the tradition. In fact, this is the only occasion in the Synoptic Gospels where the Jews try to do away with Jesus, apart from their plotting which leads to his crucifixion. The only parallels to this are in Jn 8.59 and 10.31. Both of the Johannine accounts are set in the Temple and describe attempts to stone Jesus, while Jn 8.59 is also similar to Lk 4.28–9 in that Jesus makes a surprising, possibly miraculous, escape from his attackers. For a New Testament author to attribute this degree of opposition by the Jews to Jesus indicates that there were feelings of intense antipathy between his Christian contemporaries and the local Jewish community. With John this antipathy has been caused by the actual exclusion of his audience from the synagogue. Although there is lacking in Luke–Acts the massive, sectarian introversion which one senses in John's Gospel, that Luke should also present the Jews as having the same murderous hostility towards Jesus is best explained as a reaction to the exclusion of his community from the synagogue or, at least, to a situation where it was seen as so estranged an institution as to make membership of it by Christians difficult or even impossible. Luke's interest in presenting such an estrangement to his readers is also evident in his account of Paul's first preaching, in the synagogue in Damascus immediately after his conversion (Acts 9.20–5). The Lucan version of this incident, culminating in Paul's escape from a Jewish plot to kill him, diverges from Paul's own account[38] and has a very similar pattern to the rejection of Jesus at Nazareth.[39] In both cases the depiction of Jewish hostility is part of the symbolic universe created by Luke to legitimate the decisive cleavage which had occurred between his community (many of whose members were Jews and God-fearers) and the local synagogue.

Finally, the conclusion of Acts (28.23ff.) goes some way to confirming these arguments for a decisive rupture between *ekklesia* and synagogue. This is not because the last section of Acts is the third in a series of incidents (the other two being 13.46ff. and 18.6ff.) describing Jewish rejection of the Gospel which, when taken together, indicate that church and synagogue had become separate entities by the time Luke came to write his Gospel and Acts. This interpretation, which is espoused by many Lucan commentators,[40] is incompatible with the fact, explained in Chapter 4 below, that Acts 13.46ff. and 18.6ff. do not deal with the substitution of a Gentile mission for that among the Jews, but serve to legitimate table-fellowship between Jew and Gentile in the Christian community. Nevertheless, Acts 28.23–8 is a very prominent passage by virtue of its climactic position at the end of the work and for the reason that the length of Paul's quotation from Scripture in these verses is quite unique among his speeches in Acts. Given the Jewish–Gentile mix in Luke's community, the inclusion of this motif at the end of the work is best understood as indicative of an institutional split between church and synagogue, as well as being Luke's final salvo in his long campaign to legitimate Gentiles sharing the eucharist with Jews. It is worth noting here that the tensions inevitably produced in Luke's community by its members being excluded from the synagogue which they had once attended is the best explanation for an ambivalence in Luke's attitude to Judaism which J. L. Houlden has recently discussed but explained on other grounds.[41]

From these areas of evidence we conclude that Luke's fellow-Christians would have found simultaneous membership of the church and the local synagogue difficult or impossible, so that we have satisfied the final requirement for speaking of Luke's community as sectarian within the terms of Troeltsch's typology. In the chapters which follow a number of significant features of Luke–Acts will be shown to form part of the symbolic universe which Luke erects to secure the existence of his community in view of its sectarian relationship with Judaism.

Sectarian responses to the world

The second task in establishing the broad applicability to Luke–Acts of the sociological ideas on sectarianism outlined above is to determine the usefulness of Bryan Wilson's typology of sectarian responses to the world. Many features in the text testify to Luke's interest in the relationship between Christianity and the wider social and political system in which it was located. At the literary level, for example, Luke's appropriation of Hellenistic prose style and historiographical techniques[42] indicates a sensitivity to the wider cultural context which is unique among New Testament writers. Secondly, he presents Christianity as being a significant historical phenomenon by the introduction, for example, of synchronisms setting the beginnings of the Christian era within the wider history of the period, especially of imperial Rome (Lk 1.5; 2.1–2; 3.1–2). As Paul tells Festus: 'These things were not done in a corner' (Acts 26.26). More importantly, however, Luke reveals an acute sensitivity to the status of Christianity in the eyes of Roman political, military and judicial authorities, for reasons explained in Chapter 8 below.

Since these features in the text confirm that Bryan Wilson's phrase 'response to the world' is an appropriate designation for a significant area of data in Luke–Acts, we must now proceed to consider the particular response or responses within Wilson's typology most suitable to the work. Three types of response, the thaumaturgic, the conversionist and the revolutionist, seem relevant. As for the first, there are a number of places in the work where Luke explicitly asserts the superiority of the gospel over thaumaturgic solutions to the difficulties of human existence. Cases in point are the incidents in Acts involving Simon Magus (8.9–13, 18–24), Elymas, the Jewish sorcerer in Paphos (13.6–12) and the burning of the books of magic at Ephesus (19.19). On the other hand, Luke himself occasionally includes a reference to a type of Christian healing which sails perilously close to thaumaturgy. The cures effected by the application of Paul's scarves and handkerchiefs in Ephesus (Acts 19.12) fall within this category. Nevertheless, this type of miracle is far too insignificant in Luke–Acts to displace Luke's anti-thaumaturgic theme.

The relevance of the conversionist response to Luke–Acts is self-evident, in view of its author's preoccupation with individual penance and acceptance of the Gospel in baptism,[43] which enable the believer to enter a zone of Spirit-filled experience during the period before the final consummation to be inaugurated by the returning Son of Man. But what of the revolutionist response? To what extent can that be observed in Luke–Acts? In the first century CE, when the prevailing social and economic conditions under Roman rule had produced a large degree of unrest among the population of Palestine,[44] there were groups within Israel who believed that salvation was only possible (and, indeed, was about to occur) with the destruction of the political system which oppressed them and the re-establishment of the Kingdom of Israel. Such a response to the world is, of course, very close to the revolutionist type described by Bryan Wilson. An expression of the revolutionist response *par excellence* is found in the New Testament in Revelation, although it also outcrops in Mk 13 (even if Mark is using traditions characterized by an apocalyptic fervour greater than his own)[45] and in Acts 1.6, when the disciples ask Jesus when he will restore the Kingdom of Israel. It is well worth noting that every manifestation of the revolutionist response involves a measure of hostility to the established order of things, while in its more intense forms it exhibits a violent antipathy to the existing social and political order, an antipathy evident, for example, in the celebration of Rome's imminent and fiery destruction in Rev 17 and 18.

But did Luke see the revolutionist response as appropriate for his Christian contemporaries? Or, to pose the question in the terms of current theological discussion, does Luke–Acts reveal a belief by its author in an imminent End? In *Die Mitte der Zeit* Hans Conzelmann answered this question with a decisive 'no'. He argued that the Evangelist recast Christian traditions to eliminate expectation of an imminent End and that the factor which occasioned this was the anxiety of the church caused by the delay of the *parousia*. *Fernerwartung* had replaced *Naherwartung*. For Conzelmann, in fact, Luke's 'definite theological attitude to the problem of eschatology' was the primary motivation in the composition of Luke–Acts.[46]

Before considering whether Conzelmann was correct in attributing to Luke a desire to reduce the expectation among his fellow-Christians that the End was near, three significant points arising from this statement of his broad position must be canvassed. First of all, one must raise a query over Conzelmann's endeavour to interpret Luke's theology predominantly with respect to the question of eschatology. In this book we have adopted a very different approach: namely, of examining the extent to which Luke–Acts is explicable as the product of its author's desire to explain and justify Christian belief and practice to the members of his own community, especially in view of its sectarian status with respect to Judaism and the world at large. This approach offers a far greater opportunity to account for the rich variety of data in Luke–Acts, in particular those disclosing a Lucan sensitivity to the problem of how Christians relate to the synagogue and to political authority, than Conzelmann's focus upon the single issue of the frustration of apocalyptic expectation.

Secondly, it should be noted that the basic assumption underlying Conzelmann's thesis, that it is impossible to maintain a belief in an imminent *parousia* in the face of continued delay in its arrival, is demonstrably false. There are many sects, the Jehovah's Witnesses, for example, which maintain their apocalyptic fervour over long periods of time, even in the face of frequent disappointments when the End, often predicted as due on a particular date, does not occur. Even from the New Testament itself we have the example of

Revelation, which, although containing a very powerful expression of belief in an imminent End, was probably written late in the first century.[47]

The third issue concerns Conzelmann's insistence that Luke's attitude to the problem of eschatology was 'theological'. We began Chapter 1 by registering dissent from his view that Luke's theological interests are anterior to, and dictate, his attitudes on social and political questions. The problems inherent in Conzelmann's approach are very apparent in the area of eschatology, for a little reflection quickly discloses the possibility of Luke's eschatological beliefs being dependent upon the social and political situation of his community and not vice versa. In Chapter 8 below we shall argue that there were a number of Roman officials, either military or administrative, in Luke's community and that he was attentive to their special needs and circumstances. How would they have reacted if their community had experienced an outburst of apocalypticism similar to that in Rev 17 and 18? It is beyond question that this would have put them in the impossible situation where one consequence of their faith in Jesus Christ was that they were required to glory in, and even pray for, the early and cataclysmic overthrow of the political system of which they were, in all probability, loyal and dedicated servants. In other words, eschatology has profound social and political ramifications, and even where there was an apocalyptic attitude present in the community not nearly so extreme as that in Revelation the same problem would arise. To legitimate Christianity for Roman officials among his audience, Luke would have been forced either to tone down apocalyptic fervour, even if it had not already begun to fade with the passing years, or to lend his support to any existing inclination to regard the End as not imminent.[48] This consideration disposes us in favour of Conzelmann's argument that Luke did not believe in an imminent End, and to this particular issue we now turn.

In addition to the very fact, mentioned in Chapter 1 above, of Luke's choosing to write Acts as well as his Gospel, there are many other features in Luke–Acts which indicate its author's concern to dampen apocalyptic expectation. Some of the more notable may be ventilated here. First, Luke alters earlier traditions to eliminate the notion that the onset of the Kingdom of God was near at hand. He diverges from Mark, for example, by having Jesus begin his public ministry not with a proclamation that the Kingdom was near, but what it was like (Lk 4.18–21; cf. Mk 1.15). In addition, he deletes the expression 'come in power' from Mk 9.1 to inculcate a sense of the timelessness of the Kingdom (Lk 9.27). This theme is underlined by a number of direct disavowals that the Kingdom is near or that it is proper for a disciple to be interested in the time of its arrival (Lk 17.20; 19.11; Acts 1.6–7). Secondly, Luke extricates the events surrounding the destruction of Jerusalem from the context of the End in Lk 21 and considerably postpones the *parousia* by mentioning that it will be preceded by the 'ages of the Gentiles' (Lk 21.24). This may be connected with the future of the message of salvation among the Gentiles announced in Acts 28.28. Thirdly, there is a number of miscellaneous features with the same implication. Whereas Mark, for example, has Jesus tell the Sanhedrin that they will see 'the Son of Man seated at the right hand of the Power and coming with the clouds of Heaven' (Mk 14.62), Luke merely has 'from now on the Son of Man will be seated at the right hand of the Power of God' (Lk 22.69). In the Parable of the Vineyard and the Tenants Luke adds to his Marcan source that the owner went away 'for a long time' (Lk 20.9; Mk 12.1), and this surely reflects a belief in a delayed *parousia*. Lastly, the little-noticed fact that Mary tells Elisabeth 'from now on all generations [γενεαί] will call me blessed' (Lk 1.48) is incompatible with an imminent *parousia*, even if the Evangelist is using traditional material in the Magnificat.[49]

Although Conzelmann's belief in a postponed eschatology has found many supporters,[50] other scholars have continued to discern in Luke–Acts indications of an imminent end.[51] Most of the writers in this latter group do not deny that there is a delay theme in the work, but they insist that it is balanced by a Lucan retention of *Naherwartung*. R. H. Hiers, for example, proposes that Luke attempted to show that Jesus himself did not mistakenly preach an imminent *parousia*, but that Luke wished his readers to know that they were living in the last days.[52] On the other hand, S. G. Wilson,[53] who is followed to an extent by J. Ernst,[54] sees Luke adopting the *via media* of preserving a delay theme to counter a renewal of apocalypticism and an imminence theme to prevent a loss of faith and a lax morality.

When the textual evidence relied upon to support the imminence motif is examined, however, it falls far short of this result. First of all, Lk 9.27 cannot be taken as referring to an early *parousia*. We have already commented upon Luke's omission of the phrase 'come in power' which is predicated of the Kingdom in his Marcan source. Moreover, Luke may well have expected his readers to understand that the vision of the kingdom which Jesus promises his disciples in Lk 9.27 was basically identical with that vouchsafed to Stephen in

Acts 7.56 – a vision which would lessen the sufferings of martyrdom. Alternatively or in addition, Luke may have wanted his readers to understand by 9.27 that some of Jesus' onlookers would see the Kingdom as he had described it to the Nazarenes (Lk 4.18). Good news for the poor, sight for the blind, freedom for captives and remission for sins begin during the time of Jesus' ministry, but they become virtually constitutive of the Christian community after Pentecost. That is why Luke can have the Seventy (-Two) proclaim the nearness of the Kingdom in Lk 10.9, 11 without thereby suggesting to his readers that the End is nigh. For the Seventy (-Two) preach the nearness of the Kingdom specifically in the context of healing the sick, and Luke has already interpreted the onset of the Kingdom as, at least in part, providing specific forms of redemption in the present (Lk 4.18–21).

Secondly, a number of parables in Luke's Gospel have been cited as pointing towards an imminent *parousia*. The most notable of these are the Watchful Servants (12.35–48), the stories of Noah and Lot (17.26–32), the two women sleeping and the two grinding corn (17.34–7) and the Unjust Judge (18.1–8). None of these, however, refers to an End which will come soon; they refer rather to one which will come suddenly – 'on a day which one does not expect and at an hour which one does not know' (Lk 12.46). This is true even of the Parable of the Unjust Judge. Many advocates of *Naherwartung* in Luke–Acts fix upon the statement in 18.8a that God will vindicate his elect 'quickly' (ἐν τάχει) as supporting their case.[55] This is most unwise. The parable is expressly directed towards the need for continual prayer and for not losing heart (18.1) in view of the delay of the final consummation (18.7b). Like the judge, God appears to be failing to vindicate his people 'for a time' (ἐπὶ χρόνον) (18.4a). The point of the story is that vindication will come and that faith must be maintained in the interim (18.8b). Luke is not interested in offering his readers hope of an early resolution of their difficult situation, only in counselling them in how to endure it. The phrase ἐν τάχει moreover, can be interpreted just as properly as 'suddenly', with reference to the speedy *manner* of God's vindication, as it can as 'soon'.[56]

There is only one feature of the text which defenders of an imminence theme can reasonably urge in favour of their view: namely, Lk 21.32, where Jesus solemnly avers that 'this generation (ἡ γενεὰ αὕτη) will not pass away until all things [πάντα] are accomplished'. This verse would cause little difficulty if πάντα only referred to the destruction of Jerusalem (21.20–4), but it seems also to include the coming of the Son of Man (21.25–8). Is the Lucan Jesus therefore predicting that some of his onlookers will be alive to witness the *parousia*? If this were so, it need not necessarily have been an embarrassment to Luke, as is often assumed. If he was writing in the eighties or early nineties of the first century, young children in Jesus' audience might still have had a decade or two to go before they had reached the end of their threescore years and ten (Ps 90.10). This would have given the Evangelist some room for manoeuvre in opposing an early End. Against this interpretation, is the fact that it conflicts with Mary's reference to future generations in Lk 1.48 and with the sense of futurity evident in Lk 21.24 and at the end of Acts. Another solution to the problem involves a different interpretation of ἡ γενεὰ αὕτη. For Conzelmann, this means 'mankind in general'.[57] This is not the vapid explanation that it may at first appear, since, as G. Schneider observes,[58] the four verses which follow 21.32 speak of the necessity of constant watchfulness (as was stressed in the parables mentioned above) against a fate which will come 'to all who are seated upon the face of the earth' (21.35). The moral of 21.34–6 is the need for constant prayer in the period of waiting, not that the waiting will soon be over, just as was the case with the Parable of the Unjust Judge (18.1–8). Finally, even if all these explanations were to be rejected, so that 21.32 was held to contain a fragment of imminent expectation, we would be entitled to regard it as the only exception to an otherwise uniform Lucan presentation of a delayed *parousia*, possibly arising from an inadvertent retention of a logion in Mark. The final result of this consideration of the evidence, therefore, is to confirm Conzelmann's view that Luke has eliminated a belief in an early *parousia* from his presentation of the Christian story.

The foregoing discussion of Lucan eschatology was undertaken to determine whether the revolutionist response to the world could be said to have characterized Luke's community; in view of his pervasive substitution of *Fernerwartung* for *Naherwartung*, we may be quite sure that it did not. Given the presence of Roman officials within his community, Luke would have been forced to invent a doctrine of delayed *parousia* if it had not already become current among his contemporaries. But in presenting Christianity as a faith with a future as well as a past, a future apparently extending through several generations (Lk 1.48), Luke was attending to a wider range of interests in his community than those represented merely by its

Roman members. By his firm rejection of the apocalyptic strand in the early Christian tradition, Luke establishes the future element of the symbolic universe he is erecting and thereby sets up an historical continuity within which the biographies of all members of his community, Roman and non-Roman, acquire shape and meaning.

This question of historical continuity in Luke–Acts leads us into an assessment of the usefulness of the third aspect of our sociological perspective on sectarianism in Luke–Acts, David Barrett's model for the development of an intra-church reform movement into a sect.

From Jewish reform movement to Christian sect

We have already seen that the balance of evidence indicates that Luke's community had acquired a sectarian status in relationship to Judaism. Yet the picture which Luke paints in Acts of the early post-Easter community in Jerusalem, at least as far as the end of Chapter 5, is one which highlights the continuing commitment of all its members to Judaism, especially as reflected in their involvement in the Temple cult (2.46; 3.1) and their acceptance by a large number of Jews in the city (2.47), even if they were already encountering some opposition from the Sanhedrin (4.1–21; 5.17–40). In fact, the first community, as presented by Luke, was in many ways comparable to the intra-church reform movements analysed by David Barrett in the modern African context. Here was a group, initially from depressed rural Galilee,[59] who had gathered around a charismatic leader with a message which answered their deepest dissatisfactions and longings, travelled up to Jerusalem with him and then survived the profound shock caused by his death through the conviction that he had now risen from the dead and had poured out God's Spirit upon them. They had soon begun to attract a wide following from among other Jews in the city, and this inevitably produced antipathy among the Jewish authorities, who, like the officials in modern African churches, felt threatened by the erosion of their influence or, as Luke puts it, 'became filled with envy' (5.17).

This striking discrepancy between the position of the Christian community at the beginning of Acts and its inferred position at the time Luke composed the work leads us to pose the inevitable question: how did the separation from Judaism occur, or how did an intra-Jewish reform movement become a sect? One of the most notable features about Acts is the amount of data in the text relevant to answering this question. The difficulties which the followers of Jesus have in their dealings with Judaism, especially with its institutions, is one of the most prominent themes in the work – one of the few themes, in fact, which extends from its earliest chapters to its last. Given the dramatic date at which Luke chose to end Acts, sometime in the early sixties of the first century CE, he was unable, without being guilty of very obvious anachronism, to include all the factors which led to the split. It was impossible for him to describe the immediate train of misunderstandings and circumstances which led to what David Barrett calls the 'flashpoint' being reached. The results of the Pharisaical tightening of the purity laws after 70 CE,[60] for example, had to be omitted.

But why should Luke have considered it important to publish a narrative with so much material bearing upon the early causes of the Christian–Jewish estrangement which by his time had become institutionalized? This question cannot be evaded by asserting that Luke was merely presenting the historical facts as he knew them and not just shaping history to emphasize this particular motif. The question would then become why Luke felt it necessary to record this particular history at all. For some scholars Luke's interest in this area has been motivated by a theological problem also evident in Paul's letters – how to incorporate within the divine plan the failure of Israel as a whole to respond to the Gospel.[61]

Another solution, and one which will be shown to account for the data in the text far better than this purely theological answer, begins with a consideration of some of the social realities of Luke's community. In Chapter 2 above we reached the conclusion, which is confirmed at numerous points throughout this book, that there was a significant number of Jews within Luke's community, while it is likely that many of its Gentile members had previously been in the habit of attending synagogue. Consider what would have been the effect on such persons of the split between church and Judaism. They were now excluded from the synagogue, that is to say, cut off from Israel in its primary institutional form. This must have been particularly painful for the Jewish Christians, since for them it represented a separation from their own *ethnos*, but it must also have weighed heavily upon the God-fearing Gentiles. That this experience was a cause of anguish can be seen in Luke's retention of the Q verse dealing with ostracism at Lk 6.22, in the depth of feeling present in his description of the attack on Jesus in Nazareth (4.29), in the heightening of the role of the Jewish leaders in the trial and death of Jesus[62] and in the frequent references to Jewish animosity towards Christian missionaries in Acts. External to Acts, one may cite the pain caused by exclusion from the synagogue which is very apparent in the Fourth Gospel and the Jewish action in banning Christians from synagogues, discussed above, which would not have been necessary if Christians had stopped attending synagogue of their own accord. Accordingly, there was an urgent need for Luke to overcome any anxieties and regrets over their ostracism which were troubling the members of his community. This may, indeed, have been a matter upon which Theophilus required ἀσφάλεια (Lk 1.4).

One obvious way to provide the necessary reassurance, to legitimate the sectarian status of his *ekklesia*, was for Luke to write a history of the beginnings of Christianity which pinned the blame for the subsequent split firmly on the Jews, especially their leaders, and which explained and justified early developments, such as Jewish–Gentile table-fellowship, which were still of significance to his Christian contemporaries. From this viewpoint, history is important for Luke not, as Conzelmann suggests, as a replacement for the imminent expectation of the early church,[63] but as a way of accounting for the present situation of his community. In other words, the key to Lucan historiography is not eschatology but etiology. This will become very apparent in Chapter 4 below, on table-fellowship.

But there is more to Luke's enlistment of history within his sectarian strategies than blaming the Jews for the breach between church and synagogue. It was suggested in Chapter 1 above that the defenders of a novel social order, especially in a traditional society, often attempt to legitimate it by claiming that it is actually old and established. Now there is little doubt that a high regard for traditional values and customs did characterize Greco-Roman and Palestinian society in the first century CE. This regard is reflected, for example, in the appeal Augustus made in his *Res Gestae Divi Augusti* and in the well-attested Jewish devotion to tradition. Can a Lucan interest in making use of this high estimation of ancestral values be detected in Luke–Acts? The answer is a categorical 'yes'. There is the strongest possible evidence for Luke's sensitivity to the notion that Christianity was a new faith in his redactional alteration of διδαχὴ καινή ('new teaching') at Mk 1.27 to ὁ λόγος οὗτος ('this message') at Lk 4.36. That he has nothing against the use of the word διδαχὴ is shown by the fact that he retains Mark's use of it just before this verse (Mk 1.22 and Lk 4.32). The ancestral theme actually comes to direct expression in a series of statements by Paul in the closing chapters of Acts, that he was strictly educated in 'the ancestral law' (22.3), that he serves 'the ancestral God' (24.14) and that he has done nothing against 'the ancestral customs' (28.17), to name only a few examples.

What is particularly interesting in discussing the motivation for Luke's historical impulse, however, is the realization that the ancestral theme is not merely something relied upon by Paul in an apologetic context, but is manifest throughout Luke–Acts in its author's pervasive desire to set Christianity within the history and traditions of Israel. The first two chapters of his Gospel, for example, are peopled by figures such as Zechariah and Elisabeth, Mary and Joseph, and Simeon and Anna, who are piously devoted to the traditions of their people and look forward in hope to the deliverance of Israel. Secondly, one notices the emphasis upon the extent to which Jesus is a fulfilment of Old Testament hope (Lk 4.16–30; 20.17; Acts 3.22–6; 4.11; 10.43; 13.23; 17.2–3; 28.23), just as his sufferings are in accordance with Old Testament expectation (Lk 18.31–4; 22.37; 24.25–7, 32; 24.44–9; Acts 2.25–8, 31; 3.17–18; 8.30–5; 13.27–39; 17.2–3; 26.22–3). Finally, it is worthwhile mentioning some of the many ways in which Luke underlines the continued association with, and dedication to, the Jewish faith exhibited by the early Christians, even after persecution had broken out against them (Acts 7–8). First of all, the names attributed by Christians to themselves and their movement in Acts nearly always denote a connection with, or even an intensification of, Judaism.[64] This is true of 'the disciples' and 'the brothers', the commonest terms for 'Christian' in Acts, 'the saints' (9.13, 32, 41; 26.10), 'the believers',[65] 'the saved' (2.47), the *ekklesia*, the origins of which are in Judaism,[66] even though it was used to differentiate the Christian assembly from the synagogue, 'the flock' (20.28) and 'the way' (16.17; 18.25, 26; 19.9, 23; 22.4; 24.14, 22). The only exception is 'the friends' (27.3), which appears to be a term from contemporary philosophy.[67] The Christians in Acts never specifically call themselves Χριστιανοί. Of the only two instances of the word (11.26; 26.28), it is unclear in the first if it is a self-designation, while the second falls from the lips of Agrippa. Etymological studies, such as that by H.D. Mattingly,[68] have failed in their object of showing that Χριστιανός was originally an opprobrious epithet, although the striking rarity of the word in early Christian literature certainly suggests that it was not a name eagerly accepted by Christians themselves.[69] The intra-Jewish status of Christians in Acts is also revealed in the names applied by them to Jews, such as Nazarenes (24.5) and even αἵρεσις (24.5, 14; 28.22). Translators very commonly construe αἵρεσις as 'sect'. Such a translation is quite inappropriate, however, within the sociological perspective adopted in this book, for the reason that the word is also applied in Acts to the Sadducees (5.17) and the Pharisees (15.5; 26.5), who are plainly parties or movements within Judaism and not sects whose members could no longer be said to belong to the wider Israel. As H. J. Cadbury notes,[70] Acts 24.14 suggests that Christians would disclaim the title αἵρεσις, but this may have been because it carried too philosophical a connotation, as can certainly be seen in the famous section in Josephus' *Jewish War*[71] where the author discusses the Essenes, Pharisees and Sadducees as philosophical schools and explicitly uses αἵρεσις with respect to the first two groups. The second sign of Luke's concern to indicate a continuing relationship between Christianity and Judaism is his portrayal of his great hero Paul as a punctilious observer of the Jewish law, a subject which is dealt with in Chapter 5 below. Thirdly, among a wide range of possible data, we conclude by noticing the extent to which resurrection is depicted as a belief already held among Jews, notably although not exclusively by the Pharisees (23.6–8; 24.14–15, 21; 26.6–8). The purpose of this is not to point to a possible bridge between Christianity and Pharisaism,[72] but to prove that this key Christian belief is rooted in the ancestral faith of the Jewish people.

From this examination, we conclude that central to Luke's composition of a unique history, which encompassed the Jesus story and its sequel in Acts, was an ardent desire to present Christianity as the legitimate development of Judaism. To account for this desire we must recall that the author's community contained significant numbers of Jews and Gentile God-fearers. It was largely for them, painfully excluded from the synagogue to which they had once belonged or which they had at least attended, that Luke fixed upon a legitimatory strategy which has often, both before and since, been adopted by the defenders of a new social order. He presented their new faith as if it were old and established, as the divinely sanctioned outgrowth of Judaism. It was impossible, of course, for Luke to deny that there were significant differences of belief between Christians and Jews or that the Christian faith was a recent arrival on the historical scene. His response was to interpret apparently novel features of Christianity, especially the belief in Jesus as the Messiah, as the fulfilment of promises long embedded in Jewish tradition. The notion of 'promise' (ἐπαγγελία) is a key concept for Luke, and the pervasive pattern of promise and fulfilment in his Gospel and Acts has often been noticed by scholars.[73] In other words, Judaism was a faith which carried within itself the seeds of its own transformation. So Luke could console his fellow-Christians with the message that it was not they but Jews still attending the synagogue who had abandoned the God of Abraham, Isaac and Jacob, of Moses and of David.

We shall see in Chapter 8 below that the ancestral theme also had a role to play in legitimating Christianity from a Roman perspective, by showing that it was not a new and revolutionary movement, but actually had ancient roots.

4

TABLE-FELLOWSHIP

1. Table-fellowship between Jews and Gentiles in Luke–Acts

One issue in Luke–Acts towers above all others as significant for the emergence and subsequent sectarian identity of the type of community for whom Luke wrote: namely, table-fellowship between Jews and Gentiles. An almost universal failure to appreciate the centrality of this phenomenon, both to Luke's history of Christian beginnings and to the life of his own community, is one of the most outstanding deficiencies in Lucan scholarship. It is a deficiency attributable to a methodology which is historical or theological or both, but which fails to enlist insights from the social sciences in an attempt to uncover crucial but largely unsuspected patterns of significance in the text. All Lucan commentators, of course, devote some attention to the account of the conversion of Cornelius in Acts 10 and to the Council of the Jerusalem church which discusses this event in Acts 11.1–18. Many of them even mention that Peter's fellow-apostles and disciples are concerned that he has entered a house inhabited by Gentiles and eaten with them (11.3). But this aspect of the incident is usually submerged in sweeping statements that the Cornelius account is intended to pave the way for 'the mission to the Gentiles', a catch-phrase beloved of writers on Luke and apparently expressive of his deepest intentions in the work.

There are several features in Luke–Acts which alert us to the fact that Jewish–Gentile table-fellowship had been a matter of intense controversy in the early church and was still of concern for Luke's contemporaries. The most obvious of these features is the conversion of Cornelius, but there are also the Apostolic Council in Acts 15 and the three occasions, discussed above in Chapter 2, on which Paul enjoyed the hospitality of Gentiles (16.14–15, 25–34; 18.7–11). We shall argue below that table-fellowship re-appears in Acts 27.

This phenomenon also led to the tremendous rift in Antioch described by Paul in Gal 2.11–14. There are, moreover, definite indications that the question was one which interested Mark and Matthew and therefore the communities for whom they composed their Gospels.

That our sources contain evidence of a conflict in the early church over the propriety or otherwise of Jews eating with Gentiles is of great assistance in applying a socio-redactional approach to the study of Luke's strategies and purpose. The reason for this has been well explained by Gerd Theissen. Sociological analysis interests itself in features of social situations which are usual and typical, which transcend the individual. Historical records, on the other hand, focus upon what is unusual and atypical, striking and unique. Accordingly, it is often difficult or even impossible to subject such records to sociological analysis. The importance of conflicts is that they are a form of social interaction which does figure prominently in historical records and is available for subsequent sociological examination:

> Among the unusual and singular events about which we have some knowledge, however, conflicts play a special role. Here the various customs of social groups collide with one another. In such circumstances the unusual actually sheds light on the ordinary, the dramatic conflict reveals the banal. If ever we can derive information about the social background of our historical traditions, it is through the analysis of such conflicts.[1]

Theissen himself has used the techniques of conflict analysis to great effect in his interpretation of the meaning of Paul's eucharistic teaching in his Corinthian correspondence.[2]

We must now attempt a socio-redaction analysis of the data in Luke–Acts relating to the question of Jewish–Gentile table-fellowship. We begin this with an essential discussion of how such a practice was viewed by the Jews of that period, without which it is impossible to estimate the nature of the pressures, social and ethnic as much as religious, which would be experienced by a community in which Jew sat down at table with Gentile. The result of this analysis will be to show that a theme which most writers on Luke regard as a minor one of mainly theological interest, actually has an all-important social significance as the central arch in the symbolic universe which Luke creates to legitimate the sectarian separation of his community from Judaism.

2. Jewish antipathy to dining with Gentiles

*The anthropological perspective: external threat and
purity laws*

Invaluable assistance in comprehending the significance of the Jewish
purity laws has been provided in recent years by the English anthropologists Mary Douglas and Edmund Leach, both of whom have
analysed various aspects of the Old Testament data on the subject.
In 1966 Mary Douglas published *Purity and Danger*. In Chapter 7
of that book, 'External Boundaries', she offers an explanation for
the interrelationships between the purity laws which a society,
especially Judaism, imposes on its individual members and the
external pressures experienced by that society as a whole. Her main
argument is that the human body is often used by a society as a symbol
of that society. Thus, the idea of society is a powerful image with
form, external boundaries, margins and internal structure. In all these
features it is matched by the human body, which is also a complex
structure, with definite boundaries and various parts having specific
yet interrelated functions.[3] The use of the body as symbolical of
society emerges most clearly when we see the dangers threatening a
particular social system from outside reproduced in miniature on the
human body. Accordingly, Mary Douglas strongly criticizes those
who suggest that the rituals of the human body dealing with the
avoidance of pollution are attributable to personal and private
concerns, especially of a psychopathic nature. Rather, she urges, 'to
understand body pollution we should try to argue back from the
known dangers of society to the known selection of bodily themes
and try to recognise what appositeness is there' (p. 121). In particular,
she proposes that rituals expressing concern about the body's orifices
and boundaries are a reflection of a care to protect the political and
cultural unity of a minority group. This was pre-eminently the case
with Israel:

> The Israelites were always in their history a hard-pressed
> minority. In their beliefs all the bodily issues were polluting,
> blood, pus, excreta, semen, etc. The threatened boundaries
> of their body politic would be well mirrored in their care for
> the integrity, unity and purity of the physical body.(p. 124)

Mary Douglas noted in *Purity and Danger* that there was a close
parallel to the Jewish concern for purity in the Hindu caste system.
Although this system embraces virtually all minorities, it embraces

them each as a distinctive, cultural sub-unit. In any particular locality, any sub-caste is likely to be a minority. And the purer and higher its caste status, the more of a minority it will be. 'Therefore the revulsion from touching corpses and excreta does not merely express the order of the caste in the system as a whole. The anxiety about bodily margins expresses danger to group survival' (p. 124). This view subsequently received strong indirect confirmation in Louis Dumont's *Homo Hierarchicus*, a magisterial study of the Indian caste system. In this work Dumont showed that the three essential aspects of the system (gradation of status or hierarchy, the detailed rules aimed at ensuring that separation, and division of labour) were reducible to a basic opposition between the pure and the impure.[4] There are many references in *Homo Hierarchicus* to members of specific sub-castes defining the barriers between themselves and other sub-castes by reference to particular measures of purity, especially relating to the consumption of food.[5]

The importance for the present discussion of Edmund Leach's essay 'The Legitimacy of Solomon', first published in 1966, is that it corroborates the view of Mary Douglas that the political and social problems which the Israelites experienced by virtue of their being surrounded by often hostile neighbours who disputed their title to the land were reflected in the Jewish purity regulations. Adopting the structuralist techniques of Lévi-Strauss for the Old Testament story of the succession of Solomon, Leach attempted, with a very high degree of success, to show that this story was a myth which mediated a major contradiction. On the one hand, there was the Jewish assertion of political title to the land of Palestine as a direct gift of God, which resulted in the rule of endogamy to ensure that the Jews should be a people of pure blood and pure religion living in isolation in the land, while on the other hand was the hard fact that the Jews had won the land by conquest and that to maintain the peace inter-marriage with their neighbours, exogamy, was often politically expedient.[6]

Nearly ten years after the appearance of *Purity and Danger* Mary Douglas published an essay, entitled 'Deciphering a Meal', in which she developed her earlier ideas on Jewish purity regulations with specific reference to the dietary laws.[7] One feature of her discussion is the proposal that the relevant data in the Old Testament reveal a congruence between the type of animals fit for the altar and for domestic tables and even between such animals and the humans who can enter the various parts of the Temple. She writes: 'It would seem that whenever a people are aware of encroachments and danger, dietary rules controlling what goes into the body would serve as a vivid analogy of the corpus of their cultural categories at risk.'[8]

The relationships which Mary Douglas and Edmund Leach have observed between the need for Israel to preserve its external boundaries and the purity regulations imposed upon individual Israelites also manifest themselves in the means adopted by Jewish religious movements to maintain their separate identities. The two most notable examples are the rules of the Pharisees and of the monks of Qumran. What the Pharisees and the monks of Qumran had in common was a life-style which, in varying degrees, separated them from the rest of Israel. The very name 'Pharisees' probably means 'the separated ones',[9] while part of the community rule of the Qumran monks declares that they 'shall separate from the congregation of the men of falsehood ...'.[10] For both groups the central mechanism of this separation was a zealous devotion to the Mosaic law, together with other regulations which they added to it, the Pharisees following the 'traditions of the Fathers' (an oral development of the Torah) and the monks 'acting' in obedience to the prescriptions of 'the Sons of Zadok', the sect's priestly hierarchy.[11] One aspect common to the life-styles of both was a strict prohibition against eating with outsiders.

The Pharisees were not, however, as isolated as the monks of Qumran. They founded religious fellowships (*haburot*) throughout the villages and towns of Palestine and these fellowships were like islands of purity in a polluted sea. The members of every *haburah* undertook to carry out even in the midst of less observant Israelites ritual laws which were generally neglected. They set up a barrier between themselves and the outsider, who was by definition a source of ritual defilement. In particular, they paid the priest and the Levite agricultural dues which other Jews withheld and ate their food in a state of ritual purity identical to that of the priests in the Temple.[12]

The great concern for purity of the monks at Qumran, in the splendid isolation of their settlement on a hill overlooking the Dead Sea, was also influenced by the ritual practices of the Temple priests. This emerges most obviously in their daily ritual baths and sacral meals.[13] Underlying this influence is the historical factor of the probable origin of their sect in a priestly group who had severed relations with the Temple and gone out to live in the wilderness.

Characteristic of the Pharisees and the Qumran monks, therefore, was an intimate correlation between their isolation from the rest of Israel and the heightened purity regulations imposed on individual members. This closely parallels what Mary Douglas and Edmund Leach have argued was the general position of Israel *vis-à-vis* the Gentiles in Palestine, and it is highly likely that Israel's methods of protecting itself against external threat served as a model for the Pharisees and the monks at Qumran.

Literary and historical evidence for the Jewish ban on dining with Gentiles

Although Mary Douglas does not specifically investigate the question of table-fellowship between Jew and non-Jew, one would expect that this is an issue to which her argument applies *a fortiori*. This is the case not merely because eating with outsiders carried the risk of being offered food prohibited by the food laws. No, commensality involved a most serious dereliction from the fundamental objective of preserving the separate identity of the Jewish people. How could one keep the outside world at bay and yet sit down at table with its representatives, an action expressing the warmest intimacy and respect (cf. Ps 100.5; LXX)? In a comparable way, the taboos relating to food in the Indian caste system do not merely specify what foods may be eaten, but also with whom one may eat. Among the Indian castes, moreover, inter-marriage is normally only possible between people who can also eat together without risk of defilement; in other words, there is a close coincidence between connubium and commensality. Given the antipathy of the Jews for marrying Gentiles, the Indian comparison suggests that it would be most surprising if they did not also feel a pronounced hostility towards eating with them.

It is not enough to found an argument, however, merely to demonstrate that opposition of Jews to table-fellowship with Gentiles, in the first century CE specifically, exists in the realm of anthropological probability. It is necessary to establish as a matter of historical fact that such an attitude did characterize the Judaism of this period. What then are we to make of the view of J. D. G. Dunn that in the first century CE less scrupulous Jews willingly extended and accepted invitations to meals at which Gentiles would be present,[14] or that of Stephen Wilson that it is doubtful that separation from non-Jews, including a refusal to eat with them, was 'universally practised by all Jews in this period'?[15]

Dunn makes his proposal on this matter in the context of an article on the incident at Antioch reported in Gal 2.11 – 14. After an interesting, although debatable, discussion of the socio-political background to this incident[16] and a consideration of the Jewish attitudes to table-fellowship, he reaches the conclusion that there was a diversity of attitudes among Jews of the period on the question of eating with Gentiles, with strict Jews avoiding this practice, while those less scrupulous engaged in it. From this he proceeds to suggest that what was at issue among the community at Antioch was not a Jewish–Christian demand for a complete discontinuance of table-fellowship, but merely a tightening up of the manner in which it was taking place, by insisting upon Pharisaical purity standards.[17] Two fundamental objections can be made to this theory. First, Dunn offers not a shred of evidence for Jews eating with Gentiles in this period. Material which he cites in support from the *Mishnah* and the *Talmud* is not only too late to assist him but is actually diametrically opposed to the position he is advocating.[18] Secondly, his proposal is incompatible with Paul's language and argument in Galatians. Peter had been in the habit of eating with the Gentiles (συνεσθίειν) in Antioch, but when some friends of James arrived, he stopped (Gal 2.12). For these Jewish Christians from Jerusalem there is no question of degrees of table-fellowship, there is only the stark choice between no fellowship and fellowship following circumcision and acceptance of the Jewish law. As for Stephen Wilson, he justifies his opinion with a footnote reference to an essay by G. Alon which, when examined, does countenance the existence of some social intercourse between Jews and Gentiles but lends no support whatever to the proposition that such intercourse went so far as table-fellowship.[19]

More fundamentally, the ancient evidence establishes a conclusion quite contrary to that of Dunn and Wilson: namely, that as a general rule Jews did refrain from eating with Gentiles and that this was a feature which was perceived to characterize their life-style from as early as the late fourth century BCE until far into the classical period, and not merely from the period after 70 CE, when, as Jacob Neusner has demonstrated,[20] the Pharisees induced a large number of Jews to adopt higher standards of purity modelled on those of the Temple priests in Jerusalem. The first area of evidence comes from the reactions of classical writers to Jews and Judaism.[21] One needs to exercise great caution in using this evidence because for far too long it has been thought to indicate a general hostility to Judaism in antiquity. We have shown in Chapter 2 above that Judaism exerted an enormous attraction for many Greeks and Romans, and John G. Gager has recently published a major re-assessment of the attitude of classical authors to the Jews which explains many of the reasons for this attraction and interprets some of the more hostile anti-Jewish notices as motivated by reasons other than a widespread antipathy to Jewish beliefs and practices as such.[22] Nevertheless, Gager has not managed to disprove that a strong measure of exclusivism and separatism, which was unavoidable if the Torah was to be adhered to at all, did characterize important aspects of the response of Jews to the pagan world. His sweeping reply to the viewpoint of J.N. Sevenster, that 'most Jews were not separate at all', is a serious distortion of the evidence.[23] This becomes most evident when authors who are, on his own admission, quite favourable to Judaism comment upon the anti-social behaviour of the Jews, most notably in their refusal to eat with anyone but themselves. A discussion of the significance of table-fellowship in Jewish relations with the pagan world is conspicuously absent from Gager's book, and this is a serious flaw in it.[24] Let us turn now to the evidence.

Our first author is Hecataeus of Abdera, who visited Egypt during the reign of Ptolemy I (323–285 BCE) and later wrote an *Aegyptiaca* which contained reference to the history, beliefs and customs of the Jews.[25] Under Ptolemy I the Jewish community in Egypt, which had existed there for centuries, was very substantially augmented by a wave of Jewish prisoners, mercenaries and immigrants.[26] Hecataeus was therefore an eye-witness to the reaction of a flourishing Jewish Diaspora population to the pagan world at the end of the fourth century BCE and the beginning of the third. Now this was an age which thought rather highly of the Jews, with pagan writers being inclined to regard them as a nation of philosophers.[27] Hecataeus himself, as Gager notes,[28] was not anti-Jewish and held Moses in high esteem. But this assessment only serves to endorse the accuracy of the views of Hecataeus on the life-style of the Jews when he says that the sacrifices which Moses established 'differ from those of other nations, as does their way of living [τὰς κατὰ τὸν βίον ἀγωγάς], for as a result of their own expulsion from Egypt he introduced an unsocial and intolerant mode of life [ἀπάνθρωπόν τινα καὶ μισόξενον βίον]'.[29] Thus, he attributes to the Jews a separateness from other people and an hostility towards them. Hecataeus makes no mention of whether Jews dined with Gentiles, but if they had been in the habit of so doing, either in the houses of Gentiles or in their own, it is most unlikely that they would have come to be regarded as a people who were aloof from, and hostile to, their neighbours.

Apollonius Molon was a native of Caria who made Rhodes the centre of his teaching and writing. He flourished in the first half of the first century BCE.[30] Apollonius does not appear to have had any positive feelings towards the Jews, but Stern notes that he would have had personal experience of them from his native Caria, where there were Jewish settlements in the second and first centuries BCE.[31] He thought the Jews atheists and misanthropes (ἀθέους καὶ μισανθρώπους)[32] and saw them as unwilling to associate (κοινωνεῖν) with those who had chosen to adopt a different mode of life.[33] Some invective must overlie these views, but they surely also contain a reflection of a certain exclusivism on the part of Diaspora Jews with respect to religion and social intercourse with Gentiles.

The earliest pagan author to mention a Jewish refusal to engage in such table-fellowship was Diodorus Siculus, who flourished under Caesar and Augustus and wrote a world history in the period *c.* 60–30 BCE.[34] This is another author whom Gager regards as not having been anti-Semitic,[35] yet we find him reporting the view that the Jews 'alone of all nations avoided dealings with any other people and looked upon all men as their enemies' and that they did not engage in table-fellowship with any other nation (τὸ μηδενὶ ἄλλῳ ἔθνει τραπέζης κοινωνεῖν).[36] Diodorus does not specify whether this ban applied to eating with Gentiles both in their homes and in Jewish homes, or merely to the former. It would appear to be most unlikely, however, that such a perception of Jewish practice could have arisen if Jews had been in the habit of entertaining Gentiles, especially since this would have been a simple means of reducing pagan apprehensions of Jewish separateness.

Pompeius Trogus lived at the end of the first century BCE and the beginning of the first century CE.[37] He offers an etiology of Jewish apartness by arguing that after the exodus the Jews remembered that they had been driven from Egypt for fear of spreading contagion, so in order not to become odious to their neighbours they took care not to live with strangers (*ne cum peregrinis conviverent*). In time, this rule, from having been adopted for a particular occasion, gradually became a religious institution (*paulatim in disciplinam religionemque convertit*).[38] It should be noted that Quintilian at times uses the verb *convivo* in the sense of 'to dine together' (instead of the usual *convivor*),[39] and it is not impossible that the word could also have this meaning, or a flavour of it, in Pompeius Trogus.

We will now briefly consider two other authors, Tacitus and Philostratus, to show that these perceptions of Judaism continued beyond the first century CE. Tacitus inserted an excursus on the Jews at the start of Book V of his *Historiae*, which was written in the first decade of the second century CE.[40] During the course of this famous discussion he relates that, although the Jews are extremely loyal and compassionate towards one another, towards everyone else they have a bitter enmity. He then specifies that they 'take their meals apart, they sleep apart, and, although they are as a race much given to lust, they abstain from intercourse with foreign women' (*Separati epulis, discreti cubilibus, proiectissima ad libidinem gens, alienarum concubitu abstinent*).[41] Even allowing for the animus which Tacitus undoubtedly had against the Jews, there seems no reason to doubt the correctness of his describing the Jews as neither eating with nor engaging in sexual relations with Gentiles. It is interesting, moreover, that Tacitus should so couple the very two features which general anthropological factors and the parallel with the Indian caste system suggest must go hand-in-hand if ethnic or caste identity is to be preserved.

Our last classical author is Philostratus, a sophist and writer who lived during the second half of the second century to the forties of the third century CE.[42] One of the characters in his *Life of Apollonius of Tyana* describes the Jews as 'a race that has made its own a life apart and irreconcilable, that cannot share with the rest of mankind in the pleasures of the table [οἷς μήτε κοινή πρὸς ανθρώπους τράπεζα] nor join in their libations or prayers or sacrifices ...'.[43]

This persuasive collection of testimonies from classical authors of a Jewish refusal to dine with Gentiles is amply corroborated by material to the same effect from Jewish sources, most of which dates from well before the campaign by the Pharisees for increased attention on the part of ordinary Jews to purity requirements. The background to some of the works we are about to discuss was the action of the Seleucid king Antiochus IV Epiphanes, aimed at Hellenizing the Jewish population of Palestine, and culminating in his attack on Jerusalem and virtual prohibition of the practice of Judaism in 167 BCE (2 Macc 6).[44] One element of the policy of Antiochus was to force Jews to eat swine's flesh, on pain of death if they refused (2 Macc 7.1ff.). The latest of the Old Testament books, Daniel, was composed during this emergency (167–3 BCE) and, although having a dramatic date some centuries earlier, during the Babylonian captivity, actually reflects the contemporary situation in many respects.[45] We need here only refer to Dan 1.3–17, which relate how Daniel, one of a number of Jewish boys selected to be trained for the Babylonian king's service, was assigned a daily allowance of food and wine from the royal table and was most anxious lest he would be defiled (ἀλισγέω) (1.8) by it.

So he sought, and obtained, permission to eat only vegetables and water, and on this diet he and the others flourished.

A similar attitude is revealed in the Book of Judith, which is also to be dated to the period of the Maccabean rising.[46] When Judith goes off on her mission to beguile and then slay Holofernes, she takes with her a supply of food and wine (10.5). So equipped, she graciously refuses to eat the food and wine which Holofernes offers her, 'to avoid causing a scandal' (ἵνα μὴ γένηται σκάνδαλον) (12.2), and, although she does sit at his table, she eats only her own food which is served to her by her maid (12.17–19). Each night she goes out of Holofernes' camp and bathes in a spring and, after returning to her camp cleansed (or 'pure' – καθαρά) she takes her meal (12.7–9). It is possible that she bathes before eating because she has contracted defilement by contact with Gentiles.[47]

Even in works not written at the time of the Maccabean rising – although, as Martin Hengel notes,[48] the events of that period made a lasting impression on the Jewish consciousness – there are passages which deal with the necessity of avoiding table-fellowship with Gentiles. Two apocryphal works may be mentioned first. In the Book of Esther, which is difficult to date but does not reflect the Maccabean rebellion,[49] Esther abstained from eating at the royal table or drinking the wine of libation (4.17), even though she had been brought into the king's harem and had become his favourite wife (2.15–18). Secondly, in the Book of Tobit, which was probably composed before the persecution of Antiochus,[50] Tobit reports that when he was carried off to captivity in Nineveh, he did not eat the food of the Gentiles even though his brothers and fellow-Israelites did (Tobit 1.11). It is inconceivable, of course, that only Tobit failed to apostatize; this feature of the story is added merely to underline his piety. Tobit behaves in the way which befits a loyal Jew of the Diaspora, and a significant aspect of this behaviour consists of sticking to the dietary laws.

The Pseudepigrapha are also a rich source of references on this theme. The *Letter of Aristeas*, although rarely commented upon in this connection,[51] is of particular significance. Most probably written in the early decades of the second century BCE,[52] this work, as recent scholarship has shown, does not concern itself primarily with how the Septuagint first came to be translated, a feature which occupies a fairly subsidiary place,[53] but offers a defence of Diaspora Judaism *vis-à-vis* the Gentile world or Palestinian Judaism or both.[54] Given this aim, it is clear that the information it contains about the life-style of Jews in the Diaspora (here, Egypt in particular) must be taken as typical for the vast majority of them and not as characteristic only of a small minority. We note, in the first place, that the author almost revels in proclaiming that very separateness which John G. Gager has denied to Diaspora Judaism at all. Consider how the author of the *Letter* interprets the achievements of Moses:

> [he] fenced us around with impregnable ramparts and walls of iron, that we might not mingle at all with any of the other nations, but remain pure in body and soul, free from all vain imaginations, worshipping the one Almighty God above the whole creation.[55]

In other words, the Jews have been 'distinctly separated from the rest of mankind' (παρὰ πάντας ἀνθρώπους διεστάλμεθα).[56] The most intriguing aspect of this work for the present discussion is that a substantial portion of it relates to conversations between Ptolemy Philadelphus, the Egyptian king who commissioned the translation of the Hebrew scriptures, and the Jewish translators, held at a banquet which extended over seven days.[57] At first sight, Jewish participation in this feast would appear to contradict the argument advanced so far. On closer inspection, however, this proves not to be the case, inasmuch as the banquet is held in a manner which is specifically in accordance with the requirements of the king's Jewish guests. For Ptolemy, like other kings and cities, so the author records, had a special officer to look after the Jews who were invited to celebrations and to see that everything was prepared according to their customs (κατὰ τοὺς ἐθισμούς), 'so that nothing unpleasant might disturb the pleasure of their visit'. In this case, the king's officer had separate stores under his control for use at such receptions and these he brought out for the feast.[58] Finally, we should note the table arrangements at this banquet. The only participants seem to have been the king and his Jewish guests, and these were seated in two rows, half of them on his right and half behind him.[59] The author does not specify whether food and wine were passed between the king and the Jews, but it would seem more likely that he ate his and they ate theirs. This would result in a situation similar to the way in which Judith dined with Holofernes.

In the *Book of Jubilees*, also to be dated to the second century BCE,[60] there is the following passage, forming part of an address by Isaac to Jacob:

Separate thyself from the nations,
And eat not with them: ...
For their works are unclean,
And all their ways are a pollution and an abomination and
uncleanness.[61]

This quotation is particularly significant because the prohibition
against mixing or eating with Gentiles is related not to what they eat
but to the pollution which attaches to their actions. The *Book of
Jubilees* may not be as representative of the broad range of Jewish
opinion as the *Letter of Aristeas*, since its parallels with some of the
thoughts in the Dead Sea scrolls indicate that it may represent a
narrower type of Judaism out of which that of the monks of Qumran
evolved.[62] Nevertheless, there is no reason to doubt that on the
question of the appropriate attitude to Gentiles it expressed a view
shared by many, if not most, ordinary Jews in the second century
BCE.[63]

The last work to be discussed from the Pseudepigrapha is *Joseph
and Asenath*, composed by a Jewish author, probably in the last
decades of the first century CE or the first decades of the second.[64]
Joseph and Asenath is an haggadic midrash on Gen 41.45 and
describes how Asenath, the daughter of an Egyptian priest, and
Joseph fall in love and marry, after she has turned from idolatry and
converted to Judaism. It illustrates many themes we have seen already.
Thus, it reports that Joseph had often been told by his father Jacob
to have nothing to do with foreign women, for such *koinonia* was
ruin and destruction.[65] Moreover, the author mentions that when
Joseph was entertained at the house of Asenath's parents 'they set
a table before him separately, because he did not eat with [συνήσθιε]
the Egyptians, as this was an abomination [βδέλυγμα][66] to him'.
Once again, we observe 'table-fellowship' of a very particular kind
being afforded to a special Jewish guest, and similar to that offered
by Ptolemy to the Septuagint translators in the *Letter of Aristeas*.

The last items in this survey of Jewish evidence are two passages
from the *Mishnah* and one from the *Talmud*; these, Dunn claims,
support his belief that table-fellowship occurred between Jews and
Gentiles in the first century CE.[67] In the first Mishnaic passage (m.
Berakhot 7.1) the 'Gentile' whom Dunn cites as present at a meal with
Jews is actually a Samaritan, so this example cannot support his case
unless he can show that the position of Samaritans on questions of
ritual purity had been assimilated in all respects to that of Gentiles.

The second Mishnaic passage (m. *Abodah Zarah* 5.5), which is interpreted in the Gemara section of the *Talmud* passage cited by Dunn (b. *Abodah Zarah* 8a−b), is apposite. This *mishnah* does indeed begin 'If an Israelite was eating with a gentile at a table ...',[68] but it plainly envisages that the two of them are drinking from different wine-jars (no mention is made of food), since the whole point of the passage (and of surrounding *mishnot*)[69] is how to determine if the Gentile has tampered with the Jew's wine in such a way as to make it libation-wine for his idol and therefore unfit for Jewish consumption. This can only be described as table-fellowship in a very limited sense, if at all. The corresponding Gemara in the Babylonian *Talmud* does not alter this position.[70] It does give an example of a Jew and a Gentile sitting at table in an inn and drinking wine, but once again their wine is quite separate, and the discussion revolves around how a Jew can be confident that his wine has not been polluted, which it would be, for example, if the Gentile were to touch it.[71]

We must now summarize the results of this examination, before proceeding to analyse the data in Luke−Acts on table-fellowship, in the light of other New Testament writings. In essence, the historical evidence richly endorses the anthropological insights of Mary Douglas and Edmund Leach. From the fourth century BCE right through into the second century CE and beyond there is a wealth of evidence, both from classical authors and in the Jewish sources, for the fact that the Jews were zealous in keeping themselves apart from the Gentiles by means of definite boundaries which were perceived as originating in the Mosaic code (so, in particular, Hecataeus of Abdera, the *Letter of Aristeas*, and Pompeius Trogus). Such aloofness is not, of course, incompatible with Judaism's having exuded a great attraction for many thoughtful Gentiles. But although Jews were happy to mix with Gentiles in synagogues or possibly even in market-places or streets, eating with them was a very different matter. Eating was an occasion fraught with the possibility of breaching the purity code, one of the most crucial aspects of the Mosaic law for the maintenance of the separate identity of the Jewish *ethnos*. The antipathy of Jews towards table-fellowship with Gentiles, in the full sense of sitting around a table with them and sharing the same food, wine and vessels, was an intrinsic feature of Jewish life for centuries before and after our period.

Oddly enough, there is nothing specifically in the Mosaic code forbidding such table-fellowship, just as there is nothing forbidding inter-marriage with Gentiles, except for the seven nations in Dt 7.1, though this was a practice also regarded in the sources we have considered as threatening the ethnic identity of the Jews. Yet in one way it was only a short step from the prohibitions on various foods in Lev 11 to the ban on table-fellowship, for a Jew could not safely eat any food supplied to him by a Gentile for fear that it had been stored or cooked in a vessel used for one of the forbidden foods and had thereby become ritually defiled; even Leviticus, after all, recognized that a vessel which had come into contact with some of the kinds of ritually impure creatures itself became defiled and defiling (Lev 11.31–4) and the *Mishnah* was eventually to describe various forms of purification to which utensils purchased from a Gentile had to be put before Jewish use.[72] But there also developed another reason for avoiding table-fellowship with Gentiles: namely, the fact that they were themselves ritually impure. Judith, for example, bathed in a spring every evening before her meal, as if she had become unclean through contact with Gentiles. The passage quoted above from the *Book of Jubilees*, furthermore, is unmistakable evidence for such a belief in the second century BCE. Alon has argued that the impurity of non-Jews was one of the early *halakhot*, not enjoined in the Torah, but nevertheless rooted in ancient tradition and in many respects a practical law, and that this *halakhah* was 're-established', that is, put on a firm footing, as one of the Eighteen Decrees enacted by the Sages in *c.* 70 CE.[73] Alon regarded this law as an extension of the impurity of the idols worshipped by the Gentiles to the Gentiles themselves. From the time of Ezra, as Z. W. Falk has shown, the Jews had been willing to grant legal status to prescriptions not specifically included in the Torah, although in later times dispute raged between the Pharisees and the Sadducees as to the proper ambit of such supplementary law.[74] There is a variety of evidence cited by Alon for an early belief in the ritual impurity of Gentiles, but we shall restrict ourselves here to non-Mishnaic and Talmudic examples to avoid problems over dating.[75] Most of this comes from Josephus, who reports, for example, that Essenes were required to take a bath after contact with a Gentile,[76] that Hyrcanus urged Herod not to let his Gentile soldiers enter Jerusalem while the people were purifying themselves for the feast of Weeks,[77] undoubtedly because they would defile the Israelites, and that the vestments of the High Priest had to be purified after they were removed from Roman custody,[78] presumably because they had become defiled through Gentile contact. From the period after 70 CE, when the impurity of the Gentiles was enshrined in the Eighteen Decrees, we might refer to John's remark that the Jewish leaders refused to enter the Praetorium to avoid pollution (Jn 18.28).

One consequence of this attribution of ritual impurity to Gentiles is that it is difficult to imagine how it would be possible for any genuine table-fellowship to occur even between Jew and Gentile in a Jewish home, though Dunn asserts this is not at all problematic.[79] For even before 70 CE many, if not most, Jews would have regarded Gentiles as ritually impure and therefore as defiling any vessel or cup which they put to their lips; so unless they were to come along to a Jewish home with their own vessels, and even their own food, and avoid all physical contact with their hosts, they would not be invited. In addition, they would probably have been felt to pollute the house merely by entering it, and even this form of fellowship may not have occurred. After 70 CE the Jewish antipathy to such intercourse can only have increased.

We note finally that, although we have been arguing for what was accepted Jewish practice, we do not claim that there were no exceptions and that some Jews did not breach the rules regulating their relationships with the pagan world. Acts 16.1, after all, refers to the fact that Timothy was the product of a marriage between a Greek man and a Jewish woman. An inscription from Smyrna contains a list of people called οἱ ποτὲ Ἰουδαῖοι, who were Jews who had forsworn their faith and received citizenship.[80] The point is that those Jews who permanently gave up the prohibitions which distinguished them from the Gentiles ceased to be Jews. One must assume that those Jews who did fudge the boundaries between Jew and Gentile were rightly regarded as endangering the ethnic identity of the Jewish people and came under heavy pressure to conform or to abandon Judaism altogether. In Acts 16.1–3, it is instructive to recall, Luke describes Paul as succumbing to just this sort of Jewish pressure by circumcising the anomalous Timothy and re-establishing in his case the all-important line between Jew and non-Jew. Moreover, a possible, though hardly probable, interpretation of Gal 2.3 is that, although Paul was not compelled to circumcise Titus, he did so voluntarily.

3. The attitude to table-fellowship between Jews and Gentiles in Galatians, Mark and Matthew

Before considering the sensitivity to the Jewish prohibition on dining with Gentiles evident in Luke–Acts, it will be helpful to outline the attitudes on this issue present in three other New Testament works: Galatians, Mark and Matthew. An investigation of Galatians is particularly important since it is the earliest New Testament document dealing with the subject[81] and it forms an invaluable historical control for distinguishing between history and authorial interpretation in Luke–Acts.

Table-fellowship in Galatians
In the second chapter of Galatians Paul relates that fourteen years after his first visit to Jerusalem he went there for a second time, in the company of Barnabas and Titus, an uncircumcised Greek. He laid before the leaders of the church there the gospel which he preached to the Gentiles and they had nothing to add to it. The Jerusalem leaders recognized that he had been commissioned to preach the gospel to the uncircumcised, just as Peter had been commissioned to preach it to the circumcised. Finally, James, Cephas and John shook hands with Paul and Barnabas in fellowship and asked only that they remember the poor (in Jerusalem) (Gal 2.1–10). Some time later Peter came to Antioch and at first ate with the Gentiles, apparently the accepted practice in that community, but upon the arrival of certain people from James he discontinued this fellowship, from fear of the Jews (οἱ ἐκ περιτομῆς) (2.12),[82] whereupon the rest of the Jews, even Barnabas, did the same. Paul rebuked Peter publicly for this defection, but the fact that he does not report that he succeeded in restoring the *status quo ante* strongly suggests that he failed (Gal 2.11–14). This is confirmed by the fact that those wanting Gentile Christians circumcised were subsequently powerful enough to be a considerable nuisance in Paul's Galatian churches (6.12–13), where they also instituted a reaction against the manner of Paul's evangelism, presumably by insisting on the termination of Jewish–Gentile table-fellowship. Paul may even have been forced out of Antioch altogether; he never mentions the city outside Galatians.

From our previous discussion, it is apparent that James and Peter did not break off table-fellowship with the Gentile Christians for purely theological reasons, but because such a practice threatened to destroy the boundaries which preserved the separate identity of the Jewish people; their motivations were social and ethnic, as much as theological. To an extent, the reader of Galatians is left wondering about the attitude of James and Peter to the Gentiles with whom they now refused to share table-fellowship. Did they consider that these Gentiles were still Christians and could continue to engage in table-fellowship amongst themselves, so that Antioch would have possessed groups of Jewish Christians and Gentile Christians, each with separate eucharists, or did they regard them as being quite ineligible to be Christians without first becoming Jews, by being circumcised and accepting the law? Two considerations militate against the first option, of live and let live. First, in Gal 2.14 Paul accuses Peter of compelling the Gentiles to 'Judaize' ('Ιουδαΐζειν); leaving aside the connotations of this word for the moment, there can be no doubt that Peter (and James behind him) was hoping to elicit some change in the status or behaviour of the Gentile Christians in a Jewish direction. Secondly, the wider context of Paul's argument in Galatians reveals that the essential problem he sees as facing the churches to whom he writes is the pressure on their members to be circumcised and to adopt the Jewish law. Just as in Antioch in the past, so also now in Galatia,[83] the form of Christianity which he established in the beginning, with table-fellowship between Jew and Gentile having a central place, is endangered by the forces of an orthodox Jewish reaction which insists on circumcision and the law. We must presume, therefore, that by 'Judaize' in Gal 2.14 Paul means 'to become Jews through circumcision'. This explanation precludes that of Dunn, who argues that the table-fellowship which Peter joined on his arrival in Antioch probably heeded the basic dietary requirements of the Torah by avoiding pork and meat not ritually slaughtered and that the reason for his defection and subsequent pressure on the Gentile Christians was the need to tighten up the practice of this fellowship by the adoption of the Pharisaical features of hand-washing and of tithing of the produce used at these meals.[84] Apart from Dunn's explanation representing a serious trivialization of the issues in dispute, it founders on the fact that apparently for Peter and James, and certainly for the anonymous trouble-makers in Galatia, the only way to rehabilitate this form of table-fellowship was to have the Gentiles become Jews through circumcision.

Extrapolating backwards from the events in Antioch to the agreement reached between Paul and Barnabas, and James, Peter and John in Jerusalem is no easy task. But it is hardly likely that Paul could have failed to explain his belief that the gospel and not the law was the means of salvation, a belief which enabled Jewish–Gentile commensality to occur, when he laid before them the gospel he preached to the Gentiles.

The clash between Paul and the Jerusalem church is, therefore, one between a leader who has made a revolutionary leap to the realization that the old boundaries which preserved the Jewish *ethnos* from outside contamination have, in Christ, ceased to have any significance, since 'there is neither Jew nor Greek, ... but you are all one in Christ Jesus' (Gal. 3.28), and, on the other hand, a group which, firmly believing in the election of the Jewish *ethnos*, wishes to restrict the power of the Gospel exclusively to Jews. In sociological terms, it is a clash between someone determined to establish a form of religious belief whose relationship to its mother church can only be described as sectarian, and others who see this new religious impulse as merely an intra-Judaic Messianic movement.

Table-fellowship in Mark

It is a most significant fact for an understanding of the development of the early Christian communities that Mark also presents Jesus as dismantling the barriers between Jew and Gentile by endorsing table-fellowship between them. We recall from our previous discussion that the desire of the members of a society to maintain their integrity in the face of external threat may be reflected in regulations governing personal purity. One aspect of this phenomenon is that rules as to what food one may eat will be a vital factor in deciding with whom one may eat. A decision to dine with outsiders will normally necessitate a disregard for the food laws, while a rejection of the food laws will allow one to change dining companions. The circumstances of each particular case will determine which decision comes first. What makes Mk 7.1 – 30 remarkably germane to this discussion is that these verses combine a rejection of the food laws in Lev 11 (7.1 – 23) with an incident in which Jesus himself enters into fellowship with Gentiles (7.24 – 30).

Let us begin with the words attributed to Jesus in 7.15: 'Nothing that goes into a man from outside can make him unclean; it is the things that come out of a man that make him unclean' (JB). This is almost certainly an authentic saying of Jesus. Does it, however, constitute a rejection of the food laws in Leviticus? In spite of claims to the contrary,[85] the answer is 'no'. Long before the time of Jesus, Jews had subscribed to the view that, whatever the rationale behind its various parts, the Torah was to be obeyed simply because God had commanded it.[86] Even today, this view is current among Jews. Moreover, if this saying did constitute an abrogation of the food laws, it is difficult to imagine how Jewish Christians could so ardently have advocated their preservation.[87] But the historical Jesus and the Marcan Jesus are not identical; the setting which Mark provides for this dominical saying specifically interprets it so as to abrogate Lev 11. This effect is achieved not so much by 7.19a, as by 7.19b: '[Thus] he purified all foods.' While it cannot be denied that this clause is awkwardly situated, the chief textual witnesses are virtually unanimous in its support. Accordingly, since it appears to belong to the text in its earliest form, it may reasonably be attributed to the evangelist himself.

In any event, even if 7.19b was inserted into the text after it left Mark's hands, much the same moral is conveyed by the story of Jesus healing the daughter of the Syrophoenician woman in 7.24–30. Although rarely noticed by commentators, 7.24 is quite an extraordinary verse because it describes Jesus entering a house in territory occupied by Gentiles. The text does not specify whether Jesus took food in the house, although it would seem reasonable to assume that he did. Yet even if he did not, his visit amounted to a serious attack on the boundaries which Jews had erected between themselves and Gentiles. As T. A. Burkill has observed, in 7.24–30 Jesus puts into practice what Mark describes him as having preached in 7.1–23.[88] Burkill also locates Jesus' attack on the purity laws and his residing with Gentiles within a wider Marcan desire to present the gospel in a way acceptable to the Gentile Christians among his readers.[89] In this he is surely correct, but do not the data in the text call for a more specific explanation? Is not Mark's insertion of 7.1–30 into his Gospel best explicable as a means of legitimating table-fellowship between Jews and Gentiles in the community for which he was writing? Two considerations support this view. First of all, we have seen from our discussion of the incident at Antioch described by Paul in Galatians that conservative Jewish Christians advocated a rigid demarcation between themselves and Gentile Christians and that they attempted to impose on Gentile Christians the full burden of the law. If Mark was writing for a community where conservative Jewish Christians had gained the upper hand, there would have been no table-fellowship between them and Gentile Christians and there would have been no occasion for breach of the Levitical food laws. In such a case, there would not have been any need for Mark to include material so inimical to Jewish ethnic solidarity as Mk 7.1–30. It is no answer to say that Mark was simply recording the preaching of the historical Jesus, since, as we have just seen, form-critical analysis of 7.14–23 and what we know of early church history from elsewhere indicate that Jesus himself did not announce the demise of the laws on forbidden foods. In view of all this, the most plausible reason for the inclusion of this material in Mark is that he was writing for a community in which Jews and Gentiles were in the habit of engaging in table-fellowship with one another. This practice had begun at some discrete point in the history of this community and it had become necessary immediately or soon after to counter the extreme antipathy it aroused among Jews or, more specifically, Jewish Christians appalled at this blurring of the distinction between themselves and Gentiles. It must have been perceived quite early by the advocates of commensality that one way in which such a development could be legitimated was to attribute it to the words and deeds of Jesus. This is the function of Mk 7.1–30.

A second, more particular, consideration can be summoned in support of this view. It derives from the specific details of 7.24–30. What is at stake in this pericope is whether Jesus will assist the Syrophoenician woman by exorcizing the demon from her daughter. At first Jesus declines her request for help, saying: 'The children should be fed first, because it is not fair to take the children's food and throw it to the dogs' (7.27). It is generally agreed by exegetes that here 'children' means Jews and 'dogs' Gentiles, so that Jesus is, in effect, disclaiming any interest in a Gentile mission. But the woman wins Jesus over with her reply: 'But the dogs under the table eat from the children's scraps' (7.28). In this reply there is an image of Jews and Gentiles eating bread from the same table, and since Mark establishes several connections between bread and the eucharist in this section of his Gospel (especially 6.30–44)[90] we are surely meant to see this image as a justification for the eucharistic fellowship of Jews and Gentiles in the Christian community.

Matthew and table-fellowship

On considering Matthew's treatment of Mk 7.1–23 one is immediately struck by two features in particular: first, that he has omitted Mk 7.19b (assuming that it occurred in his copy of Mark) and, secondly, that by the addition of the new verse Mt 15.20 he has drastically read down his source so that his version relates solely to the question of whether one can be defiled by eating with unclean hands. Matthew makes it crystal clear, therefore, that Jesus did not annul the Levitical code by declaring all foods pure, but merely rejected the oral tradition of the Pharisees. That this is the effect of his redactional alterations has been noted by New Testament scholars. But what has passed unnoticed is that the underlying motivation for this change was most probably the fact, of social as much as of theological significance, that table-fellowship between Jews and Gentiles was frowned upon in Matthew's community and was regarded as being in contravention of the teaching and actions of Jesus.

This conclusion is suggested by the way in which Matthew redacts Mark's story of the Syrophoenician woman (Mk 7.24–30; Mt 15.21–8). Matthew's first significant alteration is to the context in which Jesus encounters the woman. Mark describes this as happening in a house, but in Matthew Jesus and his disciples do not enter a house (15.21) and meet the woman in the open air while they are on the move (Mt 15.23). F. W. Beare, one of only a small company of commentators who remark upon this alteration, says of it: 'Matthew revises Mark's picture, perhaps because he would not have Jesus violate Jewish custom by entering a house in a heathen city.'[91] This is true, although Beare does not go far enough. For it is surely the case that Matthew, whose devotion to the Levitical code is evident in the passage immediately before this, must have been deeply embarrassed by his Marcan source attributing to Jesus behaviour which attacked the very isolation from foreigners which Leviticus was, at least in part, designed to enforce. The same embarrassment appears in a second significant alteration Matthew makes to his source: namely, in the woman's reply to Jesus' remark that it is not fitting to take the children's bread and throw it to the dogs. Mark, it will be recalled, had her reply that even the dogs under the table eat from the children's scraps and thus symbolically legitimated Jewish–Gentile table-fellowship. Matthew, on the other hand, has her speak of dogs eating the scraps 'falling from their masters' tables' (15.27). This interpretation means that the children and the dogs no longer eat the same bread and, therefore, eliminates the symbolical picture, present in Mark, of Jews and Gentiles eating from if not around, the same table.

These changes to the very features in his Marcan *Vorlage* which served to legitimate, by both the words and deeds of Jesus, table-fellowship between Jews and Gentiles seem to indicate that Matthew's community neither engaged in nor countenanced that practice. This suggests, furthermore, that his community was composed either exclusively of Jews or exclusively of Gentiles. For although it is not inconceivable that his community contained Jews and Gentiles who partook of separate eucharistic meals, this option would appear to be precluded by the fact that Matthew has included no feature in his Gospel which would legitimate the troublesome disunity that would arise from separate eucharists, and has, moreover, toughened the teaching on the Levitical food laws in a way which would be well-nigh inexplicable if there were Gentiles in his community who were exempted from their effect. This latter consideration is also, of course, a strong argument for choosing Jewish Christians as the group

exclusively represented in the Matthean community. This consideration seems to have an important role to play in determining the social
setting and composition of Matthew's community. Although such a
task is quite beyond the scope of this book,[92] it is worthwhile to note
that its notorious difficulty arises largely because of the contradictory
signals Matthew emits: on the one hand, his Gospel contains a number
of features apparently stemming from a Jewish and Torah-abiding
milieu, which were subsequently to make it the favourite Gospel of
various 'heterodox' Jewish Christian groups and individuals,[93] and
yet on the other hand it presents a number of features which indicate
some form of institutional split with Judaism (Mt 21.43; 28.15)[94] and
a mission to the Gentiles (28.19).

4. Table-fellowship in Luke–Acts

The conversion of Cornelius
The most prominent indication in Luke–Acts of the author's interest
in Jewish–Gentile table-fellowship comes in the account of events
surrounding the conversion of Cornelius, the first Gentile convert,
by Peter in Acts 10.1 – 11.18. The central issue in this narrative is not
that the gospel has been preached to Gentiles, but the far more particular fact, of great ethnic and social significance, that Peter has lived
and eaten with them. This is, after all, the substance of the complaint
against him by members of the church in Jerusalem in Acts 11.3. A
detailed examination of the text is called for, especially since this incident is frequently misinterpreted and its importance underestimated
by Lucan commentators.

The vision which Peter has just before the arrival of the messengers
from Cornelius (10.9–16) centres upon his being instructed to eat food
which is ritually impure. Lev 11 had proscribed virtually all animal
flesh except that from beasts which had cloven hoofs and were
ruminants, and here is Peter being told to eat from a collection
encompassing all quadrupeds, birds and even reptiles. To Peter's objection that he has never eaten anything profane (κοινόν) and impure
(ἀκάθαρτον), the voice in the vision replies, 'Do not call profane
those things which God has purified [ἐκαθάρισεν]' (10.15), although
it does not specify when or how God has effected this purification
of creatures banned by the Torah. Many scholars, including F.
Hauck and S. G. Wilson,[95] wrongly assert that Peter deduces from
this vision, or interprets it to mean, that God has also cleansed the
Gentiles, thereby allowing Jewish fellowship with them, as announced

by Peter in 10.28. In fact, Peter arrives at this conclusion not by the
processes of logical deduction from what he has seen in the vision,
but by the direction of the Spirit in 10.19–20. At the end of the
vision, Peter is left cogitating as to its meaning (10.19), not with any
realization of its extension from impure things to impure persons.
At this juncture, however, the Spirit tells him that three men have
arrived and he must go with them, without having any doubts,
because, says the Spirit, 'I have sent them' (10.19–20). The narrative
which follows is allusive and condensed, but it can easily be understood in the light of our previous discussion on Jewish attitudes to
the Gentiles. Peter goes down to the men, one of whom, a soldier
(10.7), is almost certainly non-Jewish, while the others are probably
Gentiles as well, and enquires about their purpose. They reply: 'The
centurion Cornelius, who is a just and God-fearing man, and highly
regarded by the entire Jewish people, was directed by a holy angel
to send for you and bring you into his house and to listen to what
you have to say' (10.22). In asking Peter to visit the house of a Gentile,
the three men obviously thought they were likely to offend his Jewish
sensibilities, for that is why they prefix their request with a statement
of Cornelius' virtues, especially his good reputation with the Jewish
ethnos, to make the notion of entering his house less shocking. That
these good qualities were not of themselves sufficient to legitimate
Peter's entering his house is manifest from our general discussion of
Jewish attitudes to such fellowship, from the particular confirmation
which that discussion receives in our analysis of the dispute between
Paul and Peter in Antioch (Gal 2.11 – 14) and from the fact that they
are entirely absent from Peter's subsequent justification of his baptism
of Cornelius before the church in Jerusalem (Acts 11.1 – 18). Peter,
however, now knows that, since the Spirit has directed him to go with
these men, and they wish to conduct him to the house of a Roman
centurion, then God himself has abrogated the Jewish ban on the more
intimate forms of fellowship between Jew and Gentile. The immediacy
of Peter's realization of this is implied in the text by the fact that he
actually invites the men into the house where he is staying and gives
them overnight lodging there.

    With all this behind him, Peter is thus able to say to the people
assembled in the house of Cornelius to hear him: 'You know it is forbidden [ἀθέμιτον] for a Jew to mix with people of another race or
to visit them, but God has revealed to me that I must not call anyone
profane [κοινόν] or unclean [ἀκάθαρτον]' (10.28). After the Spirit
has confirmed this principle by vouchsafing to these Gentiles what is

virtually a Pentecost experience (10.45 – 6; 11.15), Peter baptizes them and stays with them for a few days, presumably engaging in table-fellowship with his Gentile hosts, and all the while having the re-assurance of the vision that he may eat whatever is put before him. It is this fellowship that gets Peter into trouble on his return to Jerusalem. For Luke describes the church there as taking issue with Peter not on account of his having been responsible for the conversion of Gentiles, but because, as they bluntly put it, 'You have been visiting the uncircumcised and eating with them' (11.3). Peter must then justify his behaviour in the light of this reproach, and the role of the Holy Spirit, both in instigating (11.12) and in confirming (11.15) Jewish – Gentile fellowship, plays the central role in that justification.

The time has come to ask why Luke has placed the narrative of the conversion of Cornelius at this point in Acts and why he has treated it in such detail. For conservative scholars the answer is easy – Luke is merely rehearsing hard, historical fact. But the difficulties in the way of this are so great and have been so meticulously exposed by German scholarship in particular[96] that its persistence into the present is a cause for wonder. The primary objection to the narrative in Acts is not that it is so heavily mythological, although that characteristic is no small objection to its historicity, but that it is wildly inconsistent with the subsequent attitude of Peter (and James behind him) to Jewish – Gentile table-fellowship in Antioch (Gal 2.11 – 14). In spite of various attempts to explain such a dramatic about-turn (with I. Howard Marshall, for example, attributing it to the possibility of vacillation in Peter's character!),[97] it is just too much to believe that Peter and James, having openly accepted that Jewish – Gentile table-fellowship had been authorized by an overwhelmingly attested divine command, should later explicitly disregard that authorization and break off such table-fellowship in Antioch. It is also difficult to credit that, when Paul visited Jerusalem for the second time (Gal 2.1 – 10), he should have been regarded there as 'the apostle to the uncircumcised' and Peter as 'the apostle to the circumcised' if it had been Peter who had initiated the Gentile mission as described in Acts 10.1 – 11.18. And if, when Paul visited Jerusalem on that occasion, the church there had already sanctioned Jewish – Gentile commensality, how eagerly he would have played this trump card in his charge of inconsistency against Peter and James in Gal 2.11 – 14! But there are other serious grounds for doubting the historicity of the Cornelius story as Luke relates it. The first of these is that it has virtually been forgotten by the time of the Apostolic Council in Acts 15. Of course

Peter and James refer back to the conversion of Cornelius (15.7–11, 14), but that fails to resolve the difficulty of why people would have travelled from Judea to Antioch and urged the need for Gentiles to be circumcised (15.1) if the matter had already been settled by an earlier decision of the apostles and the brothers in Jerusalem (11.1–18). (The problems surrounding the account of the Apostolic Council itself are dealt with in the next section of this chapter.) Secondly, the Cornelius episode is very awkwardly intruded into the narrative between the persecution in Jerusalem following the martyrdom of Stephen and the subsequent mission to the Gentiles in Antioch. Acts 11.19 takes up immediately from 8.4 and does not envisage any intermediate evangelism by Peter. The text lacks any sign that the mission to the Gentiles in Antioch is a consequence of the conversion of a Roman centurion by Peter. For all these reasons, it is preferable to follow the many scholars, especially Martin Dibelius and Ernst Haenchen, who hold that Luke has abandoned an exact reproduction of history in Acts 10.1–11.18 in favour of presenting a truth of a different sort to his audience.

But what is the message that Luke is attempting to convey? Without doubt, his broad aim is to show that 'God instigated the mission to the Gentiles', as Haenchen,[98] like Dibelius before him,[99] concludes. Unfortunately, however, this solution fails to do justice to the particular issue with which Luke was concerned in the Cornelius narrative – not the legitimation of the Gentile mission in general, but the table-fellowship between Jew and Gentile within the Christian community that he presents as essential to that mission. It is for this reason that commentators, such as I. Howard Marshall[100] and R. R. Williams,[101] who find it curious that Peter is called to account by the church in Jerusalem not for baptizing Gentiles, but for eating with them, have missed the entire point of the narrative. What matters to Luke is the legitimation of complete fellowship between Jew and Gentile in the Christian community, not just the admission of the Gentiles to those communities, which could, indeed, have been legitimated by accounts of apostolic baptism of non-Jews. Moreover, although Overbeck was correct to insist that the effect of the Cornelius narrative was to show Paul's mission as 'prepared and legitimized' by the precedent set by Peter,[102] one must add the vital qualification that, for Luke, Paul's mission is not simply the broad task of baptizing Gentiles, but also that of initiating Christian communities where Jews and Gentiles share common eucharistic meals. Thus, there inevitably arises the question of why Luke, probably writing in the eighties of the first century CE, should take such pains to underline so carefully this particular theme in the work. There would appear to be a strong likelihood that this is a question with great bearing on the composition of Luke's community; which, as we argued in Chapter 2, most probably contained a significant number of Jews, as well as Gentiles. It is an issue which is also relevant to the relations of Luke's community with Judaism. But before reaching some final conclusions on these matters, the remaining material in Luke–Acts on the subject must be considered.

The Apostolic Council
The principal result of the Apostolic Council, as described by Luke in Acts 15, was that circumcision and the rest of the Mosaic law would not be imposed on Gentile Christians. But it was also agreed that the Gentiles should at least keep away from things polluted by idols, from incest, from strangled meat and from blood (15.20). This fourfold prohibition is incorporated into a letter addressed to the brethren in Antioch, Syria and Cilicia, which is joyfully received in Antioch (15.31).

There is a very strong case against the historicity of Luke's account of the Apostolic Council. Let us first consider the external grounds for this view, namely, the inconsistencies between Luke's version and the facts as we know them from Paul's letters. Acts 15 is surely incompatible with both of the trips to Jerusalem that Paul recounts in Gal 1–2, with the first because of its private nature and with the second because Paul says the leaders in Jerusalem imposed no condition on him (Gal 2.6), which indicates that Luke's presentation of the Apostolic Decree is not historically accurate. Moreover, if such a decision had been taken in Jerusalem before Paul wrote Galatians he would surely have mentioned it to strengthen this argument, since it relates to the table-fellowship question which was at the centre of the dispute in Antioch (Gal 2.12). Furthermore, although the circumcision issue did, at times, interfere with Paul's evangelism elsewhere – for example, at Philippi (Phil 3.2–3) – he never cites the decision of the Apostolic Council in Acts 15 which would have been so useful to his cause. Internal factors also confirm that Luke is not presenting historical fact in his narrative. Dibelius has drawn our attention to a number of elements in the account which show that Luke has constructed it for his readers and has not just reproduced one or more sources. Thus, the references by Peter and James to the conversion of Cornelius (15.7, 14) are so abbreviated and allusive as to have been virtually meaningless to their audience but are readily intelligible to the readers of Acts.[103] Likewise, the fact that no details are given of the signs and wonders which Paul and Barnabas claim God caused to be performed among the Gentiles (15.4) makes very little sense before the audience in Jerusalem, for whom such details may have had a decisive effect, but is readily intelligible if the statement is really directed to the readers of Acts, who have just read an account of such things in Acts 13 and 14.[104] Haenchen notes that it is very difficult to believe that the events surrounding the conversion of Cornelius could simply have been forgotten and the earlier ruling of the Jerusalem church (Acts 11.1–18) ignored by the dramatic date of the Council in Acts 15.[105] Even more damaging to any argument for the historicity of this narrative is the fact that, although Luke presents James as speaking in Aramaic (by having him refer to Peter as 'Symeon'), James quotes Amos 9.11–12 in the Septuagint version and thereby makes a point which is impossible if he had been following the Massoretic Text.[106] This feature shows quite conclusively that Luke was not using some source originating in the *ipsissima verba* of James, and may easily have drafted the whole speech himself.

For these reasons, therefore, we may be sure that the account of the Council in Jerusalem is a Lucan creation for a purpose to be discussed below. However, it seems likely that Luke did not construct the actual fourfold prohibition, because it would then be difficult to explain its narrow scope (to the Gentiles in Antioch, Syria and Cilicia), and also because there is much evidence to suggest that at least two of the prohibitions – on meat offered to idols and meat with blood in it – were still being observed by Gentiles in various parts much later.[107]

The question of table-fellowship between Jew and Gentile is not explicitly raised in Acts 15, but its presence is everywhere implied. We may confidently assume that Luke would have intended his readers to understand that what prompted the teaching by the Judeans in Acts 15.1 of the need for circumcision of Gentiles was simply the fact that they were sitting around the same table, for the eucharist especially, with Jews. This would have raised their Jewish hackles for the reasons we have already identified, especially if, as seems very likely, they too were Pharisees (15.5) or influenced by them and had accepted a much more zealous attitude to questions of purity. Circumcision was not something pressed upon Gentile Christians for some abstract theological reason; it was seen as a remedy for a situation involving grievous risk to the continued existence of the Jewish people.

Similarly, in the references to the Cornelius story made by James and Peter the reader of Acts can hardly fail to remember that the essential element of that story was not the broad notion that God had authorized the mission to the Gentiles, but the far more particular idea that what had received divine endorsement was Jewish–Gentile table-fellowship in the Christian communities. This theme is very apparent in the four prohibitions. These originate in Lev 17 and 18 as those rules imposed upon strangers living in Israel: that is to say, although such strangers are excepted from adherence to the vast majority of the commandments of the Torah, there is a small group of rules in these chapters of Leviticus which are imposed on the foreigners, obviously because they proscribe behaviour regarded as particularly loathsome to the Israelites and not to be allowed even to foreigners.[108] Now it is quite clear that these four prohibitions are singularly appropriate in a context where a Christian community has been established in which Jews and Gentiles engage in table-fellowship − a situation not unreasonably seen as parallel to the Levitical model of strangers living among the Israelites; the Gentiles have agreed to observe a code of conduct which precludes them from activities notoriously abhorrent to their Jewish brothers. On this view, the difficult verse 15.21 may be interpreted as a recognition that the fourfold prohibition goes a long way to satisfying Jewish or Jewish Christian criticism of Christian fellowship, which would otherwise be patently in breach of a well-known part of the Mosaic law: namely, Lev 17 and 18. Accordingly, Acts 15.1−31 is a passage intimately connected with the theme of Jewish–Gentile commensality, which, we have argued, is of pre-eminent importance in Luke–Acts. But before concluding our argument on this subject, we must briefly consider the remaining passages on table-fellowship between Jews and Gentiles, all of which figure in Paul's ministry to the Gentiles.

Other instances of table-fellowship between Jews and Gentiles in Acts

An illuminating reflection of the general failure of Lucan scholars to be sufficiently sensitive to the table-fellowship question in Luke–Acts is the fact that S. G. Wilson, in a discussion of Peter's entering into fellowship with Cornelius, can assert that 'it is of some interest that it is Peter rather than Paul who is allowed the one break with Jewish legal tradition'.[109] In saying this, Wilson has overlooked the fact that Luke specifically describes Paul as engaging in fellowship with Gentiles, of precisely the kind established between Peter and

Cornelius, on three separate occasions: with Lydia, a God-fearing Gentile in Philippi (16.14–15), with the Roman gaoler in the same city (16.25–34) and with Titius Justus, a God-fearer in Corinth (18.7). These incidents have already been discussed in Chapter 2 above, mainly to illustrate the type of converts which Luke describes Paul as making in the Diaspora. It is surely not without significance that all of these occasions occur after the Cornelius narrative *and* the account of the Council in Jerusalem finally approving the mission to the Gentiles in a form obviously related to the establishment of table-fellowship between Jews and Gentiles. The reason for this is that Luke does not wish it to appear that there was such fellowship until the practice has been given the most watertight endorsement by the church in Jerusalem. We saw in Chapter 2, moreover, that sense can only be made of conversion accounts before Acts 15, especially those at Antioch-on-the-Orontes and Pisidian Antioch (11.19–20; 13.13–48), on the basis that the Gentiles who converted were largely God-fearers beforehand and that Jewish–Gentile table-fellowship was a feature of the Christian communities established in those cities. In Chapter 2 it was also shown that for the Lucan Paul the expression 'from now on I will go to the Gentiles' in the Corinth narrative (18.6b) did not mean an abandonment of the mission to Jews in favour of the Gentiles, but simply the public establishment cf table-fellowship between Jew and Gentile. We are now in a better position to understand the full import of Acts 18.6b, for Paul actually says 'From now on I will go to the Gentiles καθαρός.' The word καθαρός, which has a very emphatic position at the start of the sentence in the Greek text, is often translated as an epithet signifying general moral blamelessness: thus, 'with a clear conscience' (*JB*) or 'innocent' (*RSV*). From our previous discussion of the Jewish attitudes to mixing with the Gentiles, it is very probable that this word should be taken in its cultic sense to mean 'unpolluted'. Thus, the Lucan Paul is affirming that he is ritually pure in moving into the house of a Gentile and, it is implied, will remain so thereafter.

But even though the Gentile mission and the fellowship intrinsic to it are depicted by Luke as having been twice authorized by the Jerusalem church, his presentation of Paul's role in bringing the Gospel to the Gentiles still reveals traces of embarrassment. This is apparent in Luke's suppression of specific references to Paul's eating with Gentiles before Acts 15, of course, but it is also evident in the way he presents the occasions where this does occur. At Philippi, for example, Luke notes that Lydia 'urged' or 'pressed' (παρεβιάσατο)

Paul's party to stay at her house, as a sign of their belief in her faith
in the Lord (16.15). It quite misses the point to attribute their initial
disinclination to stay with her to Paul's wish not to be a burden on
anyone.[110] Paul may have wished to work to support himself, but the
available evidence contradicts the notion that this led him to stay at an
inn rather than under someone's roof.[111] No, they are at first chary
of accepting Lydia's offer because she is a Gentile. Not unnaturally,
against their refusal from a position of Jewish ethnic solidarity she
proffers their common faith. So they accept her hospitality (as confirmed in 16.40). Luke's embarrassment over this issue is not quite
so manifest in the account of the table-fellowship in the house of the
gaoler at Philippi following the baptism of himself and all his family
(16.34), but it can, nevertheless, be detected even there. This is
probably the explanation for Luke's awkwardly describing Paul's
preaching to the gaoler and all in his house (16.32) and mentioning
their baptism (16.33), before the gaoler brings them into his house
and feeds them (16.34). By this rather artificial plot sequence Luke
avoids having Paul enter into table-fellowship with an outright pagan.
Thirdly, Luke presents Paul's moving into the house of the God-fearer
Titius Justus in Corinth, which involves his leaving the house of the
Jews Aquila and Priscilla (18.1–3), not as having been the result
of some spontaneous decision by Paul, but as a response to the
blasphemous opposition he encountered from the Jews of that city
(18.6–7).

From Luke's treatment of these three occasions on which Paul
established with Gentiles the same kind of fellowship which Peter had
with Cornelius, it is apparent that, in spite of the legitimation for the
practice provided by the Jerusalem church in Acts 11 and 15, the
subject was still problematic for Luke. Why this should be the case is
considered a little below. In the meantime, it is desirable to investigate
the possible reference to table-fellowship in Acts 27.

The nature of the meal in Acts 27.33–8
Let us consider the main features of Acts 27.33–8. It is just before
dawn. The boat in which Paul is travelling to Rome has been driven
before a storm for fourteen days but is now anchored off an island,
which turns out to be Malta. On board are Paul, his companion
Aristarchus, who is from Macedonia and may be either Jew or
Gentile, possibly some other companions of Paul, whose presence
is suggested by the first person plural narration, other prisoners on
the way to Rome, some of whom are most probably Jewish since they

were embarked at Caesarea (27.1), their Roman guard under the command of the centurion Julius, and the ship's owner and crew. At this point, Paul addresses his fellow-voyagers and urges them to eat, for this is in the interests of their deliverance (σωτηρία) (27.34). He tells them that not a hair from the head of any of them will be lost. Then, having taken bread, he gives thanks to God before all of them, breaks it and begins to eat (λαβὼν ἄρτον εὐχαρίστησεν τῷ θεῷ ἐνώπιον πάντων καὶ κλάσας ἤρξατο ἐσθίειν) (27.35). They all take heart and begin to eat. There are 266 souls on board the boat.

What does Luke wish to convey by this incident? Some scholars, who interpret the first person plural narration of Acts 27 as proof that Luke has used an eye-witness account[112] or even that he was present on board himself,[113] see in the narrative a record of historical fact. But since there is evidence that the first person plural was used as a stylistic feature by Hellenistic writers to instil a sense of vividness into descriptions of sea-voyages,[114] no such deductions can be drawn from the first person plural in Acts 27. Moreover, Paul's voyage to Rome has such a miraculous character as to counsel caution in attributing too great a degree of historicity to all the details of Luke's presentation of it.[115] For Ernst Haenchen, the whole account of the voyage has the literary intention of depicting the evangelist as 'the strong, unshaken favourite of God who strides from triumph to triumph',[116] and there is much to be said for this view.

But what of the possible eucharistic reference some scholars have discerned in Acts 27.35? Kirsopp Lake and Henry Cadbury regarded this verse as denoting nothing more than the usual Jewish custom of offering thanks before meals and derided as absurd the idea that it contained any reference to the eucharist.[117] Haenchen, too, rejects the eucharistic interpretation,[118] as does G. W. H. Lampe, albeit a little more diffidently, who comments that since 'they all partake, it evidently cannot be the Eucharist itself'.[119] On the other hand, many scholars have argued that 27.35 is eucharistic,[120] and this cause has recently been championed by Paul Walaskay.[121] Bo Reicke has published a strong defence of this position, which falls short of being totally convincing because of his failure, admittedly shared by all other writers in the field, to appreciate the connection between 27.33–8 and the Lucan interest in Jewish–Gentile table-fellowship. Reicke does make some excellent points, however. First, he argues that it is difficult to regard the meal instigated by Paul in 27.33–6 as an ordinary, everyday meal when Luke has otherwise taken such pains to present him as being quite extraordinary in his insight into the divine will (see especially 27.22–6).[122] Secondly, Reicke points to the strong similarity between the language of Acts 27.35 and other New Testament passages on the eucharist, such as Lk 22.19, Acts 20.11 and 1 Cor 11.23ff. That Acts 27.35 contains no reference to Paul distributing the bread (except in the Western Text) is hardly an obstacle to its eucharistic interpretation, since there is also no mention made of such a distribution in Acts 20.11 or in 1 Cor 11.23ff.[123] Thirdly, Reicke sensibly accounts for the odd reference to the number of persons on board the boat in 27.37, rather than at the beginning or end of the voyage narrative, on the basis of analogy with the Synoptic references to the numbers of those who were fed by Jesus during the miracles of the loaves and the fishes (for example, Mk 6.44; Lk 9.14).[124]

In spite of these arguments, however, Reicke is unwilling to regard the meal as eucharistic in the full sense, because it is shared by outright pagans ('lauter Heiden'). A view similar to this, we recall, was also expressed by Lampe, and Walaskay too gives some credit to it by speaking of the possibility of a eucharist restricted to the Christians on board. So what is Reicke's solution? He sees a close parallel between those on board and the crowds who partook of the bread miraculously produced by Jesus, whose members too were neither disciples of Jesus nor baptized, so that both groups can be said to 'participate in a prefiguration of the Christian Lord's Supper as a potential preparation for later discipleship'.[125]

The problem with this solution, of course, is that it entirely neglects to take into account the theme of table-fellowship between Jews and Gentiles so prominent elsewhere in Acts. Acts 27.33–7 is the fourth occasion in the work in which Paul enters into table-fellowship with Gentiles, thereby necessarily raising once again the problems for Jewish ethnic integrity which such behaviour entailed. In view of this, the eucharistic features persuasively expounded by Reicke are relevant, but as aspects of the fundamental social problem of the proper relationship between Jews and Christians in the Christian community, not simply in isolation as indicative of a Lucan interest in the theology of the eucharist. One might argue against this interpretation that, because Paul was taking measures in an emergency, no Jew would have found his actions objectionable, since the usual ban on eating with pagans would have been regarded as temporarily suspended. But two factors may be opposed to this objection. First, Paul could have eaten privately, but instead chose solemnly to initiate a meal involving everyone on board. Secondly, that Paul is caught up in an emergency is central to Luke's argument. This is shown by Luke's having him say 'Not a hair from anyone's head will be lost' (27.34). Although this is an Old Testament proverb (1 Sam 14.45; 2 Sam 14.11; 1 Kgs 1.52), its only other occurrence in the New Testament is at Lk 21.18, where it is used by Jesus to reassure his disciples that they will survive the troubles which await them in the period before the End. That Luke repeats this saying in 27.34 indicates that he is establishing a parallel between the situation of those on board the boat and the fate Jesus predicted for his disciples. And just as Jesus tells his disciples in Lk 21.19 that they will win their lives (τὰς ψυχάς) by endurance, so Paul can prophesy that no one on board will lose his life (ψυχῆς) in Acts 27.22. Thus, while on the literal level of the story in Acts 27 Paul takes action appropriate to an emergency, there is another level being created in which the fate of those on the boat symbolizes the experience of the disciples of Jesus after his resurrection but before the End. In one sense this is an emergency, but it is only what the disciples must expect during this time. Accordingly, the existence of this parallel and the eucharistic meaning of 27.33–7 necessitate interpreting σωτηρία (27.34) as operating on both the literal and the symbolical level, to convey survival of shipwreck and the salvation which comes from Christ for Jew and Gentile.

From this analysis, it seems highly plausible that Luke has used the story of Paul's voyage and shipwreck to communicate a message of quite specific importance to his readers. We should remember that Günther Bornkamm has shown how Matthew re-interpreted Mark's description of Jesus stilling the storm to present it as an image of Jesus' relationship to his disciples in the 'little ship' of the church.[126] Luke's interpretation is not quite the same as this, however, since not all those on board Paul's vessel are disciples or even look like becoming such (27.42–4). Nevertheless, Paul's exhortation to everyone on board (and we have argued that there were Jews as well as Gentiles) to take food, for this pertains to their σωτηρία (27.33–4), reinforces Luke's persistent emphasis on the fact that the old barriers between Jew and Gentile have been decisively shattered in the eucharistic fellowship of the Christian community and that an era of salvation for all humanity has now been inaugurated, even if there are some who do not yet realize it.

Table-fellowship and Luke's legitimatory purpose

The time has now come to locate Luke's presentation of table-fellowship between Jews and Gentiles within the wider context of his intentions and strategy. From the Jewish point of view, Jews ate with Gentiles in the Christian community only at the price of denying their *ethnos* and their faith. For Luke, it is this objection, as much social and ethnic as religious, that constitutes the main problem for the spread of Christianity throughout the Diaspora, even though he attempts to suppress its significance in the early stages, before the Council in Jerusalem recorded in Acts 15. As a description of Luke's subject in Acts, the phrase 'the mission to the Gentiles' is something of a misnomer. Even when he has Paul say 'we are turning to the Gentiles' (13.46) and 'from now on I will go to the Gentiles' (18.6), he is not suggesting that Paul is thenceforward transferring his missionary endeavours from Jews to Gentiles, but rather that Gentiles also may become part of the Christian communities, which means they may share table-fellowship with Jews.

Yet how is the table-fellowship question relevant to Luke's own community? If the most popular view as to the composition of his community were correct – namely, that its members were predominantly Gentile, with Jews either absent or an insignificant minority – it would be difficult indeed to account for the fact that his presentation of the early history of Diaspora Christianity focuses so intensely upon the relationship between Jews and Gentiles in the Christian communities and not simply on the admission of Gentiles to those communities. In Chapter 2 above, however, there was presented a body of evidence for the view that Jews were a significant component of the community for whom Luke was writing. This finding is strongly corroborated by the prominence Luke accords to table-fellowship. The most plausible explanation for why he has shown such an interest in this question is that in his community there were Jews and Gentiles who did sit down to table together and who were attracting criticism because of this. Such opposition, originating in an apprehended danger to continued Jewish identity, threatened the unity and even the existence of Luke's community and constitutes one of the prime motivations for the unique way he presents his material, in other words, for his theology.

It is possible, moreover, to chart in greater detail the dynamics of this opposition and Luke's response to it. We begin with our view that Jewish–Gentile table-fellowship was an important feature in the life of his community. Now it is clear from Paul's letter to the

Galatians (and also from Mark's Gospel) that there was a stage, early on in the spread of Christianity through the Diaspora, when such fellowship was considered permissible. However, some time in the late forties or early fifties of the first century CE there was a Jewish Christian reaction against this practice. This was initiated by Peter, at James' prompting, in Antioch, but the movement to revoke such fellowship, or to have the Gentiles taking part circumcised, and thereby to remove the offence to Jewish ethnicity it involved, then spread to other parts of the Diaspora, including to Paul's Galatian churches (whatever their exact location). Matthew's Gospel provides further evidence of this reaction. The Jewish Christian reactionaries against table-fellowship with Gentiles were able to cite as authority for their views the potent names of Peter and James, the leaders of the church in Jerusalem, and did so as far afield as Galatia. Given the non-historicity of the Council in Acts 15 and the fact that Paul does not mention in his letters that the church in Jerusalem had changed its mind on this subject, it appears that the Jewish Christians in that city were never reconciled to Jews eating with Gentiles in the Christian communities.

But in Luke's community the Pauline view on this matter had triumphed and Jews engaged in table-fellowship with Gentiles. The fourfold prohibition quoted by Luke in Acts 15 probably represents the core of a compromise agreement reached between Jewish Christians and Gentile Christians, with the Gentiles undertaking to adhere to the four prohibitions, and the Jews in return re-establishing table-fellowship. This was regarded as an arrangement which went a long way to satisfying Jewish Christian scruples, in view of the parallel to the rules enforced on foreigners living in Israel in Lev 17 and 18. We have seen that this decree did not originate in Jerusalem, but the fact that it has for its destination the brothers in Antioch, Syria and Cilicia (15.23) is best explained on the grounds that it was among the churches in these regions that the compromise agreement was reached. So Paul's opinion on the matter, probably some time after his death, was victorious at last in Antioch. Now while it is not certain in which Hellenistic city Luke's community was located, it is clear that it had either seen a restoration of table-fellowship after a period during which it had been prohibited because of Jewish–Christian hostility, or that it had maintained table-fellowship throughout the history of the community in spite of opposition from the leaders of the Jerusalem church, including Peter and James. The former alternative is probably more likely, but in either case it is evident that it was vital for Luke to legitimate, that is, to explain and justify, the practice to his Christian contemporaries. If any feature needed to form part of the symbolic universe he was creating for them in the face of the symbolic universe rooted in Jewish ethnicity, it was table-fellowship.

The particular method employed by Luke to legitimate Jewish – Gentile table-fellowship against the background of persistent opposition from the Jerusalem church in the period before the events of 67–70 CE is both simple and yet thoroughly audacious – he re-writes the history of early Christianity relating to this subject and assigns to Peter, James and the church in Jerusalem exactly the opposite roles to those which they played in fact. Thus, was not Paul known as the pioneer, if not the initiator, of the great task of bringing the message of salvation to the Gentiles, while Peter was the evangelizer of the Jews (Gal 2.1–10)? Then Luke makes Peter begin the mission to the Gentiles (Acts 10.1–11.18). Had not Peter come to Antioch and, at the instigation of James, broken off table-fellowship with the Gentile Christians there (Gal 2.11–14)? Not at all, says Luke, it was other Christians with Pharisaical links who caused the trouble in Antioch (Acts 15.1, 5), for Peter had seen Jewish–Gentile commensality as commanded by God as early as the conversion of Cornelius and this attitude had been endorsed by the Jerusalem church on that occasion and was subsequently re-affirmed by that church, under firm direction by James, during an authoritative council (Acts 11.1–18; 15.6–26). Had there not been a tremendous showdown between Paul and Peter over the table-fellowship in Antioch, with Paul failing to carry the day on that issue? By no means, Luke tells us, there was never any dispute between Peter and Paul on this or any other issue. Was not the notorious split between Paul and Barnabas after years of joint missionary work a result of Barnabas siding with Peter in Antioch (Gal 2.13)? No, the undeniable division between them was caused by their differing attitudes to taking John Mark along on a missionary journey (Acts 13.13; 15.36–40). Had not the form of Christianity developed in Antioch lacked authorization and supervision from Jerusalem? How could this be true, implies Luke, when Barnabas was actually an envoy from Jerusalem sent to Antioch very early in the history of the community there and one who was perfectly happy with what he found (Acts 11.22–3)?

That Luke should plainly feel compelled to be able to plead the support of Peter, James and the Jerusalem church, even though that meant reversing historical fact at many crucial points, tells as much about the opposition his community was encountering in maintaining table-fellowship between Jews and Gentiles. This Lucan strategy would appear to necessitate the conclusion that the names of Peter and James were being invoked by people as authorities against that practice. Such an attitude is most plausibly to be regarded as originating among Jewish Christians who held Peter and James in respect and remembered their views on Jews eating with Gentiles in the Christian community. No doubt these Jewish Christians were being influenced or even pressurized by ordinary Jews to do all they could to oppose such fellowship. In his letter to the Galatians, after all, Paul records that those advocating circumcision did so to escape persecution for the cross of Christ (Gal 6.12), and such persecution is only to be expected from Diaspora Jews alarmed at the attack on their ethnic identity involved in Jews dining with non-Jews. Some of the Jewish Christians giving Luke's community trouble could have preserved links with it, while others might have dissociated themselves from it, perhaps even by renouncing all Christian claims and returning to the synagogue. In this way we are able to see at least one aspect of both the internal and the external threat to the flock which Paul prophesied would be its lot in his speech to the Ephesian elders in Acts 20.28–30.

It should be mentioned, finally, that there is nothing in the subsequent history of early Christianity that weighs against this reconstruction of the social and religious setting of Luke's community and his response to it. There appear to have been continuous efforts in some quarters to push Christianity in a Jewish direction. Ignatius of Antioch, writing between 105 and 115 CE,[127] complains of Judaizers in the Eastern churches[128] and insists upon the importance of unity in the eucharist in a way Luke would have fully approved.[129] Later in the second century, Justin Martyr's *Dialogue with Trypho* is evidence both for the existence of Jewish Christians (46.1) and for continuing attempts to impose circumcision and the Mosaic law on Gentile Christians (47.1–2). Among some of the Jewish Christian groups, such as the Ebionites,[130] there was a strong tendency to elevate the importance of Peter, matched by a pronounced hostility to Paul. These themes emerge, for example, in the *Epistula Petri* (1.1–3) and in the *Pseudo-Clementine Homilies*.[131] Accordingly, the split in the Christian fold which opened up at least as early as Paul's confrontation with Peter in Antioch (Gal 2.11–14) appears to have persisted until well into the second century and beyond, and it is not at all surprising that Luke should have felt compelled to take a considered position on it in the eighties or nineties of the first century.

In conclusion, we have shown that a legitimation of table-fellowship between Jews and Gentiles forms a vital arch in the symbolic universe which Luke creates for his community. It was this issue that in the early history of Christianity had led to the development of a distinct Christian identity *vis-à-vis* Judaism, and it was still central to the life of Luke's Christian contemporaries.

5

THE LAW

1. Introduction

In recent years the question of Luke's attitude to the Jewish law has begun to attract increased attention in the scholarly community, as exemplified by the writings of J. Jervell,[1] S.G. Wilson[2] and C.L. Blomberg.[3] Before these incursions into the field, the subject tended to be treated only in passing in Lucan commentaries and in works on more general topics, such as the law in the Synoptic Gospels. Underlying this widespread indifference among New Testament scholars is a belief that the Jewish law was of little or no interest to the Third Evangelist, primarily because he wrote for what was predominantly a Gentile audience. This opinion had an early champion in F. Overbeck[4] and is represented more recently in the works of E. Haenchen,[5] H. Schürmann[6] and R. Banks,[7] to name only a few. Allied to this belief is the common notion that Luke does not offer a consistent treatment of the law, especially in his Gospel. B.H. Branscomb subscribed to this view,[8] and it has now been taken up by S.G. Wilson, who has argued that the law was not a problem for Luke, at least at the time he composed his Gospel, and that he was able to use inconsistent material to emphasize different themes in connection with the law − prophetic, practical or Christological − without feeling obliged to unify them.[9]

The status of the law in Acts, where it obviously plays an important role, has always been something of a stumbling-block for those who attribute to Luke a lack of interest in, or an inconsistent attitude to, the Jewish law. J. Jervell, for example, largely relying on the evidence in Acts, argued that there is a cohesive attitude to the law in Luke−Acts and that it is, in fact, the most conservative in the New Testament.[10] S.G. Wilson has attempted to cope with this difficulty by postulating that the question of Paul and the law had only become a problem for Luke after the composition of the Gospel, but before he wrote Acts.[11]

An estimation of Luke's interest in the Jewish law very different from those just mentioned is demanded once account is taken of the social, ethnic and political pressures upon his community. In the previous chapter we argued that, as far as Luke and his readers were concerned, the crucial factor in the establishment of the sectarian status of the Christian community *vis-à-vis* Judaism was the institution of table-fellowship between Jews and Gentiles, and that this was still a live issue in his own community. Such table-fellowship was quite correctly perceived by Jews as a serious threat to the existence of their *ethnos* and of the Mosaic law. Accordingly, it is hardly plausible that Luke should offer such a careful response to Jewish sensibilities outraged by the issue of table-fellowship and yet have little interest in the closely related question of the law itself. On the contrary, the conclusions we have reached so far raise a strong *prima facie* likelihood that Luke was deeply concerned with the status of the Jewish law and expressed a consistent attitude to it in his two volumes. Moreover, given the manner of his defence of table-fellowship – namely, his depiction of it as both divinely authorized and directed, and approved by the pious Jews of the Jerusalem church – it is probable that his attitude to the law was conservative rather than radical. Whatever Luke might say about the law, however, the inescapable fact was that in practising mixed table-fellowship his community had transgressed against the very sense of Jewish identity and separateness which the Mosaic law functioned to protect. We would not be surprised, therefore, if the text were found to contain unresolved tensions between Luke's programme on the law and the realities of the situation as they might appear to Jews who had not succumbed to the preaching of Christian evangelists. These alternative hypotheses must now be tested against the evidence in the text.

2. The law in Luke's Gospel

The infancy narratives

The first two chapters of Luke's Gospel, whose striking homogeneity within the overall scheme of his two volumes has been convincingly defended by P.S. Minear,[12] are peopled by a number of Jewish men and women who are characterized by their exemplary devotion to Yahweh and to his law. First of all there are Zechariah and Elisabeth who 'were both righteous [δίκαιοι] before God, walking blameless in all the commandments [ἐντολαί] and ordinances [δικαιώματα] of the Lord' (1.6). The word ἐντολαί is regularly used in the Septuagint to translate the Hebrew word *mitzvot*, to denote the individual requirements of the Mosaic law,[13] while δικαιώματα usually refers to statutes in the wider sense, including cultic and social obligations.[14] The combination of ἐντολαί and δικαιώματα is in agreement with Septuagintal usage (cf. Ex 15.26; Dt 4.40; 6.17; 10.13; 27.10). Accordingly, the adjective δίκαιος in Lk 1.6, the meaning of which is made clear in the rest of the verse, denotes complete conformity to the will of God, especially as it is expressed in his law.

The commitment of Mary and Joseph to the law, secondly, becomes most apparent in Luke's description of their presentation of Jesus in the Temple (2.22–39). In the course of eighteen verses Luke mentions that they were acting in accordance with the law no fewer than five times (2.22, 23, 24, 27, 39). It is a little ironic, therefore, that there was, in fact, no Mosaic or customary requirement that parents present their first-born in the Temple.[15] There were regulations (in Lev 12) for women to be purified after giving birth, but nothing necessitated the presentation of the child. Luke appears to have been using as his model the presentation of Samuel by his mother Hannah in the temple at Shiloh (1 Sam 1.24–8). So our evangelist has either been mistaken as to the practices in the Temple in Jerusalem on this point, which is not unreasonable given that he is writing fifteen to twenty years after its destruction, or he has deliberately created an incident and an unhistorical legal requirement to highlight the extremely conservative attitude of Mary and Joseph to the Jewish law. Either way, the impression fostered by this episode, together with their circumcising Jesus on the eighth day (2.21) and having a regular habit of journeying to Jerusalem to celebrate the Passover (2.41), is that Mary and Joseph were utterly faithful to the law which God had given to Israel through Moses.

The same must be said of Simeon and Anna. Simeon is described as δίκαιος, and this clearly relates to his obedience to the law, and as εὐλαβής (2.25), a word meaning 'devout' which is unique to Luke in the New Testament and which expresses a pious dedication to God's law.[16] Anna is not explicitly described in these terms, but their implicit application to her becomes evident in her fasting and praying in the Temple night and day (2.37).

Yet it is not just their fidelity to the law that these six Israelites have in common. All of them realize that the transformation in the fortunes of his people which Yahweh promised long before has begun; all of them are aware that the salvation of Israel is almost upon them. Thus Zechariah exults that the Lord has brought redemption (λύτρωσις) to his people and raised up a horn of salvation (σωτηρία), just as he promised through his prophets (1.68–70). Mary proclaims a very similar sentiment in the Magnificat (1.54–5). Moreover, when Simeon sees Jesus he knows that the consolation (παράκλησις) of Israel which he was expecting (2.25) has arrived, for Jesus is the Lord's Messiah (2.26), and Anna, also, recognizes in Jesus the redemption (λύτρωσις) of Jerusalem (2.38). The message that Jesus is Messiah (Χριστός) and saviour (σωτήρ) is conveyed by angels to the shepherds outside Bethlehem (2.11).

In the hymn long known as the Nunc Dimittis, however, Simeon strikes a new chord, one which will resonate throughout Luke–Acts – that the salvation revealed in Jesus will extend not only to Jews, but will also be 'for the illumination of the Gentiles' (2.32).[17] The phrase 'the light of the Gentiles' appears to derive from Is 42.6 and 49.6 and will later be used in Acts with reference to the inclusion of Gentiles in the scheme of salvation (Acts 13.67; 26.23).

Luke's depiction of these pious Jews immediately recognizing Jesus as God's Anointed for the redemption of Israel (and the Gentiles) raises issues the importance of which has been insufficiently appreciated. There is far more in these chapters than the undeniably Lucan theme of promise and fulfilment or the equally Lucan desire to present Christianity as the logical and legitimate outgrowth or continuation of Judaism.[18] The infancy narratives introduce a central feature of his reflection upon the law – that although it is God-given and worthy of the highest respect, it is incapable, *per se*, of bringing salvation to Israel. One major purpose of these two chapters is to show that the most outstanding of Jews are waiting for a redemption which the law cannot provide, and recognize in Jesus the Messiah and saviour, the agent of that redemption. This theme will later be made explicit in Acts 13.38–9. But his arrival does not involve any sharp break with their traditions, since the role of Jesus was repeatedly predicted by their ancestors. The mission of Jesus represents the culmination of the law, not its abrogation. At the very end of the Gospel there are two passages (24.26–7, 44) in which this theme is explicitly formulated, as Jesus explains to his disciples how he is the fulfilment of the law and the prophets.

Yet even in these early chapters a shadow is cast across the stage by the grim prophecy of Simeon: 'Look, this child is set for the fall and the rise of many in Israel, to be a sign that is spoken against' (2.34). In other words, while many Jews will accept Jesus, many others will not. By implication, of course, those who reject Jesus also reject

the ancestral traditions of the Jewish people which find their fulfilment in him. For if true piety and obedience to the law result in an
accurate appreciation of the identity and role of Jesus, a failure by
some to arrive at this appreciation necessarily raises a question-mark
over the integrity of their adherence to the law. We shall see that
throughout Luke–Acts the division among the people caused by the
preaching of Jesus and his disciples and the antipathy towards the
law of those who reject him are both very significant themes.

To conclude this section, it is apparent that the infancy narratives
do contain a particular perspective on the law. Luke's message on this
subject has three elements. First, the law is good but cannot provide
salvation, as Jewish tradition itself attests in speaking of a Messiah
who is to come; secondly, the most devout Israelites, without
abandoning the law, realize that Jesus is the Messiah and that the time
of salvation is at hand; and, thirdly, many Jews will reject Jesus and,
in so doing, demonstrate the illegitimacy of their beliefs and practices.
During the following discussion it will be shown that the same pattern
is present throughout Luke–Acts.

But the impression which Luke wishes to convey is one thing, the
realities of the situation are quite another. Jews antipathetic to Christianity on account of its encouragement of Jewish–Gentile table-
fellowship would hardly have been impressed by Luke's argument
that being a Christian involved no abrogation of the Mosaic law.
For there was, of course, a fundamental incompatibility between a
Christianity which included Jews and Gentiles in one closely knit
community and Judaism. That incompatibility, although not evident
in the infancy narratives, does begin to surface, as we shall soon see,
in the attitudes to the law expressed by Jesus in the Third Gospel and
is starkly uncovered in Acts (especially 10.1–11.18). Luke is obviously
discomfited by this collision between Christian gospel and Jewish law,
and his treatment of the law has a central role to play in disguising it.

In the end, however, Luke could not entirely submerge the facts
of the case. The resulting inconsistency between the Lucan programme
and the underlying reality goes a long way towards accounting for
the ambivalent attitudes to the law in Luke–Acts which have occasionally been noticed but not explained.

Jesus' respect for the law

Many passages in the Third Gospel testify to Jesus' respect for Jewish
tradition and obedience to the Mosaic code. Luke alone tells us that
Jesus was in the habit of attending synagogue on the sabbath (4.16).

On two occasions he cures lepers (5.12–16; 17.11–19) and directs
them to present themselves to the priests, a course of action prescribed
in Lev 13 and 14. He closely follows Mk 1.40–5 in the first of these
passages, but the second is unique to his Gospel. There is one particular incident in Luke's Gospel which reveals an attitude to the law
remarkably conservative in comparison with a Marcan passage which
it loosely parallels (Lk 10.25–8; Mk 12.28–34). Luke describes how
a lawyer approaches Jesus and asks: 'What shall I do to inherit eternal
life?' In the Marcan passage, Jesus' interrogator is one of the scribes
and his question is 'What is the first of all the commandments?' In
Mark, Jesus answers with love of God (quoting Dt 6.14) and love of
neighbour. But Luke has Jesus answer with another question: 'What
is written in the law?' The lawyer then replies that we must love God
and love our neighbour, to which Jesus remarks: 'Do this and you
will live.' What makes this passage so conservative is that Luke should
leave open the possibility that adherence to the Mosaic law could result
in eternal life, whereas Mark is merely interested in establishing the
correct priority among its multifarious rules and commandments.
It is possible, however, that Luke was relying upon his readers understanding this incident in the light of an aspect of his treatment of the
law developed elsewhere in Luke–Acts, that the ideal of love of
God and love of neighbour was not in fact achieved by anyone relying
only on the law. Finally, in describing the Transfiguration of Jesus
(9.28–36), Luke adds the feature that Jesus, and Moses and Elijah
appeared in glory (9.31). This results in something of an elevation
for the law and the prophets, who are inevitably diminished in Mark's
account (Mk 9.2–8) when the voice from the cloud tells the disciples
to heed Jesus and not, presumably, Moses and Elijah.

Jesus' transcendence of the law

Yet there are times when the Lucan Jesus does appear to stand above
the law. This is hardly unexpected in view of the depiction of him
in the first two chapters of the Gospel as the Messiah, the one who
will bring salvation to Jew and Gentile. Perhaps this motif is most
fully expressed in the four incidents dealing with his attitude to the
sabbath (6.1–5, 6–11; 13.10–17; 14.1–6). The first two of these
derive from Mk 2.23–8 and 3.1–6 respectively, while the remaining
two are unique to the Third Gospel. In Lk 6.1–5 Jesus defends his
disciples against the allegation of the scribes and the Pharisees that
in plucking corn they have violated the sabbath. He first cites a
precedent involving David and his followers and then asserts that

'the Son of Man is lord of the sabbath'. Luke omits Mk 2.27, but even with what remains it is quite obvious that Jesus claims the right to define the sabbath, even though he does not abrogate it. The same moral emerges from Lk 6.6–11, where, without denying the validity of the sabbath law, Jesus rejects the current interpretation of its ambit to perform a work of mercy. Later on, furthermore, he heals a crippled woman in a synagogue on the sabbath (13.10–17) and goes so far as to declare that the sabbath is just the day for healing. The same theme is continued in the fourth incident (14.1–6).

Both S. G. Wilson[19] and R. Banks[20] quite correctly insist on the Christological aspect to these sabbath stories, that is, the extent to which they reveal the authority and miracle-working power of Jesus. But Wilson surely stretches the evidence when he asserts that Luke shows little interest in the niceties of sabbath observance, because he was writing for Gentile readers for whom this would not have been a live issue.[21] Let us consider some other evidence in Luke–Acts relevant to this subject. In his passion narrative Luke relates that the Galilean women who watched where Jesus was buried had rested on the day after his death, a sabbath, 'in accordance with the commandment' (κατὰ τὴν ἐντολήν) (23.56). Only Luke specifies this detail and he appears to approve of their inactivity in view of its being required by the Mosaic code. Secondly, in Acts 1.12 he mentions that the Mount of Olives was a sabbath day's journey distant from Jerusalem. This feature presupposes an audience familiar with this distance. Thirdly, in Acts 20.7–12 he describes the events of a eucharistic gathering of the community in Troas which began in the evening of the first day of the week. The first day of the week was Sunday, which began at dusk on Saturday afternoon (Lk 23.54). Thus, the Christians of Troas came together on Saturday night. Paul's Corinthian Christians also seem to have gathered on Sunday (1 Cor 16.2).

To make sense of Luke's attitude to the sabbath it is necessary to have regard to the social and religious context of his own community. Although it was essential to the unity of Christian communities in the Diaspora that Jews forsake their ethnic identity to the extent of dining with Gentiles, this was not the case with sabbath observance. Nothing in principle prevented Jewish Christians observing the sabbath, and Gentiles, whom Luke portrays as exempted from virtually all of the requirements of the Mosaic law by virtue of the Apostolic Council in Acts 15, continuing to work on that day. The all-important eucharistic gathering on Saturday night would not be affected by different practice in regard to the sabbath. Such an approach appears similar to that endorsed by the historical Paul (Rom 14.5). This social background appears to underlie the Lucan attitude to the sabbath. He depicts Jesus as assuming the validity of the Mosaic law on this point, but as vigorously disputing with the scribes and Pharisees as to the proper scope of its application, even to the extent of using it as an occasion to work miraculous cures. Thus, the pattern of the infancy narratives re-appears. The law is good, but the arrival of the Messiah means that it must be seen in a new light. Some Jews accept the authority of Jesus over the sabbath; others, especially the members of the Jewish establishment, do not (6.11; 13.14; 14.5–6), so that Simeon's prophecy is fulfilled. Both Jews and Gentiles in Luke's community would have been reassured by this approach, the Jews because the Mosaic rule had not been revoked and the Gentiles because their failure to observe the sabbath was compatible with Jesus having transcended the law, as well as being validated by Luke's account of the Apostolic dispensation in Acts 15.

Luke's concern to indicate that Jesus both respects and yet transcends the law is also visible in one other incident – the story of the rich ruler, in which Luke follows Mark closely (Lk 18.18–30; Mk 10.17–31). This incident is somewhat similar to the one involving the lawyer, which was discussed above (Lk 10.25–8). In the present passage, Jesus is asked 'What shall I do to inherit eternal life?' and replies 'You know the commandments', before listing some of them, including the injunction to love one's father and mother. This time, however, the interrogator claims to have kept the commandments since his childhood, so that Jesus tells him that one further thing remains – for him to distribute his wealth to the poor and to follow him. Here we see a position closely aligned to that in infancy narratives; the law is a useful stage on the way to eternal life, but it will only be attained by becoming a disciple of Jesus.

Jesus' challenge to the law

Perhaps the most radical statement by Jesus with respect to the law comes in the passage where he challenges the commandment to love one's parents by telling a potential disciple wishing to put this part of the law into effect by burying his father to 'leave the dead to bury the dead' (9.60). Can this direction by Jesus, which formed part of the Q tradition Luke had at his disposal (cf. Mt 8.21–2), be reconciled with adherence to the Mosaic law? The answer must surely be 'no', in spite of the fact that Jesus elsewhere pays lip-service to this commandment (10.27–8). This incident must be seen in the light of the other passages where Jesus insists that discipleship will often clash with established familial relationships. The divisions Jesus will cause within families are starkly outlined in Lk 12.51–3, which is also from Q (cf. Mt 10.34–6). On another occasion Jesus actually announces that a *sine qua non* of discipleship is hatred of one's father, mother, wife, children and brothers and sisters (14.26). There is a Matthean parallel to this, but it is expressed in much milder language (Mt 10.37). Embedded in the traditions Luke was using, therefore, was a recurrent theme of renunciation of family ties which probably reflected the outlook of the wandering Christian charismatics of rural Palestine, whose role has been incisively analysed by Gerd Theissen.[22] Such an attitude must have been received with great hostility by ordinary Jews, for not only did it breach the Mosaic code, but it was a serious threat to the extended, yet patriarchal and close-knit families which were characteristic of Jewish society and much of Mediterranean culture as well.[23] That leaders of Christian communities felt a need to reassure their flocks against Jewish criticism on this point at quite an early stage emerges from the incident in Mk 3.31–5 in which Jesus reinterprets 'mother' and 'brother' and 'sister' to mean those who do the will of God, in other words, those who are members of the Christian community. The adoption of this solution preserves the spirit of the fourth commandment, although certainly not the letter. Not unnaturally, Luke retains Mk 3.31–5, although he eliminates the critical attitudes implied by Jesus in the Marcan passage towards his mother and brothers (Lk 8.19–21). To conclude this section, we cannot agree with S. G. Wilson that Luke seems to be unaware of the legal implications of Jesus telling the man to leave the dead to bury the dead.[24] The real position is that Luke *was* aware of them, but that this was a case where his pervasive desire to give the impression that faith in Jesus did not involve some abandonment of the Mosaic law came into collision with one of the realities of Christian life so much a part of the tradition that he could not ignore it.

Jewish paranomia *in the Third Gospel*

The prophecy of Simeon that part of Israel would, in effect, reject Jesus (2.34) is abundantly fulfilled during the course of Luke's Gospel. Our expectation that those who did so would be presented as being unfaithful to the law is also confirmed. Luke presents the leadership of Israel, especially the Pharisees,[25] scribes, lawyers and high priests, as being most resistant to the Gospel. By aiming his attacks at these Jews, Luke is probably also striking at the synagogue authorities of his own time who had brought the pressures to bear upon his Christian contemporaries which we have discussed in Chapter 3.²⁶

One point of the Good Samaritan story, a passage found only in Luke (10.29–37), is to contrast the failure of the priest and the Levite, two pillars of the Jewish establishment in the time of Jesus, to abide by the love commandment with the Samaritan's enthusiasm to do so. R. Banks errs in thinking that this story merely brings to expression Luke's interest in salvation and compassion,²⁷ since the criticism of the leaders of Israel is an integral part of it.

A similar allegation is made against the Pharisees in Lk 11.42–3, a passage from Q (cf. Mt 23.23), in which Jesus says that they are scrupulous to tithe their produce, while neglecting justice, the way one treats one's fellow-man, and love of God. It will be recalled that the possession of these two qualities was advocated as the way to eternal life in Lk 10.25–8. Luke's message is that the Pharisees' neglect of the fundamental demands of the law precludes them from enjoying eternal life.

The Parable of the Rich Man and Lazarus (16.19–31), another passage unique to the Third Gospel, constitutes perhaps the key expression of Luke's argument that the Jewish leaders have failed to follow the Mosaic law or to accept Jesus. The story is told shortly after the Pharisees have been characterized as 'lovers of money' (φιλάργυροι) (16.14) and is best regarded as aimed at them, at least in part (cf. Lk 11.42; 20.47). As Bultmann noted, there are two parts to the parable. The first part, vv. 19–26, deals with the rectification of earthly injustice in the world to come. The second, vv. 27–31, is not so straightforward. Bultmann thought that these verses meant that Moses and the prophets had made God's will sufficiently plain, so that there was no need to ask for a miracle of the resurrection of a dead man to induce belief.²⁸ Such a view is in accordance with Lk 10.25–8. Bultmann's interpretation, however, and that of virtually all other commentators, quite neglects the richly polemical nature of the text. The real point of this part of the story is that the five brothers of the rich man are leading a sinful life, just as he did during his lifetime, and the law and the prophets are not going to be effective in making them repent. But nor, says Abraham, would his brothers repent even if someone came back from the dead to warn them. In the wider context of Luke–Acts, of course, Jesus does just that. Accordingly, one aspect of the meaning of the parable is that the same Jews who refuse to recognize Jesus also fail to obey the commandments of the Mosaic law. It is difficult not to assume that Luke's introduction of a story with this point had relevance to the situation of his own community *vis-à-vis* Judaism. But more on that below.

Luke 16.16–18

The significance of Lk 16.16–18 for this investigation is that in these verses Luke comes closest to making a programmatic statement of his attitude to the Jewish law.

Although Hans Conzelmann saw Lk 16.16 as providing 'the key to the topography of redemptive history', marking the end of the old order and the beginning of the new, he also believed that the addition of Lk 16.17 meant that Luke envisaged a continuity, not a sharp break, between the old and the new, with the law and the prophets continuing during the preaching of the kingdom.[29] This is surely correct in view of the evangelist's efforts in the infancy narratives, and later, to present the salvation offered by Jesus as the prophesied fulfilment of the law, but not its death-knell. Nor can it be denied that 16.17 also expresses a vital element in Luke's total perspective. One of his main aims is to argue that Christianity does not involve the abrogation of the law, and 16.17 is directed to strengthening his case on this point. It was a position hardly likely to convince ordinary Jews, given the mixed table-fellowship of the Christian communities and the subordination of family loyalties to the demands of discipleship characteristic of the disciples of Jesus.

Nevertheless, for reasons connected with the composition of his community and the social and religious pressures upon its members, Luke still wished to defend Christian fidelity to the law. Some of the difficulties in maintaining this defence come to light in 16.18.[30] This appears to be offered as an example of the preservation of the law trumpeted in 16.17. Yet many of Luke's contemporaries must have believed that so complete a ban as that contained in 16.18 on the remarriage of anyone, male or female, who had been divorced was at odds with the Mosaic law, which did allow divorce in certain circumstances (Dt 24.1–4). This verse typifies Luke's problem with regard to the law. On the one hand Jesus was known to have taken the radical line of banning divorce (cf. Mk 10.1–12), and this has no doubt become a feature of Christian teaching. On the other hand, he was obliged to make the teaching of Jesus on divorce as palatable as possible for Jewish Christians, which he aimed to do by presenting that teaching as an intensification, rather than a denial, of the Mosaic law. He hoped to achieve this by situating a radical statement on divorce (16.18) immediately after a sweeping assertion of the permanence of the law (16.17), to give the impression that the second verse merely represented an illustration of the first. Admittedly, this must have been perceived as a fairly transparent evasion of the issue, but then it was hardly more so than his efforts to legitimate table-fellowship between Jews and Gentiles.

Finally, we have seen that the infidelity of Jewish leaders to the law figures prominently in the Lucan outlook on the subject. Now although this motif does not appear in Lk 16.16–18, it is the central issue in the verses which frame this passage, namely, in 16.14–15 and 16.19–31. Little attention has been given by Lucan scholars to the significance of this context for understanding vv. 16–18. Vv. 14–15 are very severe on the Pharisees. After noting in v. 14 that the money-loving Pharisees scoffed at the preceding words of Jesus, which largely dealt with the proper attitude to wealth (16.1–13), the Lucan Jesus then proceeds to reprimand them in v. 15. Then follow vv. 16–18 and, lastly, Luke concludes this section with the parable of the rich man and Lazarus (16.19–31). As suggested above, the point of this parable is that the rich Jews, linked to the Pharisees by the epithet φιλάργυροι in 16.14, have neither obeyed the law and the prophets, nor come to believe in Jesus. Accordingly, Lk 16.16–18 also serve the polemical purpose of asserting Christian fidelity to the law by way of contrast with the *paranomia* engaged in by the leaders of the Jews.

Lucan omissions of legal material

That Luke omits two significant Marcan passages dealing with the law (Mk 7.1–23; 10.2–12) has often attracted the attention of Lucan commentators. There is a widespread view that these omissions are explicable on the basis of Luke's having written for Gentile Christians for whom the theoretical discussion of such questions would have held little interest.[31]

Let us begin with Mk 7.1–23, or, rather, with Mk 7.1–30, since we have seen in Chapter 4 above that the incident which relates how Jesus enters the house of the Syrophoenician woman is intimately connected with the declaration of the purity of all foods in Mk 7.19. Why, then, has Luke omitted Mk 7.1–30? Our initial difficulty is that Mk 7.1–30 falls within a considerable segment of the First Gospel (Mk 6.45 – 8.26) which Luke has omitted *in toto* from his Gospel. His omission of such a lengthy, continuous section of his source has not unnaturally prompted the suggestion that it had accidentally been omitted from his version of Mark. H. Schürmann, on the other hand, has argued that Luke did have this part of Mark before him but deliberately chose to omit its various pericopes.[32] Although Schürmann's explanation is more probable,[33] it is unnecessary to decide the issue here. For whatever the reason for Luke's omission of Mk 7.1–30, the fact remains, as H. Hübner has shown,[34] that he deals with its two central issues – whether it is necessary to wash one's hands before eating and the validity or otherwise of the food laws – elsewhere in his two volumes. The question of unclean hands is dealt with in Lk 11.37–41, 44 (a Q passage: cf. Mt 23.25–8), while the status of the food laws is one of the major topics in Acts. Accordingly, since Luke is interested in these issues – and in the case of the latter acutely interested – it is hardly likely that he was writing for an audience which was not also concerned with them. We must assume a Jewish component in his audience, or, to be more precise, the presence of Jews in table-fellowship with Gentiles.

Nor does the omission of Mk 10.2–12, which is due to a redactional decision by Luke, necessarily imply a Gentile audience for his work. After all, the radical viewpoint expressed by the Marcan Jesus is preserved in a highly abbreviated form in Lk 16.18, where it is presented, albeit rather artificially, as an intensification of the Mosaic law, not its abrogation. Luke's aim throughout his Gospel and Acts is to give a general impression of the fidelity of Jesus and Christians to the law, in spite of the existence of features in the tradition, and in the life of his own community, quite at odds with this aim. In dropping the technical discussion of the divorce question in Mk 10.3–9 Luke serves the interests of both the Jews and the Gentiles among his Christian contemporaries. The details he omits would have been awkward for Jewish Christians, because they reveal a shocking disregard by Jesus of the Mosaic right of divorce evident in Dt 24.1–4,[35] while Gentile Christians would not have required a direction by Jesus on the subject to be couched in the form of Jewish controversy.

3. The law in Acts

Stephen and the law

In the first five chapters of Acts the disciples in Jerusalem, while acknowledging Jesus as Messiah, remain law-abiding Jews. Certainly, they rouse the ire of the Jewish authorities through preaching the resurrection of Jesus (4.2) and blaming them for his death (5.28), but neither charge puts them beyond the bounds of Judaism. Gamaliel regards them as Jewish and even as possible agents in the divine plan (5.34–9). Towards the end of Acts, James tells Paul in Jerusalem that the local Jews who have become Christians all zealously obey the law (21.20). In this respect, the picture of the Jerusalem community is somewhat reminiscent of the pious Jews who feature in the first two chapters of Luke's Gospel. With the account of the apprehension and trial of Stephen in Acts 6 and 7, however, this position is modified and some of the tensions as to the place of the law which can be detected in Luke's Gospel suddenly burst to the surface.

Lucan scholarship has generally found it very difficult to relate Stephen's speech (Acts 7.2–53) to the charges made against him. These charges are given in three forms in 6.11–14. Whatever the exact details, it is reasonably certain that Stephen was accused of expressing a negative attitude towards the Temple and the law and customs of the Jewish people. But what reply does Stephen make to them? For the vast majority of exegetes, none whatsoever! Haenchen's reaction is typical: 'Stephen is supposed to be answering the question whether he is guilty of the charge, but a very large part of his speech has no bearing on this at all!'[36]

Commentators of this persuasion obviously think that Stephen should have given what lawyers call 'a defence on the facts' – that is, a defence in which he actually denied that he ever did make the remarks attributed to him. That some of the accusations were made by 'false witnesses' (6.13) appears to open the door to such a defence. Now it is quite apparent that Stephen offers no factual denial of the charges. But that does not mean that he has not fully answered them. The failure of Lucan commentators to appreciate this appears to stem from a lack of familiarity with the conduct of criminal litigation. For what Stephen has done is simply to utilize the other two forms of defence available to the defendant in criminal proceedings, in addition to a denial of the facts. The first of these, referred to by lawyers today as a defence 'on the law', consists of saying, in effect: 'Even if the facts you allege are true, they disclose no breach of law.' The second is more radical. It is called a defence 'as to jurisdiction' and consists of the defendant's submitting to the tribunal before which he or she has been brought that it has no jurisdiction to hear the case. Elsewhere in Acts Luke recognizes the possibility of defences raising the issues of law and jurisdiction.[37] Although Stephen does not explicitly rely on these defences, the way he presents his case constitutes, as we shall see, an implicit reliance on them. In examining Stephen's speech from this viewpoint we shall see its close relationship with Luke's position on the Jewish law as discernible in his Gospel.

We begin with the section in Stephen's speech which deals with

Moses and the Temple (7.20–53), since these themes are raised in the charges made against him. The point of Stephen's references to Moses is quite straightforward. As F. Spitta suggested in his treatise on Acts published in 1891,[38] Moses is a type of Jesus. The Jews rejected Moses (7.27–8) and 'the living words' which he gave them (7.38–9), just as they were later to reject Jesus. The analogy is very clear in 7.25. E. Haenchen fails to appreciate the wider ramifications of this relationship when he urges against Spitta's view that the Moses-as-type theme is only present in a few verses of the speech and has little to do with the concrete accusation.[39] Stephen, at least as Luke reports him, presents Moses in this light to challenge the jurisdiction of the Sanhedrin to try him. Since their ancestors rejected Moses in the past, and since they have continued to disobey his law right into the present (7.53), they are in no position whatsoever to sit in judgement on Stephen for allegedly preaching against him. By beginning five sentences with the phrase 'This man' or 'This Moses' (7.35–8), which is a very prominent stylistic feature in the speech, Stephen's aim is to convey the ironical inappropriateness of the Jews appealing to Moses to condemn him, when Moses is the one whom they have always disregarded and who also predicted that a prophet, Jesus of course, would come after him (7.37). This last point clinches the argument, for it means that real loyalty to Moses necessitates recognition of the prophet whom he promised long ago. Thus, Stephen's aim is to dispossess the Jews of the Mosaic traditions and to re-interpret those traditions as actually vindicating his own position. This strategy was noticed as far back as 1836 by K. Schrader, who commented that Stephen, representing other Christians, is presented here as the true supporter of Moses, while the Jews are apostates who oppose their ancestral religion and do not follow Moses.[40]

This attitude taken by Stephen to the law is, of course, essentially the same as that expressed by Luke throughout his Gospel. Moreover, Stephen does not deny that, although loyal to the true meaning of the Mosaic law, he is opposed to some of its detailed prescriptions, and from the line he adopts it seems reasonable to suppose that he was. In this respect also, his defence is in accord with the tactic visible in Luke's Gospel of giving the impression of fidelity to the Torah, while simultaneously introducing facets of Christian discipleship at variance with it.

Stephen's attitude to the Temple, which is discussed in more detail in the next chapter, illustrates a defence 'on the law' to the charge that he has spoken against that institution. His reply is to say that

Solomon transgressed God's will in building him a 'house' (οἶκος), when all God desired was a tent (σκήνωμα) such as had been enough for him in the past, and that God does not dwell in the Temple (7.48–50). For this reason, it cannot be blasphemy to speak against the Temple.

But can the first part of the speech (Acts 7.2–19) be reconciled with the charges made against Stephen? M. Dibelius thought that it was impossible to find a connection.[41] An examination of these verses, however, reveals several features which are consonant with the argument of the rest of the speech and with Luke's position on the law in general. The most important of these features is the concern with setting Christianity, via Moses, firmly within the ancestral traditions of the Jewish people. In other words, the history of the patriarchs becomes the seedbed of belief in Jesus. The ancestral lineage of the salvation available through Jesus was also a principal theme of Lk 1–2. At the same time, the recital of the injustice done by the patriarchs to Joseph (7.9) is a pregnant reminder of the tendency to violence to which some Jews, pre-eminently those who oppose the gospel, are prone. Thirdly, Acts 7.2 mentions that God reveals himself outside Palestine, and this feature is related to the inclusion of Gentiles within the scheme of salvation. No longer is God concerned only with Jews (10.34–5).

No attempt has been made here to enter into the debate as to which sources, if any, Luke had at his disposal in composing Stephen's speech. We have been content to demonstrate that Stephen's attitude to the law makes explicit some of the tensions which inevitably affected Luke's community, given its mixed Jewish–Gentile membership and its sectarian status with respect to Judaism.

Paul and the law

If anything could be said to characterize the Lucan portrait of Paul, it is the apostle's total and uninterrupted fidelity to the Jewish law. Paul regularly attends synagogue (9.20; 13.14; 17.2) and exhibits a high regard for Jerusalem, as revealed, for example, in his desire to celebrate Pentecost in the Holy City (20.16), to worship there (24.11) and also to make offerings in the Temple (24.17–18). He even goes so far as to circumcise Timothy (16.1–3), to make a Nazirite vow in Cenchreae (18.18) and to become involved in the Nazirite vow of four men in Jerusalem (21.24). He expresses regret when told that he has abused the High Priest, since this is in breach of Ex 22.28 (23.5). Finally, there are a number of general descriptions of his piety. Thus he tells the Jews in Jerusalem that he studied under Gamaliel and was taught the exact observance of the ancestral law (22.3). Before the Sanhedrin he affirms that he has walked before God with all good conscience up to that day (23.1). An even more categoric assertion of his obedience comes when he tells Felix that it is according to what the Jews call 'the Way' that 'I worship the God of my ancestors, retaining my belief in all points of the law and in what is written in the prophets' (24.14; *JB*). In a similar vein, he informs the Jews in Rome that he has 'done nothing against our people or the customs of our ancestors' (28.17; *JB*).

Yet what of the Jewish case against Paul reported in Acts? The Jews at Corinth allege that he urges people to revere God contrary to the law (18.13–15).[42] Paul's fellow-Christians in Jerusalem repeat the accusation against him that he teaches 'all the Jews who live among the pagans to forsake Moses, telling them that they should neither circumcise their children nor live according to the customs' (21.21). A little after this Jews from Asia stir up the mob in Jerusalem by crying out that Paul is the man who is everywhere teaching 'against the people and the law and this place' (21.28). Finally, the case laid by the Jews before Felix against Paul is that he has caused disturbances among Jews throughout the world and attempted to profane the Temple (24.5–6), the latter charge stemming from the erroneous notion that he has brought the Ephesian Trophimus into the Temple (21.29).

There can be little doubt that Luke wants his readers to conclude that the Jewish charges against Paul were false. How could Paul have preached against circumcision, implies Luke, when he circumcised Timothy? How could he have been opposed to the Temple when he came to Jerusalem with offerings for it? How could he have been against the law in general when, by both his words and his deeds, he continually upheld it? In this respect he is identical with other Jewish Christians in Acts, such as Ananias (22.12) and the thousands of Jewish Christians whom James describes as all zealously devoted to the law (21.20).

The same cannot be said of the Jews, however. In Acts Luke greatly amplifies the message he has begun communicating in his Gospel: that the Jewish opponents of Jesus and his teaching have themselves forsaken the Mosaic law. He does this principally by mentioning a number of incidents which starkly reveal their willingness, first evident in the treatment of Jesus in the synagogue at Nazareth (Lk 4.29–30), to get rid of their opponents by murdering them. Thus, they plot to kill

Paul in Damascus (9.23) and Jerusalem (9.29), they stone him in Lystra (14.19) and make another attempt on his life in Jerusalem (21.31). A group of Jews even takes a vow to do away with him, with the full knowledge and connivance of the High Priests and elders (23.12 – 15). Another sign of *paranomia* manifested at the highest level of the Jewish establishment occurs when the High Priest orders Paul, who is making his defence before the Sanhedrin, to be struck on the mouth. This prompts Paul to ask him: 'Do you sit judging me according to the law and yet in contravention of the law order someone to strike me?' (23.3).[43]

The Jews also set themselves at odds with the law by not recognizing Jesus, whose coming has been predicted in the law and the prophets long before. They fail to realize that loyalty to the ancestral Jewish traditions means belief in Jesus. Philip points this out to the Ethiopian eunuch (8.35), as does Peter to Cornelius (10.43). There are several occasions, moreover, on which Paul ventilates this argument (13.23 – 6, 32; 26.6 – 7, 22 – 3, 27).

On the other hand, Luke is quite open in Acts about the limitations of the law which arise inevitably from the fact that Jesus brings salvation, not the law. In his address to the synagogue in Pisidian Antioch, for example, Paul explicitly states that everyone who believes in Jesus is justified in a way impossible under the law (13.38 – 9), and mentions that salvation is now available through Jesus (13.23, 26). Secondly, Peter exhorts the Council in Jerusalem not to lay on the neck of the Gentile disciples the yoke (of the law) 'which neither our fathers nor ourselves have been able to bear (βαστάζειν)' (15.10). E. Haenchen believes that in this verse Luke has lost sight of the continuing validity of the law for Jewish Christians, which it appears from Acts 21.21 he does not contest. According to Haenchen, in 15.10 we have 'the law seen through Hellenistic Gentile Christian eyes, as a mass of commandments and prohibitions which no man can fulfil'.[44] A convincing refutation of this view, however, has been published by J. Nolland.[45] By means of a careful contextual and semantic study, Nolland has shown that the words 'yoke' (ζυγός) and 'bear' (βαστάζειν) do not carry the implications of oppressiveness demanded by Haenchen's opinion, and that the meaning of the verse is simply that the law did not bring the experience of salvation to the Jews.

The truth of the matter, however, is that the Lucan Paul goes far beyond merely preaching that the law has been transcended in Jesus Christ. For the Jewish case against Paul was, in one vital respect,

correct, and as a result of this Luke's presentation of his allegiance
to the law is revealed as the energetic advocacy of an impossible brief.
Whatever Luke might say about Paul, he could not obscure the fact
that he lived and ate with Gentiles, thereby endangering the separate
existence of the Jewish *ethnos* and almost certainly renouncing the
Levitical food laws. There are explicit references to this in Acts 16.15,
34 and 18.7 and Paul's letters confirm that this was an aspect of his
evangelism (Gal 2.11–14; 1 Cor 10.27–8; Rom 14.20). Such historical
evidence stands in stark and irreconcilable opposition to the assertions
by the Lucan Paul that he has done nothing against 'our people or
the customs of our ancestors' (Acts 28.17) and that he has retained
his belief in all points of the law and the prophets (24.14). On the other
hand, the Jewish claims that he has urged people to revere God
contrary to the law (18.13) and has taught Jews not to live according
to their customs are perfectly accurate, at least as far as the grave
offence of living and eating with Gentiles is concerned.

Although rarely, if ever, commented upon by scholars in the field,
so striking a dichotomy between Luke's picture of Paul's fidelity to
Jewish law and Jewish tradition and the facts of the case is certainly
a phenomenon of great significance for an understanding of the
author's strategy and intentions in Luke–Acts. This is especially so
when we consider that the historical Paul, as known from his own
letters, displays no reticence about revealing the extent of his rejection
of the Jewish law, even though his residual loyalty to it causes him
some pain and occasionally leads him into theological inconsistencies,
in the manner amply documented by E. P. Sanders.[46] We must now
offer an explanation for this dichotomy between Lucan intention and
historical fact within the wider context of Luke's total perspective on
the law.

4. Conclusion

At the beginning of this chapter, after a review of existing scholarly
opinion on the treatment of the law in Luke–Acts, a number of
alternative hypotheses were proposed, all of which were extrapol-
ations from the conclusions reached in earlier chapters of this book.
These alternative hypotheses have now been significantly confirmed.
During the course of this chapter, it has emerged that Luke was deeply
concerned with the status of the Jewish law and that he had a consistent attitude to it, an attitude which was extremely conservative.[47] In
brief, Luke portrays the law as good and as continuing into the

Christian epoch. The coming of Jesus bearing salvation for Jew and Gentile, an event predicted by the law and the prophets long before, fulfils, even transcends, the law but does not result in its abrogation. Those who recognize Jesus for what he is and follow him are truly loyal to the law, while the Jews who reject him are the ones who contravene the Mosaic traditions in other respects as well. This pattern is present in the infancy narratives in the first two chapters of the Gospel and in the treatments of the attitudes which Jesus, the early church in Jerusalem, Stephen and Paul all express to the law.

Yet Luke's keen desire to depict Christian fidelity to the law runs up against the hard facts of the case. This happens first in the Gospel, in those passages where the demands of discipleship run counter to the law, and then in Acts, where the existence of table-fellowship between Jews and Gentiles substantiates the Jewish claim that Paul has opposed Moses and the customs of the Jewish people. It is quite incorrect to say, as S.G. Wilson does,[48] that Luke's attitude to the law was 'ambiguous' or 'ambivalent', as if Luke was unable to make up his mind on the question or could tolerate in his work the existence of two contradictory views of it. Luke presents a consistent programme on the law. His problem, however, was that this programme came into collision with essential features of the Christian tradition and with the fact of Jewish–Gentile eucharistic fellowship.

Why, then, does Luke go to such lengths to argue what is ultimately an impossible case for Christian beliefs and practices involving no breach of the Mosaic law? The only probable answer to this question is that Luke was shaping the sources and traditions at his disposal in such a way as to satisfy some need of the community for whom he wrote. Such a conservative attitude to the law – and one marked by a consistent claim that it was the Jews, especially their leaders, and not Christians, who had renounced Moses – really only makes sense if there were a significant number of Jews in his community whose grip on the gospel was under threat on account of criticism from Jews, or from conservative Jewish Christians, that they were endangering the Jewish *ethnos* and the Mosaic law. Luke's legitimatory strategy consists of assuring them that Christianity and Judaism are not incompatible and that the very Jews who are worrying them are themselves unfaithful to Moses. At the same time, Luke avoids excessively technical discussion in presenting his case on the law, and this serves the needs of the Gentiles who were also members of his community.

From the examination carried out in this chapter, therefore, it is apparent that Luke's treatment of the law is another area of his theology which has been vitally influenced by the social and ethnic, as well as the religious, pressures upon his community.

6

THE TEMPLE

1. The prominence of the Temple in Luke–Acts

Few features more consistently typify Luke's unique approach to his material, both in his Gospel and in Acts, than the prominence he accords to Jerusalem and the Temple. For Luke Jerusalem is 'the city of destiny for Jesus and the pivot of salvation for mankind',[1] and within Jerusalem the Temple is the pre-eminent institution for the emergence of Christianity. There are many treatments of this subject in the literature,[2] so only a summary is necessary here. The first two chapters of the Gospel are replete with incidents which take place in the Temple. Luke's Gospel actually begins, excluding the dedication to Theophilus (1.1–4), inside the very sanctuary of the Temple, with the appearance of Gabriel to Zechariah (1.5–20). After the birth of Jesus, Mary and Joseph bring him to be presented in the Temple, where they encounter Simeon and the prophetess Anna (2.22–38), the remarks of both of whom will reverberate throughout the work. In these early sections the Temple is presented as the place where Israel realized the imminent onset of the good news of salvation which it had long been awaiting. Later comes the incident when Mary and Joseph accidentally leave Jesus in Jerusalem and three days later find him seated in the Temple, engaged in discussion with the teachers of Israel (2.41–51). Only Luke, of course, includes these stories of Jesus' infancy and youth. When he takes up the Q story of Satan's threefold tempting of Jesus, Luke has the temptation for Jesus to throw himself down from the Temple last, as opposed to Matthew, in whose version this temptation comes second and is followed by the one in which Satan invites Jesus to worship him and receive in return all the kingdoms of the world. The order in Matthew is almost certainly original. T. W. Manson takes the opposite view, for the reason that 'Matthew's arrangement works up to a fine dramatic context' and 'it is difficult to imagine what could have induced Luke to alter it'.[3]

131

This misses the point that Luke has put the plainly less significant temptation at the climax of the passage simply because it is set in the Temple.

One of the most often noticed aspects of the Third Gospel is that its author has deliberately highlighted in its central section the motif of a journey to Jerusalem (9.51–19.27).[4] The significance of Jerusalem as the place where Jesus would be taken up (i.e. into heaven) is mentioned a little earlier when, in a detail of the transfiguration pericope peculiar to Luke, Moses and Elijah speak to Jesus of his 'exodus', which he is to accomplish in Jerusalem (9.31). So Jesus comes to Jerusalem, a city which kills the prophets (13.34) and will reject the king (19.11–27), a city which will be destroyed because it did not recognize the time of its visitation (19.41–4).

Unlike the Gospels of Mark and Matthew, in the final sections of which the disciples are directed to meet Jesus in Galilee (Mk 16.7; Mt 28.6), Luke's Gospel ends with them remaining in Jerusalem. For it is from Jerusalem that the mission to the Gentiles is destined to begin (Lk 24.47; Acts 1.8), and it is here that the first Christian community is formed, whose members remain, by and large, faithfully devoted to the Temple, as shown by the fact that they go there to pray and teach within its precincts.[5] The one exception to this devotion is the apparently negative attitude of Stephen, and presumably the circle around him, which is discussed below. Even after Christian communities in the Diaspora have begun admitting Gentiles, Jerusalem is the site of an important conference to determine to what extent, if any, these new converts must obey the law (15.5–29). Later still, Luke has Paul relate that he once had a vision in the Temple during which God despatched him to the Gentiles far away (22.17–21). Finally, the action in the last third of Acts is set in motion by Paul's apprehension in the Temple by Jews provoked to violence upon hearing a false allegation that he has profaned its holy precincts by bringing in Greeks (21.27–31).

In this chapter the focus is upon the Temple, rather than Jerusalem. The data in Luke–Acts concerning the Temple are susceptible of separate treatment because of its presentation by Luke as the institution of Judaism most closely involved with the announcement and beginnings of the Gospel. Moreover, the striking prominence of the Temple in Luke–Acts is, without a shadow of a doubt, a phenomenon which must be taken into account in attempting to understand Luke's purpose and strategy. Yet this fact had not been entirely obvious to many scholars who have considered the matter. Often they have been content to describe the ways in which the Temple is emphasized in the work without exhibiting much interest in why Luke should have bothered to work such an emphasis into his presentation.[6] In fact, however, it appears a particularly promising field in which to adopt the socio-redactional approach outlined and defended in Chapter 1 and applied in Chapters 3, 4 and 5 above. Although the Temple was the pre-eminent institution in Jerusalem and in Judaism as a whole, the attitude to it of anyone who revered the God of the Jews had profound social, as well as religious, implications, as will appear below. This raises the possibility that an exegesis inspired by a sociological imagination may be capable of accounting for Luke's presentation of the Temple — which we will soon see is decidedly ambivalent — as a response to the social and religious significance which the Temple continued to hold for his fellow-Christians at least a decade after its destruction.

In tracing the links between Luke's theology of the Temple and the experience of his own community, it will be necessary to offer something of an historical reconstruction of the realities of worship in Jerusalem *vis-à-vis* the beginnings of Christianity in that city. This foray into the historical situation of the first generation of Christians is admittedly exceptional in this book — which focuses on the position of Luke's community forty or fifty years later. It is necessary in this chapter, however, because the attitude to the Temple evident in Luke–Acts, and present in the community for whom Luke was writing, is best explained (as shown below) as a continuation of an experience of one segment of the early church in Jerusalem whose feelings for the Temple, given its social and religious impact on them, were profoundly ambiguous.

2. Luke's ambivalent attitude to the Temple

Many of the references to the Temple in Luke–Acts portray that institution in quite a favourable light; in particular, it plays an important role in the proclamation of the good news of salvation from the appearance of Gabriel to Zechariah in the first chapter of the Gospel right up to the evangelism of the church in Jerusalem in the early chapters of Acts. Taking his cue from such passages, F. D. Weinert goes so far as to assert: 'Throughout Luke–Acts the main impression which emerges is Luke's positive regard for the Temple … in his eyes and throughout his work the Jerusalem Temple consistently remains worthy of Christian respect.'[7]

The attitude to the Temple expressed in Stephen's speech (7.2–53, especially at 7.48) is quite inconsistent with this rosy view, but Weinert attempts to explain away this inconsistency. Even M. Bachmann, the author of a detailed monograph in which he argues that Luke understood the Temple as the centre of Jewish worship and the earthly locus of all Jewish life and hope,[8] fails to concern himself with any negative feelings Luke may have had towards that institution.

Weinert and Bachmann not only have in common that they attribute to Luke an extremely positive regard for the Temple, but they also lack any interest in asking *why* Luke should have subscribed to this attitude, let alone in attempting to relate it to the experience of the community for which he was writing. Now if these two scholars were correct in their assessment, it would not be impossible to suggest a way in which Luke's elevation of the Temple to such a prominent place in his work might have had a social function in his community. It could be argued that in depicting the Temple as so significant for the beginnings of Christianity Luke has re-created it for his audience in a symbolical mode. As such it becomes a substitute for the now-destroyed Temple in Jerusalem, a substitute from which the Jews could not drive Luke's Christian contemporaries as they appear to have done from the synagogues. That is to say, since the Temple no longer existed in fact, Luke could insinuate it into the history of the church and even the biography of individual Christians and thereby establish it as a central component in the symbolical universe he erects in his Gospel and Acts.[9]

The problem with this approach, however, is that it is predicated upon a more favourable attitude to the Temple than can actually, *pace* Weinert and Bachmann, be found in Luke–Acts. The shoal upon which all attempts to argue for a totally favourable attitude to the Temple in Luke–Acts must inevitably founder is the inclusion of the text of Stephen's view on the matter:

> But the Most High does not live in dwellings made by human hands
> (ἀλλ' οὐχ ὁ ὕψιστος ἐν χειροποιήτοις κατοικεῖ) (7.48)

The force of this statement, discussed further below, is reinforced by the fact that in the Septuagint the word here used for a dwelling made by hand (χειροποίητος) is reserved exclusively for pagan idols,[10] and that it is reminiscent of the words Stephen has just used of the golden calf (7.41).[11] Thus, Stephen is not just entering the fray on the much-debated question of the sense in which God could be said to dwell

in the Temple; he is making the radical statement that the very notion
of God dwelling in a man-made temple is actually idolatrous. What
underlines the broader significance of this opinion in the overall
scheme of Luke—Acts is that exactly the same sentiment is later
expressed by Paul in his address to the Athenians on the Areopagus:

God ... does not live in dwellings made by man

(ὁ θεὸς ... οὐκ ἐν χειροποιήτοις ναοῖς κατοικεῖ) (17.24)

Paul's use of the word χειροποίητος here is a close substitute for the
word τὰ σεβάσματα ('objects of worship', 'idols') immediately
before (17.23). That this same view should outcrop in two speeches
plainly invested with great thematic importance in the work should
give pause to those, such as C. H. H. Scobie and M. Simon, who wish
to explain away Stephen's negative attitude to the Temple as a unit
of discordant tradition which Luke includes out of fidelity to his
sources rather than because it accords with his own views on the
subject.[12] The explanation for the importance of the Temple in
Luke—Acts which is offered in the rest of this chapter will take into
account both the positive and the negative aspects of Luke's attitude
to it.

3. The explanation for Luke's attitude to the Temple

Historical reality and Lucan redaction in Acts 6.1 – 8.3

Introduction

By the end of this chapter we aim to have explained Luke's presentation of the Temple as a facet of the way he has shaped the traditions
at his disposal in response to the pressures on his community. Our
search for the explanation of his attitude to the Temple begins with
the antipathy Stephen expresses towards it in Acts 7.48, in the hope
that an investigation of this element, which is claimed by many to
be at odds with the rest of Luke's views on the subject, may actually
result in a far more accurate and comprehensive understanding of
Luke's outlook on the Temple. To analyse Acts 7.48, however, it is
necessary to set the verse in its context – the narrative in Acts
6.1 – 8.3.

Unfortunately, we do not possess any sources Luke may have used
in writing the narrative in Acts 6.1 – 8.3 and no earlier account than
his of these events exists for the purpose of comparison. This makes
redactional analysis difficult. Nevertheless, it is possible to use

Acts 6.1–8.3 both to attempt a reconstruction of part of the history of the first Christian community in Jerusalem and, from certain awkward transitions and other tell-tale signs of Lucan redaction, to suggest how and why he has modified that history.

The narrative in Acts 6.1–8.3 begins with a conflict within the Christian community (Acts 6.1) and proceeds to a conflict between Jews and Christians which culminates in the martyrdom of Stephen and the expulsion of part of the Christian population from the city. With the dual and related aims of historical reconstruction and redactional analysis we must first identify the two groups of Christian actors in the conflict, the Hellenists and the Hebrews, and then investigate the nature of the struggle between them and the reason for the eventual expulsion of the former group from Jerusalem.

The identity of the 'Hebrews' and the 'Hellenists' in Acts 6.1

Few verses in the New Testament cause one more surprise than Acts 6.1. For after all the initial images of unity and harmony among the early Christians, even to the extent of their having had community of goods, we suddenly find Luke, without any warning, describing a dispute within the Jerusalem church, with the 'Hellenists' murmuring against the 'Hebrews' because their widows are being neglected in the daily distribution. What are we to make of this indication of disunity, or even conflict – especially in view of the other manifestations of conflict in Acts 6.1–8.3? F. C. Baur wisely conjectured long ago that there must have been a deeper ground for disagreement between Hellenists and Hebrews underlying this discontent over poor relief.[13] But another response has been simply to ignore the problem. F. F. Bruce, for example, includes no comment on this remarkable transition from the original seamless unity of the church in his commentary on Acts.[14] This reflects a British approach to Acts, unwisely glorified by W. W. Gasque,[15] which first erects a false dichotomy between the investigation of linguistic, historical and archaeological background on the one hand, and the question of the unique pattern Luke has given to his materials on the other, and then proceeds to devote nearly all its attention to the first, while writing off the second as 'German' and ultra-critical. The correct position is that *Actaforschung* needs both these lines of enquiry, pursued closely in conjunction with one another, and in few places is this more imperative than in Acts 6.1–8.3.

Many suggestions have been made as to the identity of the Ἑλληνισταί and the Ἑβραῖοι referred to in Acts 6.1. We begin with

H. J. Cadbury, who argued that the *Hebraioi* were Jews and the *Hellenistae* Gentiles.[16] The principal objection to his theory is that some, at least, of the only people named in the text who are almost certainly to be regarded as Hellenists − namely, the Seven appointed for the ministry at tables in Acts 6.5 − are Jewish.[17] That Stephen, for example, was a Jew is shown by his trial before the Sanhedrin and the numerous occasions during the course of his speech before that body in which he refers to the shared ancestry of himself and its members. Secondly, Nicholaus, the Antiochean proselyte (Acts 6.5), was Jewish, because proselytes were regarded as full Jews in almost every way, including their right to enter the Temple.[18]

The fact that Paul, the pre-eminent evangelizer in the Greek-speaking Diaspora, called himself an *Hebraios* (2 Cor 11.22; Phil 3.5) does not necessarily favour Cadbury's position, since, as C. D. F. Moule has pointed out, *Hebraios* could perhaps be interpreted to mean one who knew Greek in addition to Aramaic, while *Hellenistes* was reserved for someone who only knew Greek.[19]

But if Cadbury goes astray in seeking to explain the distinction as simply involving a split between Jews and Gentiles, for the reason that there were certainly Jews among the *Hellenistae*, we should be careful not to conclude from this that were no Gentiles in this group as well. The attempt of scholars such as E. C. Blackman and C. D. F. Moule to rule out Cadbury's suggestion simply because it postulates Gentile members of the Jerusalem church at an impossibly early date[20] will be shown later to rest upon an inadequate perception of the social and historical realities of the beginnings of Christianity.

One rather eccentric approach to the problem came from A. Spiro, who wanted to interpret the *Hebraioi* as Samaritan Christians but also thought Stephen was a Samaritan Christian.[21] Although there may be some Samaritan influences in Stephen's speech, Spiro goes far beyond the evidence in interpreting the *Hebraioi* or Stephen as Samaritan Christians. As we have just seen, Stephen was a Jew, whatever else he may have been.

The next two suggestions as to the identity of these groups within the early church have in common a belief that the Hellenists were Jews, but of an unorthodox kind, as opposed to the Hebrews, who were orthodox Jews. Oscar Cullmann argues in *The Johannine Circle* that both Hebrews and Hellenists came predominantly from Palestinian Judaism, but that the latter group had split off from official Judaism prior to their becoming Christians and pursued more or less esoteric tendencies with a syncretist stamp.[22] The principal objection to this view, that the Hellenists were ordinary Diaspora Jews prior to their contact with Christianity, is explained below. The keynote of M. Simon's suggestion is that the Hellenists were Greek-speaking Jews from the Diaspora whose background had resulted in their having a less favourable attitude to the law and the Temple than Jews from Palestine.[23] Many scholars believe that Jews in the Diaspora were less rigorous in their dedication to the law and the Temple. Unfortunately, this view is usually regarded as one of the assured results in the field and is rarely thought to require a reasoned defence. Simon's opinion, for example, rests largely upon an interpretation of merely a few verses of the Septuagint which adopt different expressions to refer to God dwelling in heaven and in the Temple, and which therefore, he suggests, indicate a Diaspora criticism of the Temple in Jerusalem, its ritual and sacrifices. This is too shaky a foundation upon which to base such an edifice, since the few verses he singles out are susceptible of other explanations and are not shown to be typical of a more widespread tendency in the text.[24] In fact, the notion that Diaspora Jews were lax in their devotion to the law and the Temple is not only a suspicious one from the viewpoint of sociology but is also disproved by the history of the period, for the reasons outlined later in this chapter.

The last suggestion as to the identity of the Hellenists and Hebrews to be treated here is the traditional one that the Hellenists were Greek-speaking Jews, while the Hebrews were Aramaic-speaking Jews from Palestine. In a recent essay, Martin Hengel has marshalled some persuasive arguments for this view.[25] Hengel quotes the concise statement of Chrysostom on the matter: Ἑλληνιστὰς τοὺς Ἑλληνιστὶ φθεγγομένους λέγει (Homily 21, on Acts 9.29).[26] He argues that this is linguistically the only answer possible in the context. The etymology of Ἑλληνιστής, in particular, exclusively supports the meaning 'Greek-speaking', without any syncretistic or even derogatory associations; the word comes from Ἑλληνίζειν, which almost always – from Thucydides and Plato to Plutarch, Sextus Empiricus, Lucian and Cassius Dio – means 'speak Greek (perfectly)' and, occasionally, 'translate into Greek'. The few examples with a wider significance (i.e. 'to live or to act like a Greek') are relatively late, appearing as isolated instances in Plutarch, Diogenes Laertius, Eusebius and Libanius. Hengel interprets Ἑβραῖοι as Aramaic-speaking Jews: that is, those Jews who spoke Ἑβραϊστί (Jn 5.2) or Ἑβραΐδι διαλέκτῳ (Acts 21.40; 22.2; 26.14).[27] He correctly notes that this interpretation of *Hellenistae* is in accord with the meaning of the word at Acts 9.29, where it plainly refers to Greek-speaking Jews. He regards the correct reading at 11.20 as Ἕλληνας, not Ἑλληνιστάς, and this view has also been accepted by C. D. F. Moule.[28]

Therefore, the best explanation for the distinction between the two groups mentioned in Acts 6.1 is a linguistic one; the *Hebraioi* spoke Aramaic (though some of them may also have known Greek), while the *Hellenistae* spoke Greek exclusively. Furthermore, that some of the Hellenists were Jews who had returned to the Holy City from the Diaspora is highly probable. Stephen and Nicholaus, the proselyte from Antioch, were certainly Jews. But the evidence does not necessitate assuming that there were no Greek-speaking Gentiles among the Hellenists. Lastly, we may be confident that Hellenists and Hebrews did constitute distinct groups within the first Christian community in Jerusalem and that Luke's audience was aware of the distinction between them.

Having established the identity of *Hebraioi* and *Hellenistae*, the way is now open to consider the two areas of conflict in Acts 6.1–8.3. We shall begin with the clash between Jews and Christians which led to the martyrdom of Stephen and the expulsion of part of the Christian community from Jerusalem, because more data are available in the text for the investigation of this area, and then proceed to the more opaque dissension within the Christian community itself (6.1).

The expulsion of the Hellenists from Jerusalem

A notable feature of the narrative in Acts 6.1–8.3 is that, although Luke records that on the day of Stephen's death 'there was a great persecution of the church in Jerusalem, and all were scattered ... except the apostles' (8.1), it seems highly probable that the only Christians to be expelled from the city were the *Hellenistae*.[29] This is suggested initially by the most unlikely feature that only the apostles were exempt from expulsion. As M. Simon pertinently remarks, governments do not rid themselves of the rank and file of seditious movements and leave the responsible leaders alone.[30] The true explanation must be that the group or party represented by the apostles, most probably the Aramaic-speaking *Hebraioi*, were not persecuted by the Jews, while the *Hellenistae* were.

That this is the correct explanation is confirmed by considering what led the Jews to expel some of the Christians from the city. The only indication as to the motivation for the Jewish attack comes in the charges made against Stephen and his reply to them. In essence,

Stephen is charged with uttering blasphemy against the Temple and the law, not just with being a believer in Jesus (6.11–14). Luke, moreover, does present Stephen as having a negative attitude to the Temple (7.48). Now, whatever the historicity of the actual words attributed to Stephen in Acts 7 – and debate still rages around that issue[31] – the charges against him and his reply must surely contain the germ of the motivation for the persecution.[32] Some members of the church must have said or done something to bring down the wrath of the Jews upon their heads, and whatever it was must have gone beyond believing in Jesus as Messiah, since that was a belief also shared by the Christians who were not expelled. The only thing likely to have produced such a reaction is precisely that described by Luke – a perceived opposition to the Temple and the law. In Jerusalem, of course, opposition to the Temple could be expected to raise a great deal of the most profound Jewish antipathy, for the reason that the whole socio-economic well-being of the city depended upon the wealth attracted to it for the continuation of the Temple cult.

Now it is precisely on the question of the Christian attitude to the Temple that a cleavage must have existed within the Christian community. For the early chapters of Acts indicate that the apostles were devoted to the Temple, not merely inasmuch as they used it as a site for daily preaching and teaching (5.42), but even to the extent that they attended the afternoon *tamid* sacrifice (3.1).[33] Moreover, the rather curious note by Luke that a great number of priests became obedient to the faith (6.7), which is often ill-advisedly taken as evidence of a link between the church and Qumran,[34] makes good sense as an indication of the pro-Temple attitude of much of the Christian community in Jerusalem. There is no hint in the text that the priests gave up their priesthood in becoming Christians – a step which would have meant forgoing their rights to a share in the tithe. On the other hand, unwillingness to attend sacrifices in the Temple, or even more extreme gestures of defiance, presumably characterized the opposition of Stephen and the other Hellenists to that institution. Put simply, the *Hebraioi* were pro-Temple and the *Hellenistae* were anti-Temple and this probably explains why the latter were expelled from Jerusalem and the former were left in peace.

We have still not attempted to explain this cleavage, but the fascinating possibility arises that there may be some connection between the reason the Hellenists were persecuted and the deeper cause of discontent underlying the dispute about the treatment of the Hellenists' widows in Acts 6.1.

The conflict between Hebrews and Hellenists

Investigating this possibility involves ascertaining the facts behind the incident reported in Acts 6.1ff. There can be little doubt as to the historicity of a conflict between Aramaic-speaking Christians and Greek-speaking Christians lying behind Acts 6.1ff., since the events described are so destructive of the picture of peace and harmony in the church presented by Luke prior to this. One senses that here was a feature of early Christian history which, although unsavoury, was too well known for the author to suppress. But he has certainly sought to lessen the embarrassment it caused.

As Luke presents it, we have a complaint by the Hellenists against the Hebrews over the administration of the 'ministry at tables' (ἡ διακονία ἡ καθημερινή), which is resolved by the Twelve, who summon an assembly of the disciples to select suitable persons to look after the 'ministry at tables' (διακονεῖν τραπέζαις). The result is that seven men are chosen for this purpose: Stephen, Philip, Prochorus, Nicanor, Timon, Parmenas and Nicholaus, the Antiochean proselyte.

One feature of this account in particular arouses an immediate suspicion as to its accuracy: the fact that after this assembly there is never any mention made of the Seven being engaged in such a ministry. All we ever hear of them regards the proselytizing of Stephen in Jerusalem and its tragic consequences (6.8−7.60) or the evangelical work of Philip amongst the Samaritans and with the Ethiopian eunuch (8.4−13, 26−40) and his later status as an evangelist (21.8). This apparent anomaly is only likely to be explained through very careful attention to the social realities underlying Luke's version of the facts.

First of all, we must ask who were the Seven. It is widely agreed that they were *Hellenistae*, that is to say, Greek-speaking Christians, probably Jews, though some of them may have been Gentiles. This view is supported by the fact that they all have Greek names (although this itself is not conclusive), that Stephen and Nicholaus certainly spoke Greek and Philip probably did,[35] and that Stephen and Philip were certainly involved in the persecution, which, as we have seen, only affected the Hellenists. Of course, it is not impossible that Prochorus, Nicanor, Timon and Parmenas, who are otherwise unknown, were from the *Hebraioi*, but the chances of this being the case are minimal.

Given the likelihood that the Seven were from among the Hellenists, the next question to arise is whether we are to understand that they were given responsibility for the 'ministry at tables' for the whole community, as Luke's account is usually taken to mean, or whether they merely ensured a proper treatment of their fellow-Hellenist Christians. The narrative seems to allow either alternative, as C.D.F. Moule has noted.[36] Sociological reflection, however, suggests that the Seven could not have performed this ministry with respect to the *Hebraioi*. In the first place, this would have involved Greek-speakers having to attend to people of whom some at least only knew Aramaic. Whatever the precise nature of the 'ministry at tables', a linguistic difference such as this would not have been conducive to its smooth administration. In the second place, it is unlikely that the Hebrews, who had previously been mistreating the Hellenist widows by means of the power they wielded over the community's purse, would have consented to give up this power and put themselves in a position where they were exposed to exactly the same treatment from the very people who may still have nursed a sense of grievance for their previous mistreatment.

But to probe a little more deeply than this, let us consider another example of a dispute within a religious community over alms, so that by using it as a distant comparison with Acts 6.1ff. we may be able to ask some new questions of the text, in the manner explained in Chapter 1 above. B. Hartmann and J. Boyce have recently published a book about life in a contemporary village in Bangladesh, which they have called 'Katni' to protect the privacy of the villagers. For some time the Moslems of Katni were in the habit of attending the mosque in the neighbouring village of 'Borobari'. In general, the people from Katni were less well-off, as measured by the size of their landholdings, than the people of Borobari. On special occasions, representatives from the mosque would collect money from Katni and Borobari and distribute it as alms to the poor of both villages. But a dispute arose, since the Moslems from Katni always felt that their poor received far less than those of Borobari. In the end the Katni Moslems decided that they would keep their money and distribute it to their own poor. The Borobari response was to forbid them to use their mosque, so Katni had to erect its own.[37]

All that Luke tells us of the dissatisfaction of the Hellenists with the Hebrews was that their widows were being overlooked in the daily ministry. The Katni comparison suggests, but does not, of course, prove, that this would have been accompanied by a sense of grievance that the Hellenists were not getting a fair share of what they, too, had contributed to the community's purse for alms-distribution. It is hardly likely, after all, that they did not also contribute for this purpose. The most significant question, however, which the comparison with Katni prompts is whether the dispute over alms actually led to a decisive break between the two Christian groups, so that it would be more accurate to speak of Christian communities in Jerusalem, rather than of one community. Martin Hengel has observed that the Aramaic–Greek linguistic difference would probably have resulted in separate liturgies in the two languages at quite an early stage in the history of the church in Jerusalem, this being facilitated by an early translation of some tradition about Jesus into Greek.[38] Thus there would have been a liturgical split between the two groups after a short time, although there must also have been some degree of unity, especially in the pooling of property for alms-distribution. Yet we also know from the fact that the Jews expelled the Hellenists from the city, and not the Hebrews, that a fundamental differentiation between the two groups persisted until the end of the Hellenists' presence there. This indicates that the unity and peace which Luke presents as being established between them in 6.2ff. probably did not characterize their relationship.

We may now outline, to explain the historical facts underlying Luke's narrative, an hypothesis which both takes into account its awkward aspects and also incorporates some of the insights which flow from a sociological approach to the text. Early in the history of the Jerusalem church two groups sprang up within it which were recognizably distinct by the fact that one used Aramaic in its liturgy and the other Greek. During the first period both Hebrews and Hellenists contributed to the common funds of the church and, although the Hebrews controlled the purse, there was a fair distribution of alms to the poor of both groups. However, after a while this changed. For some reason, examined in detail below, the attitude of the more powerful Hebrews altered, and those of them running the poor relief of the church began to neglect the Hellenists' widows. This caused great dissatisfaction among the Hellenists, and their leaders (the Seven listed in 6.5), who were already outstanding for their evangelism in Jerusalem, instituted a new system whereby the Hellenists set up a separate common fund and used this to support their own poor. This act deepened the separation which had already existed between the two groups at the levels of language and liturgy, so that henceforth there were two Christian communities in the Holy City, only one of which was eventually to be persecuted and driven out by the Jews.

Some external evidence for this reconstruction exists in the collection which Paul organized for the poor Christians in Jerusalem

(Gal 2.10; Rom 15.25–7; 1 Cor 16.1–4; 2 Cor 8–9). What was Paul's motivation for this project? The idea that the collection was a Christian analogy to the half-shekel Temple tax paid by adult Jews can be ruled out, principally because it would have been an unambiguous sign of the subjection which Paul avoided in his discussions with the leaders of the Jerusalem church (Gal 2.6–10).[39] Furthermore, it is unlikely that Paul saw the collection solely as a fulfilment of the Isaian prophecies that in the last days all the nations would stream to the mountain of Yahweh in Jerusalem, bringing their wealth with them (Is 2.2–3; 60.5ff.; cf. Micah 4.1–2).[40] Although this idea may have figured in Paul's thinking,[41] it is quite absent from Gal 2.10 and Rom 15.25–7. This leaves the most likely explanation: that the collection was designed to express the unity of the church.[42] On the assumption that the Hellenists did set up a separate alms-fund in Jerusalem, this explanation may be accepted in general, but subject to a critical qualification. Paul's visit to Jerusalem, recounted in Gal 2.1–10, may well have been aimed not merely at gaining accreditation for his interpretation of the Gospel, but also at healing a division between Hellenists and Hebrews dating from before the expulsion of the former group from the Holy City. If one of the causes precipitating the original split had been the withdrawal of the Hellenists from the common fund and their establishment of their own distribution system, the deal struck between Paul and the Jewish Christian leaders at last recognized the legitimacy of preaching to the Gentiles, but only in return for a restoration of payments by the Hellenists to the fund for the poor in Jerusalem. Moreover, even though the behaviour of Peter in Antioch (Gal 2.11–14) probably amounted to a repudiation of the agreement by the leadership in Jerusalem, Paul continued to perform his side of the bargain (Rom 15.25–7; 1 Cor 16.1–4; 2 Cor 8–9). His actions, however, may well have been interpreted by the Jewish Christians as motivated by a hostile intent – to draw the attention of the Christian world to the fact that they had reneged on the agreement. Their antipathy may explain why Luke does not mention that Paul was bringing money from his communities on his last journey to Jerusalem (Acts 21.1ff.), and even why Luke describes the financial aid which was sent from Antioch to Jerusalem not as part of an agreement between Paul and the leadership in Jerusalem, but as *ad hoc* assistance during a famine (Acts 11.27–30).

So much for historical reconstruction; what about Lucan redaction? Why has Luke shaped the facts as he has in Acts 6.1ff? Elsewhere in Acts his desire to have Peter and the Jerusalem church legitimate some aspect of the Christianity vital to his community is evident in the text. This is particularly so with regard to the legitimation of table-fellowship between Jew and Gentile in the narrative of the conversion of Cornelius. The split between *Hebraioi* and *Hellenistae* must have been a cause of some embarrassment to himself and his readers. For they adhered to the traditions of the Hellenist Christians who had formed a community in Jerusalem separate from that of Peter and the apostles, yet at the same time they wanted the Aramaic-speaking side of the church to be seen to have endorsed those traditions. On this particular occasion, Luke's course was clear. He knew of the split, and he had among the traditions at his disposal information relating to the decision of the Seven, the Hellenists' leaders, to set up a separate alms-distribution system. What was needed was that this initiative be attributed to the Twelve and the whole assembly of the disciples. Thereafter, he could forget all about the 'ministry at tables' and move on to a description of the martyrdom of Stephen and the evangelism of Philip, both heroes of the Hellenists and of Luke's community.

But at this point we must return to a question already raised: what was the cause of the Hebrews' turning sour on the Hellenists to the extent of neglecting their widows, and was there any relation between this and the negative attitudes to the law and the Temple which the Hellenists seem to have held and which led to their persecution and expulsion from Jerusalem? The time has come, therefore, to consider just why the Hellenists adopted a critical attitude to the law and the Temple, as distinct from the Hebrews, who did not. Having presented an explanation for this historical problem, we shall suggest why the issue continued to be important for Luke's community.

Temple, God-fearers and Gospel

The attitude of Diaspora Jews to the Temple and the law
The most popular explanation for the negative attitude of the Hellenists to the Temple and the law is that which sees this group as composed of Diaspora Jews whose exposure to Greek ideas in Hellenistic cities had led them to a lower opinion of these institutions than Palestinian Jews *prior* to their contact with the Gospel. Such a view has been adopted by, for example, M. Simon and E. Haenchen.[43] We must now justify our earlier assertion that the notion of Diaspora Jews having been lax with respect to the Temple

and the law is a dubious one in terms of sociological theory and is, in fact, contradicted by the history of the period.

A little sociological reflection on what is generally known of the life-style of Jews in the Dispersion strongly posits the likelihood of their having been enthusiastic for the law and the Temple. A considerable body of sociological literature exists on the ways in which an ethnic minority group may respond to the larger culture in which it is located. Possible responses of the minority range from a total breakdown of the group's boundaries, leading to complete assimiliation, on the one hand, to a tight maintenance of its separate identity on the other.[44] It is remarkable how consistently the Jews scattered around the Greek cities of the Roman East preferred the latter option to the former. Although there were some apostates to Hellenism, it seems that the vast majority of Jews earnestly strove to maintain their identity and distinctiveness in the sea of Gentiles which surrounded them.[45] This phenomenon, manifested both in their life-style and in the geographic separation involved in their living in distinct quarters of Diaspora cities, led Max Weber to coin the phrase 'pariah people' to describe them, by which he meant 'a guest people who were ritually separated, formally or *de facto*, from their social surroundings'.[46] From these considerations, one would expect to find among Diaspora Jews a devotion to the law and the Temple even greater, if anything, than that of their cousins in Palestine. For the Jews of the Diaspora the practice of circumcision, the observance of the Sabbath and the festivals, adherence to the dietary code and refusal to dine with Gentiles, and devotion to Yahweh in his Temple in Jerusalem would have served to preserve the boundaries between themselves and the surrounding pagan culture and religion. Palestinian Jews, on the other hand, did not need to be so strict to maintain their Jewish identity, since it was supported by other factors, such as their not being embedded in a Gentile majority and their speaking a Semitic language in a land hallowed in the biblical record.

This sociological reflection is amply confirmed by the historical record. A number of factors indicate that Diaspora Jews had a high regard for the law and the Temple, even though they used a Greek translation of Scripture which often Hellenized important concepts and expressions in the Hebrew original.[47] To begin with, much of the evidence presented in Chapter 4 above to show the Jewish disinclination to dine with Gentiles came from the Diaspora, so that it cannot be said that the Jews outside Palestine were lax in their adherence to the dietary code. That Diaspora Jews observed the sabbath is plain from the numerous references to this institution in pagan authors.[48] The general loyalty of these Jews to the law is evident in the number of Roman decrees, recorded in Josephus, which order Greek cities to allow Jews to live in accordance with their ancestral customs.[49] One of the most ardent defenders of the law mentioned in the New Testament, after all, was Saul of Tarsus. It is quite clear, moreover, that Jerusalem and the Temple were held in high regard by Diaspora Jews. Large numbers of them went on pilgrimage to the Holy City for the great feasts of Passover, Pentecost and Tabernacles.[50] J. Jeremias has estimated that the number of visitors, many of them Jews from abroad, during the Passover was several times the population of the city (which he puts at 25,000 – 30,000).[51] Even Philo, the great allegorizer, made at least one pilgrimage to Jerusalem.[52] Many Diaspora Jews returned to live in Jerusalem (Acts 2.5).[53] The Jews outside Palestine also showed no hesitation in paying the annual half-shekel tax payable by every adult Jew to the Temple. So much money was despatched by their communities in Greco-Roman cities to Jerusalem that special precautions had to be taken for its safe delivery.[54] Josephus cites a number of Roman decrees which direct certain Hellenistic cities not to interfere with the despatch of this money.[55]

Accordingly, sociology suggests and history confirms the dedication of the Jews of the Dispersion to keeping the law and honouring the Temple. But what makes the efforts of Lucan scholars to argue the opposite even more surprising is the fact that Acts itself contains considerable evidence of the loyalty of Diaspora Jews. It must not be forgotten that the very people whom Luke describes as commencing proceedings against Stephen in the Sanhedrin are Jews from an undoubtedly Greek-speaking synagogue or synagogues in Jerusalem (Acts 6.9–12). External evidence exists for Greek-speaking synagogues in the city[56] and there is even extant an inscription from the first century CE commemorating the erection of one by Theodotus, son of Vettenus, who was both a priest and an *archisynagogus*. The synagogue of Theodotus provided lodgings for foreign visitors, presumably Jews from the Diaspora.[57] There have been attempts to identify this synagogue with that mentioned in Acts 6.9, but a degree of uncertainty remains.[58]

Further evidence as to both the existence of Diaspora Jews in Jerusalem and their devotion to the law emerges at Acts 9.29, where Paul, on his return to the city from Damascus after his conversion, is described as preaching to and arguing with the 'Hellenists', by which

Luke here means Greek-speaking Jews, who respond by trying to kill him. Throughout the course of Acts the congregations of synagogues in the Diaspora manifest a keen interest in defending the law of Moses against what they perceive to be a Christian threat to it. It is, moreover, Jews from Asia who stir up the crowd in Jerusalem against Paul, alleging that he preaches against the Jewish people and the law and has defiled the Temple by bringing a Gentile, Trophimus, into it (Acts 21.27–9).

The opposition to Stephen originates, therefore, primarily or even exclusively among the usually conservative Diaspora Jews in Jerusalem. This fact disqualifies all theories which attempt to locate the origin of Stephen's position on the Temple and the law in some form of Palestinian syncretism. For this reason we must reject the views of Oscar Cullmann already mentioned, as well as other theories which seek to relate Stephen's position to that of the monks of Qumran.[59]

So where are we left? Our task is to explain how it happened that there arose among a group of Jews normally characterized by the most profound allegiance to the law and the Temple attitudes antipathetic to both institutions in the Holy City itself. It appears that the only viable way forward is to reconstruct the realities, social as well as religious, of Temple worship for a Diaspora community in Jerusalem, and then to assess what effect the message of Jesus would have had upon these realities. In sociological terms, this task involves factor analysis – that is, the manner in which social setting affects the establishment and maintenance of belief – and function analysis – that is, the effects of belief and the behaviour associated with it upon the social setting.[60] We begin with an account of the Temple and its cult.

The Temple and the cult

To those approaching Jerusalem from a distance Herod's Temple appeared like a snow-clad mountain, from the whiteness of the stone used in its construction and the quantity of gold with which it was adorned.[61] There is a fleeting evocation of the overwhelming visual impact of the Temple at one point in Luke's Gospel, when the author diverges from Mark to describe it correctly as 'adorned with beautiful stones and votive offerings' (Lk 21.5; cf. Mk 13.1).

Herod began his tremendous reconstruction of the Second Temple and the buildings which surrounded it in 20/19 BCE,[62] but the work was not finally completed until the governorship of Albinus in

62–4 CE.[63] It is possible to obtain from the sources a reasonably clear understanding of the lay-out of the Temple and the other buildings on the Temple mount.[64]

The surface area of the Temple mount had been considerably enlarged over the centuries, and Herod carried this process further by constructing large stone retaining walls and levelling off the extra space.[65] F. J. Hollis calculates that the roughly rectangular area of the mount so produced was 929 feet wide on the south side, 990 feet on the north, 1,186 feet on the east and 1,226 feet on the west.[66] Magnificent porticoes, with tall marble pillars, entirely surrounded the Temple mount, and at their north-west corner was located the fortress Antonia, garrisoned by Romans.[67] The stoa on the eastern side bore the name 'Solomon's Portico'[68] and appears to have functioned as a meeting-place for the early Christian community in Jerusalem (Acts 3.11; 5.12). Under and in front of these porticoes took place the bustling activities of the Temple mount. Here merchants sold animals for sacrifice and money-lenders conducted their trade, especially the exchange of Greek and Roman coinage for the half-shekels with which Jews paid the annual Temple tax.

A small distance within the stoas on all four sides was a low stone wall called the *soreg*, which effectively divided the surface area of the mount into an inner and an outer court. At regular intervals along this barrier stood slabs containing inscriptions, some in Latin and others in Greek, prohibiting foreigners from passing beyond the *soreg*, under penalty of death if they did.[69] One of these slabs has been discovered with the inscription virtually intact; the text reads: 'No foreigner [ἀλλογενής] is to enter within the balustrade and embankment around the sanctuary. Whoever is caught will have himself to blame for his death which follows.'[70] Samaritans almost certainly came within the terms of this prohibition, since there is strong evidence that from the beginning of the first century CE they were regarded as being on a level with the Gentiles in all things ritual and cultic.[71] Furthermore, the word for foreigner in the inscription (ἀλλογενής) is used by the Lucan Jesus with respect to a Samaritan in Lk 17.18. The underlying rationale for the prohibition was that the Gentiles (and Samaritans) were unclean and would thereby defile the Temple precincts by their presence.[72]

The Temple itself was situated inside the area delineated by the *soreg*. In essence, it consisted of a walled complex of unroofed courts, within the innermost of which the tall roofed sanctuary had been erected. This complex was roughly rectangular in shape and was orientated along an east–west axis. As only Jews could pass beyond the *soreg*, only Jews, of course, could enter the Temple. The first court, from which there was access to the rest of the Temple, was the Court of the Women. The main gate to this court was on the eastern side, adjacent to Solomon's Portico. Women were not allowed to go any further. On the western side of the Court of the Women was the flight of stairs leading up to another gate, beautifully decorated with Corinthian bronze,[73] and beyond this gate lay the Court of Israel, open only to Jewish men. Inside this court there was another to which only the priests had access. Within the Court of the Priests was the altar of sacrifice, and slightly west of this the sanctuary itself.

The sanctuary towered to a height of ninety cubits, while its base measurements were fifty cubits long and twenty wide. Its interior and exterior walls were covered with gold plates. The gate opening into the sanctuary was also overlaid with gold; above its golden doors were golden vines, and before these there hung a splendid Babylonian tapestry which typified the universe.[74] The effect of these features on the Jewish men able to observe them from the close range of the two innermost courts must have been overwhelming. The sanctuary contained two chambers.[75] The first was furnished only by a seven-branched menorah, a table used for the shewbread and an altar of incense.[76] To the west of this chamber was another only half its size and separated from it by a veil, which the Synoptics describe as having been split in two when Jesus died. The chamber behind the veil was the Holy of Holies, the *debir*, and it was entirely empty.[77] The only person who ever entered it was the High Priest, and even he did so only once a year, on the Day of Atonement.[78] The Holy of Holies was probably situated directly over the sacred rock, the highest point on the Temple mount.[79] In rabbinic tradition the sacred rock was called *'eben sh^{e}tiyyah*, the 'foundation stone', and it was regarded as the foundation stone of heaven and earth.[80] Some Jewish thought, especially in certain apocryphal writings and in Hellenistic authors such as Philo and Josephus, went even further, beyond the explicit affirmations of the Old Testament, and endeavoured to find a cosmic symbolism in the Temple, whereby it was seen as the centre of the world.[81]

The central element of the cult which was carried on in this magnificent setting was the *tamid* service (*tamid* originally meaning 'always' or 'daily'), the holocaust offering of two lambs, one in the morning (shortly after dawn) and the other in the mid-afternoon. Individuals were only allowed to offer their sacrifices between these two communal offerings. The central features of the *tamid* were the opening of the sanctuary gates to the sound of trumpets, the slaughtering of the *tamid* lamb and its preparation of sacrifice, the offering of incense on the altar of incense, the blessing of the people by all the assembled priests (cf. Nb 6.23–5) and the burning of the slaughtered lamb on the altar.[82]

The afternoon *tamid* took place at about the ninth hour.[83] Several aspects of the *tamid* are reflected in Luke–Acts. As already mentioned, Zechariah had drawn the lot to put incense on the inner altar prior to the actual sacrifice of the lamb (Lk 1.8–9). In Acts 3.1 Peter and John are described as going up to pray in the Temple at the ninth hour. This means that they had chosen to enter the Temple specifically to be present at the afternoon *tamid* sacrifice, not just to pray.

But what was the significance of the *tamid* for those who were present, or of the individual sacrifices to those who offered them? There were three broad categories of sacrifice:[84]

1. Holocausts (Hebrew *'olah*), in which the entire victim was burnt, except for the skin, and nothing was given back to the man who offered it or to the priests. The *tamid* took this form, of course, but holocaust offerings could also be made by individuals. The morning and afternoon *tamid* lamb was offered on behalf of all of Israel to Yahweh in a perpetual renewal of its covenant with him.

2. Communion sacrifices (Hebrew *zebaḥ shᵉlamim*, or *zebaḥ*, or *shᵉlamim*), which were characterized by the fact that the victim was shared between God, the priest and the person offering it, who later ate it with his family and friends, in a state of ritual purity, as a holy thing. The covenant between the worshipper and his God was sealed by this sacrificial meal.[85] There were three types of communion offerings, the sacrifice of praise (*todah*), the voluntary sacrifice (*nᵉdabah*), offered out of sheer devotion, and the votive sacrifice (*neder*).

3. Expiatory sacrifices, which aimed at re-establishing the covenant with God after it had been broken by sinful men. Almost half the sacrificial code of the Second Temple concerns this type of sacrifice.

The prohibition on Gentiles (and Samaritans) entering the Temple meant that they could neither be present for the *tamid* sacrifice nor enter the central courts to slay their sacrificial animals or lay their hands on their heads, which were two acts performed by Jewish men offering individual sacrifices. Nevertheless, there was specific provision in the Torah for them to offer sacrifice (Lev 22.18), and this must have been effected through Jewish intermediaries. But the type of sacrifices they were allowed was strictly limited to voluntary and votive offerings,[86] and even these were of a very unusual kind, since Gentiles were not allowed to eat any part of the offerings though this was a central feature of communion sacrifices.[87] To allow Gentiles to partake of a communion victim would have been to concede the possibility of communion between Yahweh and a people not his own. This would have struck a death-blow to the whole notion of Jewish election, so eloquently emphasized by the court-within-court arrangement of the Temple and the area around it. In spite of these restrictions, many Gentiles did come to Jerusalem to offer sacrifices in Herod's Temple.[88] How Gentiles excluded from the cult in this way felt about the matter is considered below. It is reasonable to suppose, however, that there must have been a marked difference of attitude as between those Gentiles who just saw Yahweh as one of a large number of gods around the East in whose temples it was useful to offer sacrifice and those, on the other hand, who had formed some sort of attachment to Judaism, perhaps to the extent of adopting its faith in Yahweh as the one and only God.

We must now consider the more general religious significance of the elaborate arrangement of zones of steadily increasing holiness in the Temple and the progressive narrowing of the type of person who could proceed further into its depths. Mircea Eliade has convincingly argued that for religious man space is not homogeneous: it is divided into space which has been made sacred by some manifestation of divinity, and secular space, the formless expanse lying outside this area of sanctification.[89] 'Every sacred space', he writes, 'implies a hierophany, an irruption of the sacred that results in detaching a territory from the surrounding cosmic milieu and making it qualitatively different.'[90] When Jacob, for example, had his dream in Haran of a ladder with angels ascending and descending on it and heard God speaking to him from above it, he said: 'How awe-inspiring this place is! This is nothing less than a house of God; this is the gate of heaven!' (Gen 28.10–19; *JB*). So he named the place 'Bethel', meaning 'House of God'. In such a sacred place man comes closest to God, for it is here that a route of communication is opened up between earth and heaven.[91] Temples are pre-eminent sacred places because they are seen as the houses of the gods. The reason that temples, such as the one in Jerusalem, were so often built on mountains was that such a position put them closest to heaven and, therefore, made communication with the gods easier.[92]

The notion of the Temple as the place where God resides on earth was deeply, if ambivalently, implanted in Jewish religion. When the Ark of the Covenant had been installed in Solomon's temple, we are told that the cloud (of Yahweh's presence) filled the place and Solomon said:

> Yahweh has chosen to dwell in the thick cloud.
> Yes, I have built you a dwelling,
> a place for you to live in for ever. (1 Kgs 8.12–13; *JB*)

On the other hand, there was a more sophisticated appreciation, at least in some quarters, that the transcendent God could not be contained in a Temple built by man. Did not Solomon himself also say:

> Yet will God really live with men on the earth? Why, the heavens and their own heavens cannot contain you. How much less this house that I have built! (1 Kgs 8.27; *JB*)

One solution to the paradox was to have God listening from heaven while his people prayed from the Temple (1 Kgs 8.30); another was to say that it was the Name of Yahweh that dwelt in the Temple (1 Kgs 8.17, 29). Last of all, Judaism evolved the notion of the *shekinah*, 'the dwelling', which was an attempt to express the gracious presence of God among his people without detracting from his transcendence.[93] However Israel grappled with this problem, there is no doubt that a belief in Yahweh's albeit mysterious presence in the Temple was the whole reason for the worship carried on there, in both sacrifice and prayer. Accordingly, the unqualified assertion by Stephen in Acts 7.48 that the Most High does not live in dwellings made by human hands is best understood as outside the mainstream of Jewish opinion on the matter and fully consonant with a rejection by Stephen of the Temple and its cult. Even the sectarian monks of Qumran were less extreme than this, for although they regarded the priesthood of their day as totally corrupt, they were not opposed in principle to the worship of Yahweh in the Temple or to the idea of that being in some way his dwelling.[94]

A few final remarks may now be made as to the more general significance of the sacrificial cult in the Temple. It inevitably follows that if the Temple was where God 'lived' on earth, then that was the place to carry on a service of prayer and sacrifice to him. As Eliade says, 'This is as much as to say that every religious man places himself at the Center of the World and by the same token at the very source of absolute reality, as close as possible to the opening that ensures him communication with the gods.'[95] The sequence of gradated zones of holiness in the Temple is eloquent proof of the importance attached by Judaism to proximity to the Holy of Holies and to the God who in some way dwelt therein. The Temple and its cult were for Israel and individual Israelites a most beautiful and potent place and mechanism of purification. Here, in the presence of God, sin was purged and the Covenant with Yahweh was perpetually maintained. The one word which most completely denotes this process is 'atonement', as understood in its original sense, for it was within the inner courts of the Temple in Jerusalem that Israel was put at one with its God.

Marginalized God-fearers in Jerusalem

But what of the Gentiles in the outer court of the Temple? What of any God-fearers who may have been present? The Jews in the inner courts must have experienced a great sense of satisfaction at being so close to the centre of their world, but what was the reaction of any God-fearers who were excluded from this experience by the *soreg*? We shall now show that there were God-fearers in Jerusalem, assess their attitude to being forbidden to enter the inner courts of the Temple, and then apply our findings to interpreting Acts 6.1ff.

There is abundant evidence for the presence of Gentiles in Jerusalem in the New Testament period. That they were to be found on the Temple mount is clear, for example, simply from the fact that the *soreg* was erected to prevent them from entering the Temple. There were many reasons why Gentiles came to Jerusalem. The first was for the purposes of commerce. As J. Jeremias has meticulously demonstrated,[96] Jerusalem was heavily dependent upon the import of animals and other products, many of them from abroad, for the maintenance of the elaborate Temple cult. This trade inevitably brought foreign merchants into the city. Secondly, the status of the city as a centre of government meant the presence both of Roman military personnel and also of foreign diplomats, such as the Athenian visitors mentioned by Josephus.[97] But it was the third reason, the religious significance of the city, that probably attracted the largest number of Gentiles. We have already noted that Gentiles did come to Jerusalem to sacrifice in the Temple. E. Schürer even devotes an appendix of *The History of the Jewish People in the Age of Jesus*

Christ to 'Gentile participation in worship at Jerusalem'; it begins: 'It is a well-attested fact that despite the rigid barrier erected between Jews and Gentiles in regard to religious matters, Gentiles participated in Temple worship in Jerusalem.'[98] Much of the evidence for this is found in Josephus, who mentions, for example, that among the people not permitted to partake of the Passover sacrifice in Jerusalem were 'the foreigners, who were present in great numbers for worship'.[99] There is interesting corroborative evidence for this passage in John's Gospel, where he speaks of 'Greeks' (i.e. Gentiles) who were going up to Jerusalem to worship at the Passover (Jn 12.20). Finally, it is worthwhile to note the testimony of Josephus that the altar in the Temple was 'venerated by all Greeks and barbarians'.[100]

The oddity of Schürer's discussion of this subject is that he explicitly restricts its ambit to 'real Gentiles': that is, not God-fearers, not 'people who to some degree also accepted the Jewish religion and for this reason demonstrated their respect for the God of Israel by offering sacrifices', but those who 'whilst sacrificing in Jerusalem, wished in no way to make thereby a confession of faith in the *superstitio Iudaica*'.[101] Now it is quite true that some of the Gentiles sacrificing in Jerusalem did come within this latter category and would have been just as comfortable offering sacrifice to Artemis in Ephesus or to Zeus in Olympia. But it is quite untenable to restrict the Gentiles in Jerusalem solely to this type.[102] It is scarcely credible that from among the large numbers of Gentiles whom we have seen to associate themselves with the Diaspora synogogues there was not a significant proportion who made pilgrimages to Jerusalem as a natural consequence of their faith. The Gentiles, referred to by Josephus in *AJ* 3.318–19, who were not permitted to partake of their sacrifices and yet showed great respect for the Mosaic law were almost certainly God-fearers.

This last point introduces an issue of considerable importance in what follows. We have already seen that there were synogogues for Greek-speaking Jews in Jerusalem, synagogues which seem, moreover, to have catered for Jews from particular regions of the Diaspora. We must now ask whether these synagogues would have been attended by the God-fearing Gentiles whom we have concluded were to be found in Jerusalem. Although there appear to be no data directly on this issue, one is surely justified in answering the question in the affirmative. It is difficult to accept that Gentiles who had been in the habit of frequenting synagogue services in their own cities would not also have gone along to a synagogue in Jerusalem – especially one used by Jews from their own cities, some of whom they may have already known – even if their association was limited by the Jewish dietary laws. The presence of Gentile God-fearers in the Greek-speaking synagogues in Jerusalem is, accordingly, assumed in what follows.

The stage is now set to examine the attitude of God-fearers such as these to the Temple and its cult. Let us conduct a modest socio-logical experiment by considering the case of one of these, whom we shall treat as broadly typical of the rest. Let us, then, set him down on the eastern side of the Temple mount, so that he stands, with Solomon's Portico behind him, gazing up through the gate towards the glories of the Temple, which lie beyond the *soreg* barring him from further access. It is the ninth hour and the afternoon *tamid* sacrifice is in progress. He has seen Jews, some of whom he knows, go by him and up into the sanctuary for this service. Within the inner courts the covenant between Yahweh, the God he reveres, and Israel, to which he does not belong, is being magnificently renewed. His attitude to the Temple is fundamentally ambivalent. On the one hand, he experiences great satisfaction that he has come to the Temple of his God and has viewed its overwhelming beauty; on the other, at the same time, he is greatly dissatisfied that he is prevented from approaching as closely as possible to the presence of God on earth and being a full participant in his cult. As he stands there, the very architecture of the place brings home to him that, for all his devotion, he is an outsider and will remain so unless he undergoes circum-cision, an operation which is both painful and utterly at odds with his Hellenic distaste for self-mutilation in any form. In sociological terms, such a person is 'marginalized'. He stands on the boundary of Judaism 'neither completely belonging nor suffering outright rejection'.[103] Back in his own city, where he could attend synagogue services almost as freely as the Jews, and where he always had the social support of his pagan friends to rely upon, this may not have mattered so much, but in Jerusalem the awareness of his marginal-ization is greatly enhanced.

Nor does the Judaism of his day offer him any resolution of this basic ambivalence, short of his taking the major step of conversion. Perhaps he takes solace in the words of Isaiah, that the holocausts and sacrifices of Gentiles 'will be accepted on my altar, for my house will be called a house of prayer for all peoples' (Is 56.7). But nothing leads him to think that this Isaian vision belongs to anything other than the most distant future; nothing in contemporary Judaism suggests that the barriers between Jew and Gentile, visibly evident in the arrangement of the Temple, are about to be broken down.

The impact of the Gospel

Such, then, was the experience of large numbers of God-fearers who came to Jerusalem for business reasons or on pilgrimage. They were drawn to Jerusalem, stood before the Temple and returned to their own cities. As an exercise in what sociologists call factor analysis, let us ask the all-important question: given the socio-religious position of Diaspora Jews and God-fearers in Jerusalem, what was the effect upon them of the first proclamation of the Christian message there? Caution is necessary here, since we are not sure what was the nature of the earliest proclamation. Judging from the pre-Pauline creed in 1 Cor 15.3ff., however, it probably contained reference to the death and resurrection of Jesus. Perhaps reference was also made at an early date to some of his sayings. This new message, of Jesus as Messiah, may have been heard initially in the outer courts of the Temple. Anyone present, Aramaic- or Greek-speaking Jew, God-fearer or pagan, would have encountered the preaching. At this time there must have existed in Jerusalem the earliest Christian community, the leaders of which were Aramaic-speaking Jews, most of them probably from Galilee. Certain simple liturgical events characterized this community, such as a memorial meal in honour of the death of Jesus, now risen. In other respects, the members of the community remained Jews and continued to attend the services in the Temple, even the *tamid* sacrifice at the ninth hour. Some of the members of this community were Greek-speaking Jews from the Diaspora. Like Christians later in the first century, they were enthusiastic to preach the Gospel to their fellows from the Diaspora in the synagogues in Jerusalem which catered for them. Such preaching is clearly implied from what Luke says in Acts 6.9. But what of the God-fearers whom we consider must as surely have been present in these synagogues as in those of their own cities? How did they react to this Messianic preaching? There are sociological parallels for the interest of such marginalized individuals in joining smaller, even sectarian, religious groups which offered some relief from their marginalization.[104] If they were swayed by the arguments of men like Stephen and other Hellenists, would they have been accepted as members of the community gathered around Peter, James and the other original disciples? Were their requests for admission rebuffed on the basis that what principally differentiated the community from the rest of Judaism was the memorial meal which many, if not most, Jews would have been loath to share with Gentiles?

In attempting to answer these questions, we must remember first of all that bonds existed between the Diaspora Jews and God-fearers at both the linguistic level, since they all spoke Greek, and the level of their common attendance of synagogues in Jerusalem. Between some of them there may even have existed friendship formed in the Diaspora cities from which they came. Such bonds did not exist, however, between Aramaic-speaking Jews and the Gentile God-fearers. For this reason, it is highly likely that only the Diaspora Jews would have been open to persuasion by their God-fearing friends that these should be admitted to the circle of disciples of Jesus. Now even these bonds may not have been enough to achieve this end if the traditions of the sayings and actions of Jesus had not contained material which seemed to go right to the heart of the marginalization felt by the God-fearers – concerning the role of the Temple and of adherence to the law in the divine scheme of salvation. Had not Jesus said that he would destroy the Temple and in three days rebuild it? Had not he also taken a flexible attitude to the law and actually dined with the ritually unclean? With these aspects of the traditions about Jesus, all of which are almost certainly historical,[105] we must assume that the Gentile God-fearers sought to persuade their Jewish friends of their right to become members of the community. They were also able to appeal to the behaviour of the Aramaic-speaking Jews, such as Peter and John, who persisted in attending the sacrifices in the Temple. What was the point of the death and resurrection of Jesus, and how was he a source of forgiveness, they may well have asked, if the original disciples felt it necessary to preserve their links with the machinery for atonement provided by the Temple? It is, indeed, very difficult to imagine how a theory of the atoning death of Jesus, already present in Paul and Mark and, indeed, in pre-Pauline and pre-Marcan traditions,[106] could have arisen among Jews who preserved close links with the sacrificial cult.

From this discussion we are able to suggest an hypothesis which, it is submitted, explains more aspects of the historical situation underlying the narrative of these chapters of Acts than the existing theories. Our hypothesis is that the God-fearers were successful in convincing their Greek-speaking Jewish friends who had become disciples that they, too, should be admitted to discipleship. This is not the first time that it has been proposed that there were Gentiles among the early community or communities in Jerusalem,[107] but it does seem to be the first time that the reasons which would have led them into the early congregation, and the effect that this would have had on the other disciples, have been assessed. Let us now test this hypothesis.

We have already argued, following Hengel, that there were probably separate Aramaic and Greek liturgical groups among the first community from quite an early point in its history. For the Diaspora Jews to let in the God-fearers meant that they were willing to have table-fellowship, culminating in the eucharist, with them. This would have given grave offence to the other Diaspora Jews in their synagogues who did not accept Jesus as Messiah, since it represented a breaking-down of those barriers between Jew and Gentile which were all-important for the maintenance of separate Jewish identity in the Greek cities of the East. They would naturally have accused those responsible (Stephen, for example) of changing the customs and the law which they had received from Moses (Acts 6.11 – 14). Furthermore, the Greek-speaking Jewish disciples most probably saw that in their situation the antipathy of Jesus towards the Temple, whatever its original socio-religious context, was an attitude that they should adopt in solidarity with their Gentile friends, for whom exclusion from the Temple was such a painful issue. This may have led them actually to forsake attendance at Temple services and even to develop a theology which attributed to Jesus, rather than to the sacrificial cult, the central role in the forgiveness of sin. Accordingly, the anti-Temple statement of Stephen in Acts 7.48 rings true as an expression of the attitudes of the Hellenists, and is an admission of that part of the charges against him relating to the Temple. The Epistle to the Hebrews, moreover, may be an expression of a theology close to that of the Hellenists.[108] In time, the opposition to the Hellenists from the orthodox Jews in the synagogues built up to such a pitch that a persecution was launched against them and they were driven out of the city. But the Aramaic-speaking Jews, of course, had remained orthodox in their Judaism, especially by not engaging in table-fellowship with Gentiles and by continuing in their devotion to the Temple. For this reason they represented no threat to the Jewish authorities in the city or to Greek-speaking Jews and were not included in the persecution when it broke out.

We may safely assume that the Hebrews were strongly opposed to the negative attitude of the Hellenists to the Temple, this being quite at variance with their own views and even more hostile to the sharing of the eucharist with Gentiles. But since there were probably separate liturgies for Greek- and Aramaic-speakers, this may not have presented a problem at the level of eucharistic celebration. However, there was one activity of the community where this question could lead to practical problems – the daily distribution to the poor. Unfortunately, we are not able to say exactly what form this distribution took. It is described as the 'daily ministry' and as 'ministry at tables' (Acts 6.1–2). The latter expression is often understood metaphorically, as an administrative task, but if it is to be understood in its literal sense, it may hold the key to what set off the dispute between the two groups. Assume, therefore, that the early poor were given relief in the form of actually being sat at a table and provided with food, which is the literal implication of 'ministry at tables'. Possibly there were Hellenists and Hebrews around the same tables, or perhaps there were separate tables (in separate places?) for the poor of both groups. In either case, however, the Hebrews who originally administered the distribution may have been most unhappy to serve the Hellenists at table once they had become ritually impure by breaking bread with Gentiles. This would, in all probability, have led them to 'overlook' the Hellenists' widows, with the drastic results which we have already discussed. This cannot be proved, but it does get behind the surface of the text in a way which is sociologically and historically plausible.

The usefulness of this hypothesis also extends to explicating several other features of the text. That it has this explanatory power says much for its accuracy. First of all, after the expulsion of the Hellenists from Jerusalem Philip preaches the gospel in Samaria, and his evangelism is subsequently confirmed by Peter and John. Then Philip encounters and converts the Ethiopian eunuch. Why, we ask, are these two incidents related first? The answer may be that they have in common a feature which intimately connects them with what we have just discussed – the fact that neither Samaritan nor eunuch was allowed into the Temple.[109] Samaritans, moreover, were almost certainly not regarded as ritually pure for the purposes of table-fellowship. Thus, we see Philip evangelizing among people marginalized by the sacrificial apparatus of Israel in virtually the same way as Gentile God-fearers. Luke has probably been influenced here by Is 56.3, where hope is offered to 'foreigners' (ἀλλογενεῖς – a word used by Luke of the Samaritans in Lk 17.18) and eunuchs. But whereas Is 56.4–8 envisaged these two groups obtaining access to the Temple, Luke shows that the promise has been fulfilled quite differently. The historicity of the confirmation of Philip's work in Samaria by Peter and John is doubtful. It probably represents an effort by Luke to have the Hebrews seen to legitimate an action which was probably not something they would have approved.

The next feature explicable on the basis of our hypothesis is the beginnings of a Gentile mission in Antioch (Acts 11.19ff.). As Luke describes it, the first disciples who arrived in Antioch after being expelled from Jerusalem preached only to Jews; then some disciples of Cypriot and Cyrenean extraction arrived and also began preaching to Greeks, that is, to Gentiles. If this two-stage mission is historically accurate, the initial evangelism for Jews only may have been due to the reluctance of Diaspora Jews, who had already been persecuted once for making Gentile converts, to risk the same fate in Antioch. For some reason, however, the Jews from Cyprus and Cyrene, perhaps because they were more involved with the Gentiles in their own cities, did commence preaching to Gentiles in Antioch. The problem with the account as it stands is that Luke offers no motivation for this widening of the scope of the mission. In his account, nothing happens between the Hellenists' expulsion from Jerusalem and their arrival in Antioch to explain this mission to the Gentiles. We have argued elsewhere, of course, that the Cornelius incident has been inserted artificially by Luke as a *post factum* means of having the Jerusalem church endorse a mission which began quite independently of them. Accordingly, it seems reasonable that the pro-Gentile attitude of these latter arrivals at Antioch was already present in Jerusalem, for the reasons already explained, and that the Gentile mission did not begin in Antioch at all.

4. Conclusion: Luke's redaction and the needs of his community

We have now presented an outline of the history of the first Christian community in Jerusalem, as it can be reconstructed from Acts 6.1– 8.3; this offers the marginalization experienced by God-fearers as a result of their exclusion from the Temple as the critical feature of that history. But what of Luke's interpretation of these early events in the life of the church? Why, in particular, has he disguised the beginnings of a Gentile mission in Jerusalem? Why should that subject and its links to the Temple cult be important to his audience? What, finally, is the relationship between his redaction of earlier traditions and the needs of his community?

Let us begin answering these questions by considering how Luke relates the conversion of that prototypical Gentile convert, Cornelius

(Acts 10.1–11.18). The vision, in which he is instructed by an angel to get in contact with Peter comes to Cornelius at about the ninth hour (Acts 10.3). This was, of course, the hour of the evening sacrifice. Furthermore, when the angel speaks to Cornelius, he says, *inter alia*, 'Your prayers and your alms have ascended as a memorial before God' (ἀνέβησαν εἰς μνημόσυνον ἔμπροσθεν τοῦ θεοῦ) (10.4). The last expression, 'ascend as a memorial before God', is very unusual but has close parallels in the Septuagint, in connection with the fragrance of sacrifice rising before Yahweh.[110] Putting these two features together, then, we see that Luke is suggesting that the prayers and the alms of this Gentile were accepted by God in lieu of the sacrifices which he was not allowed to enter the Temple to offer himself. In other words, God has acted to break down the barriers between Jew and Gentile by treating the prayers and alms of a Gentile as equivalent to the sacrifices of a Jew. Confirmation for this way of interpreting the incident comes with the first words of Peter to Cornelius: 'Truly, I understand that God is not partial, but that in every nation he who fears him and acts justly is acceptable to him' (10.34–5). This is an astonishing leap in understanding, for the Temple remorselessly proclaimed by its very architecture just the opposite. Prior to the onset of the gospel, Yahweh was a God totally partial to Jews alone, but now the path of salvation is open to Gentiles; that it is salvation which is the fundamental issue in all this is shown by the way in which Peter's message to Cornelius is described as words by which he and all his house would be saved (11.14). Thus Luke shows that for Gentiles as well the words of Is 56.3–8 have been fulfilled, but in a way quite contrary to that envisaged by Isaiah. The Temple has not been opened up to non-Jews; it has been replaced.

The Cornelius narrative operates at a different level from Luke's version of the history of the early church in Jerusalem. We have seen that, although what actually happened with respect to the Hellenists can be deduced from the text, Luke has certainly disguised some of the harsher realities and has not, in particular, explicitly gone into the marginalization experienced by the Gentile God-fearers in Jerusalem. Yet he has obviously felt able to bring this theme to the surface in dealing with the events surrounding the conversion of Cornelius. Why is this? In Chapter 4 above we argued that Luke inserted the Cornelius episode into its present position to legitimate the incorporation of Gentiles within the Christian fold by having it appear that this development was inaugurated by Peter and approved by the Jerusalem church even before the gospel was preached in the Diaspora.

From this we may deduce that it was important for his community that such legitimation be provided and that Luke found it necessary to eliminate or greatly to reduce all signs of disagreement between the *Hebraioi* and the *Hellenistae*, who were no doubt looked back to by his Christian contemporaries as the founders of their form of Christianity. Accordingly, Luke suppressed, as far as possible, reference to the grievous separation between the two groups which had occurred in Jerusalem and, in particular, omitted all reference to the specific issue, acceptance of Gentiles by Hellenists, which had caused this split. But in dealing with the conversion of Cornelius Luke was not under such constraints and felt free to bring to the attention of his readers the underlying motivation for the initial conversion of Gentile God-fearers – their marginalized status in the sacrificial cult of Israel.

It is now possible to make some broad observations about the attitude of Luke and his Christian contemporaries to the Temple. When he wrote his work, the Temple had lain in ruins for ten to twenty years. And yet many of his community must have remembered the time when the Temple was in existence and when it had the central place in the Judaism to which they belonged or were loosely attached. Some of them may even have visited it. So for Luke's community the ambivalence towards the Temple which God-fearers had experienced as they stood gazing up at it from beyond the *soreg* was also part of their own experience. Their affection for the memory of the Temple was tempered by the recognition that their Christian faith ultimately sprang from a rejection of the Temple and its cult. So, in the end, Luke could have his cake and eat it. He could trade upon this affectionate memory by setting his Gospel more closely than any of the others in the Temple, and thereby attaching it to the ancestral traditions of Israel, and, at the same time, he could include a veiled recognition that the mission to the Gentiles only got underway when a few Jews in the Holy City were far-sighted enough to see that continued devotion to the Temple cult and to the Messiahship of Jesus were fundamentally incompatible.

7

THE POOR AND THE RICH

1. A theology of the destitute in Luke–Acts

In Luke's Gospel Jesus begins his public ministry in the synagogue at Nazareth (4.16–30). His first words are a quotation from Isaiah:

> The spirit of the Lord is upon me,
> because he has anointed me
> to proclaim good news to beggars ... (4.18a)[1]

Among Lucan commentators there is a fairly general agreement, in which we concur, that the Nazareth episode serves a programmatic function within Luke–Acts as a whole.[2] If so, what significance attaches to the fact that pride of place in the inaugural preaching of Jesus is given to 'beggars', which, as we shall see, is the correct rendering of πτωχοί in the Greek, a word whose force is eviscerated by the translation 'the poor', which appears in nearly all English versions? And when Jesus continues the Isaian quotation by saying that he has been sent 'to announce freedom for captives, sight for the blind and liberation for those suffering oppression' (4.18b), we are led to ask what role these deprived groups have within the Lucan programme. If, moreover, scholars are correct in seeing in the references to the widow of Zarephath and to Naaman the Syrian in Lk 4.25–7 a prediction and authorization by Jesus of a future Gentile mission, what are we to make of the widow's being numbered among the poor who were on the brink of death by starvation (1 Kgs 17.12)?

Throughout this book our aim has been to assess the extent to which features of Lucan theology have been motivated and influenced by the social and political constraints experienced by his community. In this chapter the focus is upon Luke's attitude to poverty and riches and their place in the Christian life. In this task our first duty is to confirm that this is a subject in which Luke was interested and did have his own particular view to express, rather than being content merely to rehearse earlier Christian traditions. That he sets those suffering economic and other forms of destitution in the limelight in the Nazareth episode does predispose one in favour of his having had a distinctive theology of property, but several scholars have denied this, and the case therefore needs to be proven. Once the arguments in favour of Luke–Acts containing a unique and emphatic teaching on poverty and riches have been set out, it will be possible to relate that theology to the social realities of Luke's community.

Considerable disagreement exists among Lucan commentators on the question of whether the evangelist did have a special interest in poverty and riches, as opposed merely to repeating the emphasis in his sources. Many say that he did, but many others say that he did not. Among the latter group are to be found A. Plummer,[3] H. Conzelmann[4] and D. L. Mealand.[5] Of these, D. L. Mealand offers the most recent and extensive case against the existence of a special interest in poverty and riches in Luke–Acts, so that we shall begin with him. According to Mealand, Luke retains much which he has inherited from his sources, including some fiery denunciations of the rich, but his own redactional activity on Mark and Q suggests that he did not accentuate this theme of hostility to riches. Since he can find no consistent tendency on Luke's part to increase the severity of Mark and Q towards riches, Mealand attributes the large amount of Lucan special material on poverty and riches to loyalty to tradition, rather than to any particular interest in the subject on Luke's part.

A number of serious objections must be made to Mealand's position, even before we commence a detailed analysis of the text. Even if Mealand were correct in asserting that Luke had not accentuated the Marcan passages relating to poverty and riches, that would not prove that Luke was not himself keenly concerned with the issue. It might mean merely that he found that Mark had expressed himself with a severity adequate for his own needs and that there was no need to alter or amend his source. Worse than this, Mealand makes Luke a slave to tradition. He gravely underestimates the freedom with which Luke chose additional pericopes and sayings to insert into his work over and above what he found in Mark and Q. The ultimate weakness of Mealand's argument, however, resides in the fact that Luke does intensify what his Marcan and sayings sources, especially the former, have to say on riches and poverty. Let us begin with Mark.

The first point of interest noted by Mealand in Luke's redaction of Mark[6] is that he retains virtually all passages or sayings which reveal an antipathy for the rich and a sympathy for the poor. These are: the section in the interpretation of the Parable of the Sower which

mentions the tendency of riches to choke the development of the Word
(Mk 4.19; Lk 8.14), the instruction to the Twelve to take little or
nothing with them on their journey (Mk 6.7–13; Lk 9.1–6), the
saying about gaining the world but losing one's soul (Mk 8.36;
Lk 9.25), the incident of the rich young man (Mk 10.17–22; Lk
18.18–23), the immense difficulty the rich have in entering the
Kingdom of Heaven (Mk 10.23–7; Lk 18.24–7), the rewards which
will crown the disciples' renunciation of possessions and families
(Mk 10.28–31; Lk 18.28–30), the condemnation of the scribes who
swallow the property of widows (Mk 12.38–40; Lk 20.45–7) and,
lastly, the efficacy of the poor widow's offering (Mk 12.41–4; Lk
21.1–4). On the other hand, although it is a feature not noticed by
Mealand, Luke does omit a pericope which, in its Marcan form,
reveals a notable prodigality with respect to possessions. This is the
incident of the woman anointing Jesus with precious ointment while
he is being entertained by Simon the leper in Bethany (Mk 14.3–9).
The disciples object that this ointment could have been sold for three
hundred *denarii* and the money given to the beggars (τοῖς πτωχοῖς).
The purchasing power of this sum of money can be conveniently
gauged from a comparison with Mk 6.37, where two hundred *denarii*
are specified as the amount needed to provide a meal for five thousand
men. But Jesus overrides the objections of his disciples; he tells them
that they have the beggars (τοὺς πτωχοὺς) with them always and that
they will be able to assist them whenever they wish (ὅταν θέλητε).
Wherever the gospel is proclaimed, he concludes, the woman's action
will be recounted in memory of her. Luke does have an account of
a woman who anoints Jesus, but its location and features are very
different from Mark's (Lk 7.36–50). It is uncertain whether the Lucan
pericope is a free reworking of Mk 14.3–9, or whether he has drawn
upon a different tradition. In either case, it is noteworthy that Luke's
version has no reference to the value of the ointment, or to the fact
that it could have been sold to assist those utterly destitute, or that
such people would be with the disciples always and that helping them
was a voluntary, rather than an obligatory, feature of the Christian
life. Why Luke should have been loath to include a passage which
contained these features will become evident later in this chapter.

Finally, there are a number of passages in Luke which reveal an
intensification of the attitude to riches and poverty present in Mark.
The first and most significant of these is the first occasion on which
Jesus preaches in the synagogue in Nazareth. In Mark this incident
occurs well into the public ministry of Jesus (Mk 6.1–6), but Luke

has transferred it to the beginning of that ministry (Lk 4.16–30). We began this chapter with the emphasis Luke's version places upon the utterly destitute as the recipients of the good news, and this emphasis is significant even if Luke has utilized other traditions in retelling the events of Nazareth. The focus upon the destitute is even more emphatic, however, if Luke has relied only on Mark for his version. J. Fitzmyer has argued that Lk 4.16–30 is a free re-working of the Marcan parallel, and this seems to be the best solution.[7] Those who favour non-Marcan sources, H. Schürmann,[8] for example, normally attempt to demonstrate the existence of Aramaisms in Lk 4.16–30, but features in the text so labelled are generally explicable in other ways. Whatever the truth of this matter, the fact remains that Luke has chosen to diverge from his Marcan source in quite a radical fashion by beginning his description of the public ministry of Jesus with an incident which highlights the special place the poor have in the scheme of salvation. This incident, the significance of which for his subject Mealand has unfortunately failed to appreciate, is alone enough to invalidate his view that Luke does not intensify the hostility to wealth which came to him from his sources.

A number of other redactional changes point to Luke's concern to sharpen the impact of his Marcan source in this area. Luke adds to Mark's description of the call of the first disciples the detail that they left everything (πάντα) to follow Jesus (Mk 1.18, 20; Lk 5.11). He amends his source on the call of Levi to add the detail that he too left everything (καταλιπὼν πάντα) (Mk 2.14; Lk 5.28). Similarly, in Luke the rich young man is told to sell all that he has (πάντα ὅσα) (Mk 10.21; Lk 18.22). The attempt of Mealand to diminish the cumulative effect of these changes by referring to Lk 18.28, where the evangelist reports Peter as saying 'we have left τὰ ἴδια', as compared with Mark at this point, who has 'we have left everything' (πάντα) (Mk 10.28), is unsuccessful.[9] The reason for this is that the meaning of τὰ ἴδια in Lk 18.28 is provided by the list of what they have renounced in Lk 18.29, which is much the same as the parallel list in Mk 10.29. That is to say, τὰ ἴδια in Lk 18.28 has virtually the same meaning as πάντα in Mk 10.28, and, since it covers both family and possessions, it is probably best translated, with the Jerusalem Bible, as 'everything'.

To assess whether Luke has accentuated the features of Q dealing with riches and poverty is inevitably rendered difficult by the uncertainty as to whether, in any given case, the original text is represented in his Gospel or in Matthew. Nevertheless, a measure of probability can be reached in most cases. There is really only one example of Luke having sharpened a relevant Q reference. This is the saying 'give to him who asks you' (Mt 5.42a), which appears in Luke as 'give to everyone who asks you' (Lk 6.30). T. W. Manson plausibly suggests that Luke has added the 'everyone' here, since this is a favourite word with Matthew and it is unlikely that he would have left it out had it stood in Q.[10] A number of other features in Luke, on the other hand, are probably closer to their Q form than the Matthean parallels; examples of these are the saying that 'man does not live by bread alone' (Lk 4.4), to which Matthew adds 'but by every word which proceeds from the mouth of God' (Mt 4.4),[11] and the beatitudes (Lk 6.20–2), which Matthew spiritualizes by having, for example, 'Blessed are the destitute in spirit' (Mt 5.3) instead of 'Blessed are you who are destitute', and 'Blessed are they that hunger and thirst after righteousness' (Mt 5.6) instead of 'Blessed are you who hunger now' in Luke. In both these beatitudes the Lucan form seems to appeal to physical forms of deprivation and is certainly more direct by being expressed in the second person. Finally, Luke's version of the Parable of the Great Feast probably reflects Q more closely than its Matthean parallel (Lk 14.15–24; Mt 22.1–10).[12] Now although Luke is closer to the original in these instances, we shall see below that these passages fit in well with Luke's broad attitude on the question of poverty and riches and that if they did not he could easily have altered them, just as Matthew has done. Finally, there is one place where Luke does appear to spiritualize Q; this is at Lk 11.13, where he says that the Father will give 'the Holy Spirit' to those who ask him, whereas Mt 7.11 reads 'good things' instead of the Holy Spirit. Luke's interest in the Holy Spirit makes it more likely that he has altered the original Q form of the saying, which is represented in Matthew. For reasons to be given below, this redactional change must not be interpreted as a sign of a general Lucan belief in a purely spiritual salvation, but rather as the sharpest reminder Luke gives his audience not to see salvation only in materialist terms, as they might otherwise have done, given the way he handles the question of poverty and riches.

Having established by redaction analysis how pronounced is Luke's concern to sharpen the preference in his sources for the utterly destitute and the virtues of renouncing wealth, it is useful to mention the large number of sayings and pericopes among the material unique to his Gospel which deal with this subject. The more important of these are the Magnificat (1.47–55), the preaching of John the Baptist

(3.10−14), the woes of the rich (6.24−6), the exhortation to lend without hoping for repayment (6.34−5), the friend at midnight (11.5−8), the Parable of the Rich Fool (12.13−21), the instruction on whom to invite to banquets (14.12−14), the connection between discipleship and total renunciation of possessions (14.33), the Parable of the Unjust Steward (16.1−9), the accusation against the money-loving Pharisees (16.14), the story of the rich man and Lazarus (16.19−31) and the conversion of Zacchaeus (19.1−10). Nor should we forget that this theme is continued in the early chapters of Acts, in the descriptions of the donations of property by richer members of the community for use by all (2.44−5; 4.32−7) and of the difficulties which arose in connection with this κοινωνία (5.1−11; 6.1).

The only plausible conclusion to be drawn from this examination of Luke's redaction of Mark and Q and his introduction of a large body of material relating to the question of riches and poverty is that this was a matter of vital concern to him. In other words, it represents an important element of his theology, which we may now examine to ascertain the extent to which it has been motivated and shaped by the social setting of Luke's own community.

2. Luke's theology of poverty and its social setting

There is a widespread belief among scholars in the field that Luke−Acts was written in a city of the Roman empire, probably in one of its Eastern provinces, and this view was accepted in Chapter 2 above. In spite of this consensus, it appears that no Lucan commentator has ever attempted to relate Luke's attitudes on riches and poverty in anything like a systematic manner to the realities of life in a Hellenistic city of the Roman East towards the end of the first century CE. In fact, the very idea that such an enterprise might be necessary has only occurred to one or two scholars.[13] This represents an astonishing and lamentable hiatus in Lucan studies. It is absolutely essential in understanding Luke's perspective on this subject that we ask such fundamental questions as: What was it like to be poor in such a context? Or rich? Who were the rich and the poor? What civic or private means, if any, existed for the relief of poverty in these cities? What resonances, accordingly, were raised in the minds and hearts of the poor members of Luke's community by the words of Jesus in Lk 4.18−19, or by the other passages in Luke−Acts promising the destitute alleviation of their plight? Did Luke's community provide relief for its poorer members? And so on. L. T. Johnson, in fact, proceeds full-speed in the opposite direction, by arguing that Luke's material on possessions is really just a metaphor in telling his story 'of the Prophet and the People'![14]

To his credit, H.-J. Degenhardt at least compares the Lucan teaching on alms-giving with the provision of charity in the Hellenistic world,[15] but this is only a fraction of the study of social setting which needs to be done. Some other Lucan scholars, it is true, have investigated the Isaian background to the quotation in Lk 4.18–19:[16] for example, as to the significance of 'the Lord's year of favour'. But what is the point of asking what this expression meant for the rural Palestinians for whom Third Isaiah was writing in the sixth or fifth century BCE,[17] while ignoring its impact on the urban Christians of the first century CE who constituted Luke's audience? The assumption behind such egregious neglect is, of course, that the social realities of the community for whom Luke–Acts was composed are quite irrelevant to the task of understanding the theology of that work. To appreciate how such an assumption could have flourished in the field so vigorously and for so long, one turns to H. Richard Niebuhr's discussion of the middle-class church, for whom, he writes, the 'problem of personal salvation is far more urgent ... than is the problem of social redemption'.[18] For the middle-class church sin is 'not so much the evil with which the whole social life and structure is infected as it is the personal failure of the individual'.[19] And in the symbolism of this church 'conceptions of heaven in which individual felicity is guaranteed are much more important than the millenial hope of the poor man's faith'.[20] The ingrained disregard among scholars for the social and economic setting of Luke–Acts, and their corresponding enthusiasm, discussed below, for its alleged spiritual and individualistic approach to salvation, originate in a clear middle-class bias. Generations of scholars, in their seminaries and universities, have been so successful in making Luke's message on possessions palatable for bourgeois tastes that its genuinely radical nature has rarely been noted. Having succeeded in spiritualizing the good news announced by the Lucan Jesus to the destitute, the European scholarly establishment should not be too surprised that during the last 150 years the working classes have abandoned the leading Christian denominations in the West in their droves.

To allow the real Luke to speak through this layer of *embourgeoisement*, we must examine his message in the light of what it was actually like to be rich or poor in the Hellenistic cities of the Roman East. On this subject there is a vast amount of literary, archaeological and epigraphic evidence, so that it will only be possible here to cut an exploratory trench through it.

3. The rich and the poor in the Hellenistic cities of the Roman East

Social stratification

When Rome began establishing provinces in the East, its policy was to place groups of autonomous communities in particular areas under the military control of Roman magistrates. These communities were called *civitates* or πόλεις; each of them consisted of an urban centre occupying a defined area of land, its territory.[21] Common to virtually all the cities of the Empire was the general pattern of elective annual magistrates, a council (*curia* or βουλή) and a popular assembly (ἐκκλησία). The members of the council were called 'decurions' or βουλευταί. In the West there were normally one hundred decurions on a council, but this figure was often much larger in the East, where councils with six hundred members were not unknown.

In each city the decurions and the magistrates (who were nearly always elected from among the decurions)[22] constituted the local aristocracy. The decurions were actually classified as an *ordo*, that is to say, a social category having an official definition.[23] The two *ordines par excellence* were the senatorial and equestrian *ordines* in Rome. Senators and equestrians comprised, respectively, the upper and lower strata of the Roman nobility, whereas the decurions were the local gentry in the provincial cities. Only a tiny percentage of the population was included within these *ordines*. According to Ramsay MacMullen, of the fifty million or so inhabitants of the Empire in Tacitus' day, the senatorial stratum amounted to approximately two-thousandths of 1%, while the equestrians probably totalled less than a tenth of 1%.[24] The proportion of decurions in the populations of the provincial cities no doubt varied considerably, but it could rarely have been more than 5%. Attached to all three *ordines* were property qualifications. A Roman senator had to possess 250,000 *denarii* and an *eques* somewhat less than half that amount,[25] while a typical figure for a decurion was 25,000 *denarii*.[26] The immensity of these amounts can be seen by comparison with the daily wage earned by labourers – one *denarius*.

The primary fact for understanding the social system at Rome and in the provincial cities is the immense gap that existed between the aristocracy – the members of the *ordines*, be they senators, equestrians or decurions – and the rest of the population. Social stratification, as W. G. Runciman has recently confirmed,[27] can be assessed in terms of the three variables of economic class (meaning one's access to wealth and the means of production), status (meaning prestige, noble birth, etc.) and power. These variables were maximized among the Roman and provincial aristocrats to a remarkable degree. The aristocracy, in common with the elites in virtually every other pre-industrial society, preferred to keep their property in the form of land.[28] Although they normally resided in the cities, they owned country estates largely worked by slaves, the surplus from which allowed them to live a life of leisure and luxury in town.[29] It is worth noting that the mustering-out bonus of an officer in the Roman legions (a centurion, for example) was large enough to allow him to enter the council of a large provincial city.[30] As to our second variable, status, Romans and Greeks, like the members of other pre-industrial societies, went to great lengths to advertise where they stood in the social scale. Peter Garnsey has drawn attention to the fact that the privileges of decurions in the provinces were comparable with those of senators at Rome. They sat in special seats at the games and in the theatre, they dined at the public expense, they received more than others in the distribution of gifts, they wore distinctive dress, and high-sounding epithets were applied to the *ordo* as a whole.[31] As for our third variable, political power, the institution by Octavian of the Principate had largely deprived the Senate of the ability to shape events to its will. Nevertheless, individual senators and equestrians could be invested with considerable delegated authority, and the decurions and magistrates in provincial cities, although subject to the Roman governor, exercised significant power.

Accompanying the firm grip which this tiny elite kept on the social resources of wealth, prestige and power was their disdain, often bordering on loathing, for the mass of the population, who were allowed little, if any, access to those resources. The elite regarded themselves as morally superior to the rest, an attitude which is nicely illustrated by the use of the word *boni* to refer to them during the late Republican period. During the Empire the upper classes came to refer to themselves as *honestiores*, possessors of *honos*, or esteem, while the rest were simply *humiliores*, those of lowly birth and status.[32] The aristocracy continually reminded the others of their superior position, by their conspicuous consumption, their entourages in the cities, their dress and their titles, by offering their clients in-ferior food and wine at banquets, and even by the fact that the law discriminated positively in their favour.[33] On this latter point, Peter Garnsey has pointed out that decurions were exiled rather than punished for capital crimes, while crucifixion, exposure to wild beasts, work in the mines and other public labour, chastisement and torture – in short, all 'plebeian' penalties and punishments – were ruled out for themselves and their children.[34] The ruling elite of Greco-Roman society looked down on the vast mass of the population, especially because they had to rely upon manual labour or on trade and commerce to earn a living.

Which groups were to be found in the vast majority of the population who constituted the *humiliores*, the people Cicero could describe as *sordes urbis et faex*, the filth and dregs of the city?[35] The most fortunate were probably the wealthier merchants and traders, who could normally earn a reasonable living, even though they were barred from sitting on the provincial city councils because they were thought to engage in a degrading livelihood.[36] Then there were the artisans and those who engaged in service industries, such as hauliers and bargemen. The members of these three broad groups frequently formed themselves into *collegia*, or 'guilds', which, by and large, had a social rather than a political or economic role; they rarely pushed their commercial interests as the medieval guilds were later to do.[37] Usually, each *collegium* bore the name of a god and had a human patron who had benefited the membership in some way,[38] most typically by donating enough money for them to construct their meeting-hall, where the *collegium* met on a number of special occasions each year to share celebratory meals. The *collegia* had numerous officers to whom they applied titles which often imitated those of municipal officials.[39] One result of this system was, as W. A. Meeks has observed, that the *collegia* gave those who were unable to participate in the politics of the city itself a chance to feel important in their own miniature republics.[40]

After the merchants and traders came the unskilled workers, both free men and freed men, citizen and peregrine. They were dependent on finding employment in the cities, often on a day-labour basis.[41] The construction of public buildings provided much work for day-labourers, but this was an activity subject to great fluctuations.[42] Other areas of employment in pre-industrial cities, such as those in the Roman East, included burden-bearing, message-carrying, animal-driving and ditch-digging.[43] Large sectors of the populace must have eked out a slender livelihood by hawking various foodstuffs to passers-by, just as they do in cities throughout Turkey and the Middle East today.[44] For those of the free poor who were unable to work, such as the blind, the crippled or the mentally disturbed, the only means of livelihood was begging (πτωχεία) or support by relatives.

There was another group of people in the Eastern provinces whose plight was particularly unfortunate – those who had been deprived of their liberty by creditors to whom they were unable to pay their debts. G. E. M. de Ste Croix has usefully applied the term 'debt bondsmen' to debtors such as these and 'debt bondage' to their condition. They were not slaves in the technical sense; if the debt was repaid they could regain their freedom without the need for anything in the nature of manumission.[45] Although the creditor appears to have had no legal right to make the debtor work off the debt, this must have been the usual course. There would have been very little point in seizing a defaulting debtor and then incurring the expense of keeping him in idleness, except if he were thought to have concealed assets or compassionate and moneyed relatives.[46] A convincing body of evidence has been gathered by de Ste Croix for debt bondage having been a very widespread phenomenon in the Greco-Roman world.[47] In an important passage in his *Res Rusticae* Varro includes among the categories of people engaged in agricultural labour a group called *obaerarii* (debt bondsmen) and says that there were considerable numbers of these in Asia, Egypt and Illyricum.[48] Debt bondage is also found in the New Testament, most notably in the Parable of the Unmerciful Servant (Mt 18.21–35), but also in a brief Q passage (Mt 5.25–6; Lk 12.58–9).

The last component of the population comprised the slaves. In terms of status they were certainly at the very bottom of the social scale. In terms of subsistence, however, they were likely to be better off than the free poor. For slaves at least had owners to whom they might look for food and shelter.

A number of passages in the classical authors show that occasionally the poor returned the hatred which they received from the ruling elite. Sallust, for example, notes that the Roman plebs favoured Catiline's conspiracy.[49] For the most part, however, the poor accepted their lot, as we may infer from their passivity, in silence and deference. Some of them, however, took care to ensure that their souls at least rested peacefully at the conclusion of their struggles in this life by joining associations which provided a decent burial for their members.[50] Such associations charged an entrance fee and a small monthly subscription[51] and were allowed by law to meet no more than once a month.[52] During the first and second centuries CE, according to Waltzing, associations of this kind, which came to be called *collegia tenuiorum*, were to be found in great numbers in all parts of the empire.[53]

The experience of poverty

It is now necessary to examine a little more closely what it was like to be poor in a Hellenistic city of the Roman East. Then, as now, the urban poor had two basic needs: food and shelter. The most important food at the time was bread baked from wheat,[54] so that the poor had to ensure that they had enough wheat, together with some olive oil for cooking and lighting, to supply themselves and their families. This may not have been too difficult for merchants and artisans, but for unskilled labourers things were very different. Their problem was that they were often hired on a daily basis and failure to obtain work meant that the labourer and his family went hungry the next day. For the urban poor, accordingly, existence was a day-by-day struggle to obtain enough food to live, and hunger was an ever-threatening reality. Nor could the poor look to public or private charity to alleviate their condition.

In the first century CE there was no general system of wheat-distribution in the cities of the Roman East. Rome of course, did have a public corn-distribution system, which has been analysed by D. van Berchem[55] and by G. Rickman.[56] But the *frumentum publicum*, although provided free, was limited to a fixed number of Roman citizens who were residents of the capital.[57] Resident foreigners, such as Jewish expatriates, whose catacombs have survived to this day,[58] were ineligible. But even with this limitation, the system at Rome was, at least during the first and second centuries CE, quite unique. There is no evidence that there were similar distributions elsewhere, and a number of factors, which have been usefully set out by G. Cardinali,[59] suggest that there were not.

The situation changed in the third and fourth centuries CE. As a result of some admirable papyrological analysis by J. R. Rea, we now have considerable documentation concerning the corn dole for resident citizens in Oxyrhynchus during the reigns of Claudius II and Aurelian.[60] At the beginning of the fourth century there were systems of distribution in Alexandria and Constantinople, and possibly elsewhere.[61]

If the urban poor in whatever city Luke–Acts was written did not receive the benefit of free corn supply by the state, were they eligible for any other forms of assistance? There is no doubt that rich individual citizens in the provinces occasionally distributed corn *gratis* to the inhabitants of their own cities.[62] A. R. Hands has shown that in the ancient world gifts such as these were made from motives which were hardly disinterested. Those who gave to their social equals, even to the extent of inviting them to banquets, did so in the hope of receiving benefits in return or to cement valuable friendships. Gifts to one's social inferiors, on the other hand, resulted in the donor gaining *honos* or τιμή, honour or prestige.[63] Numerous inscriptions testify that the motivation for particular gifts was φιλοτιμία[64] and there is even a passage in Plutarch where a public benefaction is described as a φιλοτίμημα.[65] Whatever the motive, of course, the recipients still benefited from the gift. Unfortunately, however, such benefactions were quite irregular in occurrence and variable in scope, and could therefore not be relied upon to provide any permanent solution to the problem of obtaining enough food to live. The same must be said of the system, which was common in the Eastern cities in the first century, of having a special corn fund set up under officers called σιτῶναι, which was used to stabilize the price at which corn was sold in the local markets.[66] Although this was a useful device, it only assisted those who had the money to purchase corn at the set price. Those without went hungry.

Nor did the professional and burial associations mentioned above play any significant role in the alleviation of urban poverty. Although they held regular meetings at which the members enjoyed a banquet paid for out of membership fees or by some wealthy patron or benefactor, such meals were too infrequent to be a permanent solution to the problem of hunger. From a careful survey of the evidence Waltzing has shown, moreover, that neither the professional nor the burial *collegia* had a charitable purpose; it was not their practice to come to the aid of sick or indigent members. None of the many *collegia* inscriptions speaks of assistance being provided to such members *per se*. The use of the funds of *collegia tenuiorum* for any other purpose than the provision of burials for their members was, in fact, forbidden by the *senatusconsultum* which permitted them to be established. Occasionally, of course, distributions to all the members were made possible by benefactions, but that such distributions had no charitable purpose is eloquently revealed by the fact that often those who had less need, such as office-holders in a more fortunate economic position, received a greater share of whatever was distributed.[67] Finally, it should be recalled that, since both types of associations charged membership fees, the poorest sectors of the population, especially beggars, could not have afforded to be members, even of the *collegia tenuiorum*.

The picture we have sketched so far assumes the normal situation where there was enough corn available in a city for those with the money to buy it. In fact, serious shortages of corn, with famine as the result, were a common feature of urban life in the cities of the empire. Ramsay MacMullen has written that no 'large percentage of the people in the Roman empire can have lived their lives through without at least once wondering where the next meal was to come from'.[68] At present, there exists no extensive and systematic treatment of famines in the empire. Ancient historians, with a few notable exceptions,[69] have shown little interest in this subject. We must now outline some of the reasons for the frequency of famines, and the consequences of these for the urban poor. Rome relied upon enormous imports of grain from Egypt, Africa and other areas to feed its population, but in this it was an exception. The provincial cities, as a rule, drew their supplies from the agricultural production of their own territory,[70] often leaving local peasants destitute as a result.[71] Even in times of good harvests, the hinterlands of the cities barely produced enough grain, so that in the event of crop failure, which happened frequently, given the irregular rainfall of the Mediterranean climate,[72] the results tended to be catastrophic. True, grain could be imported from elsewhere, but this was not as uncomplicated as it might sound. Inland cities came up against the high cost of land transport. In a famous calculation, A. H. M. Jones estimated that a wagon-load of wheat doubled its price on a journey of 300–400 miles.[73] This was a serious problem for inland cities such as Pisidian Antioch (which experienced a severe famine during the reign of Domitian),[74] Iconium, Lystra and Derbe. Cities on the coast were able to import by sea. This was much cheaper: G. Rickman has estimated that freightage of wheat from Alexandria to Rome, for example, only increased the price by 16%.[75] Yet even here there were problems. The grain ships were often lost in storms, such as the one in 62 CE which sank nearly two hundred ships already in the harbour at Ostia.[76] Secondly, the import of grain from Egypt, the nearest granary to the Eastern cities, was subject to imperial licence, which was very sparingly granted.[77] In both inland and coastal cities, moreover, local grain merchants and landowners were only too willing to buy up all available corn in times of shortage, hoard it in their warehouses and only release it at an enormous profit. In times of famine, the plight of the urban poor, which was difficult at the best of times, became desperate. Often corn simply could not be purchased, and when it was available was likely to be on sale at a much higher price than normal.

The second need of the urban poor, shelter, can be dealt with more briefly. Those without any form of income except begging probably adopted the practices of the urban homeless which can be seen even today in cities from London to Bombay: taking advantage of any form of cover, natural or man-made, under which the civic authorities suffered them to remain. During the last decades of the fourth century CE, John Chrysostom reported that the homeless in Antioch-on-the-Orontes were sleeping on straw in the colonnades of baths and temples.[78] Gregory of Nyssa wrote of the beggars who thronged the cities: 'The open air is their dwelling, their lodgings are the porticoes and streetcorners and the less frequented parts of the market-place.'[79] There is little reason to believe that this would not also have been the case in the first century CE throughout the Eastern cities. The slightly better-off members of the urban poor may have lived in small one-storey huts constructed in the parts of the cities furthest from the comparatively grand central sections where the public buildings and the residences of the rich were located.[80] Finally, we come to those among the urban poor who had enough money to rent premises closer to the centres of cities. In Rome and other places, especially Ostia,[81] there were multi-storey tenements called *insulae* containing several apartments which were leased out to tenants. The nature of these buildings and the quality of life of those who inhabited them have been well described by L. Homo. Some of the *insulae* were well built, but the poorer ones were not. There was a constant danger of their collapsing or being destroyed by fire. Those used by the poor were overcrowded, dark and insanitary, usually without running water or toilets.[82] It seems that at Rome, where urban overcrowding was intense, the *insulae* were higher than elsewhere, sometimes reaching six storeys, as opposed to the three-storey examples known from other cities.[83] That Luke was familiar with dwelling-houses having three floors emerges in the passage relating the misfortune of Eutychus, who fell from the third storey of a building in Troas (Acts 20.9).

Wherever the poor lived in the Eastern provincial cities – under colonnades, or in huts or tenements – we may be sure that they were bedevilled by ill health, just like the poorer inhabitants of virtually all pre-industrial cities. Overcrowding, and often polluted water supplies, enabled diseases to sweep through their ranks. The poor – and particularly the children of the poor – suffered from high morbidity and high death rates. Life expectancies were low.[84] For the rich, of course, the outlook was much brighter. In the cities they tended to live in *domus*, low, four-sided buildings constructed around a courtyard open to the air, which were altogether more salubrious residences than those occupied by the poor. Moreover, they could afford an adequate diet and the best medical assistance, such as it was, and if plague of some sort threatened the city they could always retire to their country estates.

Conclusion

From this brief survey of social stratification and the experience of poverty in the provincial cities of the empire, it is clear that the urban poor suffered extreme forms of economic, social and political deprivation. For them life was a very grim business. Ill-fed, housed in slums or not at all, ravaged by sickness, precluded from all access to social prestige and power over their own destinies, and having virtually no hope of improvement in their condition, they went through life with little if any confirmation that they, as much as the tiny elite who lorded it over them, were creatures with personal dignity and respect, entitled to share in the fruits of the earth. Let us now turn to Luke–Acts to see if its author has shaped the gospel traditions in such a way as to respond to this experience of deprivation.

4. The Lucan version of the Nazareth pericope in its Hellenistic setting

We began this chapter with the proclamation by Jesus of good news to beggars in the synagogue at Nazareth. It is now possible to relate what Luke has Jesus say on that occasion to the social situation in which his own community must have found itself. This discussion of the Nazareth incident will open up a number of issues which will be further investigated below.

The social strata represented in Luke's community

In the previous section of this chapter we described the intensity of social stratification in the Hellenistic cities – the immense distance separating the aristocratic and wealthy elite at the top from the utterly destitute at the bottom. Given this social setting, that Luke has Jesus refer to the widow of Zarephath and Naaman the Syrian as examples

of non-Jews who had, in times past, experienced the loving-kindness
of the God of Israel acquires added significance (Lk 4.25–7). For
these two represent both extremes of the social spectrum: the widow,
one of the urban poor on the brink of death by famine (1 Kgs 17.12),
and Naaman, the rich and powerful army commander of the king of
Aram (2 Kgs 5.1–5). It is widely agreed that Luke's selection of these
two characters is related to his desire to present the gospel as open
to the Gentiles (although, as we have seen, in fellowship with Jews).
Accordingly, it must be considered likely that Luke is making the
further point that Jesus has predicted and authorized the presence
within the Christian community of both the rich and the poor.

There is nothing in Lk 4.25–7 to indicate whether the existence
of both extremes within Luke's community led to tensions and, if so,
how they were resolved. Other verses in the Nazareth pericope do,
however, hint at such difficulties and also the Christian solution to
them. More significantly, both the problem and its solution are amply
dealt with in the rest of Luke–Acts.

Luke 4.18–19 and the experience of poverty

The Isaian passage quoted by Jesus in Nazareth is drawn from Is
61.1–2, with the exception of the words ἀποστεῖλαι τεθραυσμένους
ἐν ἀφέσει, which come from Is 58.6. The primary stress in Lk 4.18
falls upon the proclamation of good news to beggars (εὐαγγελίσασθαι
πτωχοῖς). In the Septuagint version of Is 61.1 the word πτωχοί is a
translation of *'anāwīm* in the Hebrew text. E. Bammel has noted that
the word *'ānī* primarily denotes a condition of being an inferior in a
relationship, rather than expressing a state of social distress.[85] In the
Old Testament the *'anāwīm* are pre-eminently those who throw themselves humbly before Yahweh for rescue from their oppressors. With
this background, it would be incorrect to translate *'anāwīm* at Is 61.1
as 'beggars'. In a Greco-Roman city in the first century CE, however,
πτωχοί did mean 'beggars'. The word πτωχός is related to πτώσσω,
meaning to 'cringe' or 'crawl'. There were other Greek words, such as
πένης or ἐνδεής, to describe someone who was poor without being
destitute. According to A. R. Hands, words such as these were applied
to the vast majority of the people in the cities who, having no claim
to the income of a landed estate, lacked the leisure and independence
enjoyed by the ruling elite.[86] Luke's interest in 'beggars' in the socio-
economic sense, as understood by his Greco-Roman contemporaries,
appears on a number of other occasions in his Gospel, and these are
discussed below (14.13, 21; 16.20, 22, for example).

Consider, therefore, in the light of the stratification which characterized Hellenistic society, how extraordinary it must have sounded to an audience in a Greco-Roman city for the Lucan Jesus to begin his public ministry by specifying beggars and a number of other groups of people at the very bottom of, or rather right off, the social register, as the primary recipients of the gospel! For such a perspective entailed a radical upheaval in prevailing social attitudes. The urban dregs, who to the ruling elite were almost too inconsequential to be worth despising, were being offered first place in the Kingdom. This inversion of traditional values must have been startling even for those Gentile members of Luke's congregation who had previously been exposed to Jewish Scriptures, with their positive attitude to the *'anāwīm*, during their time of association with the synagogue. For it is inevitable that the God-fearers had been socialized to accept the stratification which characterized their society.

In its original context in Is 61.1 the phrase 'to proclaim freedom for captives' (κηρύξαι αἰχμαλώτοις ἄφεσιν) (Lk 4.18) appears to rely upon imagery drawn from the release of slaves in the Jubilee Year, as prescribed in Lev 25.10.[87] It also appears that the reference in Is 61.2 to 'the Lord's year of favour' (ἐνιαυτὸν κυρίου δεκτόν) uses imagery appropriate to the Year of Jubilee. Yet what meaning did the notion of 'the release of captives' have for Luke's audience? Apart from its two appearances in Lk 4.18, the word ἄφεσις is used on eight other occasions in Luke–Acts, in the phrase ἄφεσις ἁμαρτιῶν (Lk 1.77; 3.3; 24.47; Acts 2.38; 5.31; 10.43; 13.38; 26.18). Should we deduce from this pattern of usage that the 'captives' in Lk 4.18 are merely those who have given up their liberty to sin? The answer is 'no'. While it may be the case, as R. Bultmann suggested,[88] that ἄφεσις here *includes* the thought of forgiveness, it would be a serious distortion of Luke's intentions to regard this as its only meaning. We say this because by his redactional changes and additional material Luke plainly manifests a desire to relate his Gospel to both physical and spiritual aspects of human bondage. When Luke speaks of the destitute, the blind and the lame, for example, he is speaking of them as literally and physically such (cf. Lk 6.20; 7.22; 14.13, 21; 16.20; 18.22; 19.8; 21.3). The alleviation of destitution and disabilities is a vital aspect of Luke's Gospel preaching, even though, as we shall see, it is not the only one. Thus, the liberation promised in the programmatic verse 4.18 must be so interpreted as to cover the salvation at a physical level which commences with the ministry of Jesus.

In fact, it is possible to suggest two contexts in which the release of captives could have had a very particular point in the Hellenistic cities of the period. S. Applebaum maintains that after the Roman conquest of Palestine in 70 CE there were thousands of Jewish slaves scattered around the East.[89] This view is consistent with what Luke says at 21.24: αἰχμαλωτισθήσονται εἰς τὰ ἔθνη πάντα ('They will be led off captive among all the nations'). Some of these slaves may have become Christians, and their communities could have been in the habit of manumitting them. If so, Luke would be endorsing this practice in Lk 4.18. Secondly, it is possible that Luke's audience understood αἰχμάλωτοι as a reference to the debt bondsmen we discussed above. If this is the case, Luke's community may have undertaken to pay off the outstanding debts of some of these people, presumably those with links to the community, and so secure their release. In both classical and Septuagintal usage, the word ἄφεσις is used for the discharge of debts.[90]

The announcement by Jesus of 'sight for the blind' in Lk 4.18 is more straightforward. For many, if not most, people afflicted with blindness in the Roman East, begging was likely to be the only form of livelihood. Luke retains from Mark the story of the blind man who sat begging outside Jericho (Mk 10.46–52; Lk 18.35–43). The promise of 'sight for the blind' made by Jesus in Nazareth is fulfilled in a literal way during the Gospel (7.21; 18.35–43). At the same time, Jesus issues an instruction that the blind are to be invited to the banquets of the rich (14.13), upon which more will be said below.

Lastly, mention should be made of the widow of Zarephath (Lk 4.25–6). Although not totally indigent, since she owns a house with an upper room (1 Kgs 17.17, 19), a long famine has left her with only enough flour and oil to make one last meal for herself and her son before they die. As we have seen, famine was still a common feature of city life in Luke's time and must have struck a chord of recognition in his audience. In 1 Kgs 17.14–16 the widow and her son receive an unfailing supply of meal and oil. In other words, the mercy of Yahweh is manifested to them in the physcial satisfaction of their hunger. That Luke should mention the widow suggests that in the salvation inaugurated by the coming of Jesus, hunger will cease to affect the poor on whom God's favour rests.

Conclusion

During the course of this discussion of the Nazareth pericope, a number of elements in the Lucan perspective on poverty and wealth have emerged which we expect, given the nature of Lk 4.16–30, to find further developed in the rest of Luke–Acts. Thus, it appears likely that Luke's community encompassed individuals from the top and bottom strata of Hellenistic society, but that his presentation of the gospel radically elevates the destitute to a position of pre-eminence. The Lucan Jesus promises to alleviate the extreme physical deprivation suffered by the beggars, the blind, the lame, the imprisoned and so forth, without, however, ignoring the spiritual aspects of salvation. It is now possible to see if a detailed examination of Luke–Acts supports these findings.

5. The rich and the poor in Luke's community

It was suggested above that the reference by Jesus to the starving widow of Zarephath and to Naaman, the Aramean army commander, in Lk 4.25–7, pointed to the presence in Luke's community of representatives from either extreme of the socio-economic spectrum. The rest of Luke–Acts must now be investigated to ascertain if it contains other evidence to confirm this suggestion. For it is apparent that it would be difficult to appreciate Luke's perspective on riches and poverty without having a broad outline of the socio-economic standing of the various members of his community. Our primary interest is to identify the highest and lowest strata represented among his Christian contemporaries. This has the result that it is unnecessary to become involved in the lively and long-standing debate as to the *predominant* social level of the early Christians.[91]

The upper socio-economic strata in Luke's community
In 1 Cor 1.26 Paul tells his Corinthian Christians that at the time of their conversion not many of them were wise according to earthly standards, not many of them were powerful and not many were of noble birth (εὐγενεῖς). G. Theissen is surely correct in holding that these negative statements carry the inevitable implication that there were a few of them who were wise, powerful and well-bred.[92] Although Theissen does not mention it, the only people appropriately described as εὐγενεῖς in a Hellenistic city, barring the presence of senators or equestrians from Rome, were the decurions and magistrates: that is, those at the very top of the local social, economic and political hierarchy. Were there people such as these in Luke's congregation? That they were to be found in the Corinthian community in the fifties of the first century CE does not, admittedly,

prove that they were present in Luke's community in the eighties or early nineties. It does, however, mean that it is not unreasonable to expect to find them there. More importantly, a number of features in the text suggest that some of Luke's audience were wealthy and influential, possibly even decurions.

First of all, the high literary style of parts of Luke–Acts, especially of the Prologue (Lk 1.1–4) and of the sea voyage and shipwreck description in Acts 27, implies that its author came from the upper segment of Greco-Roman society. According to A. H. M. Jones, the literary education offered by the Hellenistic cities was largely inaccessible to the lower orders.[93] This means that behind the artifice of some of Luke's Greek there lies a large amount of leisure devoted to literary pursuits only possible among the upper reaches of his society. It is, moreover, unlikely that Luke was the only member of his community with this background; there were, presumably, others capable of savouring his occasional recourse to excellent Greek.

Secondly, there is Luke's focus upon converts of elevated status, economic position and political power. On three occasions Roman centurions express their openness to the ministry of Jesus or readiness to accept the Gospel (Lk 7.1–10; 23.47; Acts 10.1ff.). The conversion of the third of these, Cornelius, is actually depicted as inaugurating and authorizing the inclusion of Gentiles within the Christian communities. Centurions had considerable social status and their mustering-out pay was, as mentioned above, sufficient to allow them entry to the *ordo decurionum*. Other individuals from the ruling elite whom Luke portrays as favourable to the gospel and to its preachers, often to the extent of converting, include Joanna, the wife of Herod's steward Chuza (Lk 8.3), the Ethiopian Eunuch (Acts 8.26–39), Manaen, 'who had been raised with Herod the Tetrarch' (Acts 13.1), Sergius Paulus, the proconsul of Cyprus (Acts 13.7), Greek women and men of noble birth from Beroea (Acts 17.12) and the Ephesian Asiarchs, who are described as Paul's friends (Acts 19.31).[94] With the exception of Sergius Paulus, who was of senatorial rank, all these individuals must have had a status equal to that of decurions. The care which Luke takes to mention them is best explained as indicating that there were members of his community who could identify with these early heroes of the faith by virtue of having a similar, or perhaps slightly inferior, position in society.

The presence of wealthy Christians among Luke's audience is confirmed, finally, by those passages in the Third Gospel where Jesus warns the rich to mend their ways. These passages include the Parable of the Rich Fool (12.13–21), the command to sell one's possessions and give alms (13.33), the instruction to invite beggars, etc., to banquets (14.12–14), the saying about making friends out of unrighteous Mammon (16.9) and the story of the rich man and Lazarus (16.19–31), all of which occur in Luke's special material, and, lastly, the incident of the rich ruler (18.18–30), which is taken over from Mark with one or two significant modifications. This last incident is particularly interesting because in Luke's version the man does not depart after he has failed to accept the radical invitation which Jesus has offered him, as he does in Mark (cf. Mk 10.22 and Lk 18.23). The effect of this change, as S. Legasse has noted,[95] is that the rich man and his problem are presented by Luke as being within the Christian community.

The poor in Luke's community

Some commentators deny that Luke was addressing his message to the poor. According to E. Bammel, for example, 'Luke neither thinks from the standpoint of the poor nor really seeks to address them.'[96] Proponents of this viewpoint do not necessarily deny that there were poor in the Lucan community, but if they do not make this denial they are confronted with a problem as to explaining why Luke directed his two volumes to only one section of the flock. In fact, an examination of the evidence reveals both that Luke does address the poor, even the utterly destitute, and that they constituted part of his congregation.

On external grounds, first of all, it is impossible to believe that the urban poor were not at all represented in a Hellenistic Christian community such as Luke's. Why should we imagine that his community was utterly different from Paul's in Corinth thirty years earlier, where only a few Christians were learned, powerful or well-bred (1 Cor 1.26)? But above all it is difficult to credit that the emphasis placed on the poor throughout Luke's Gospel was not balanced and even motivated by the presence within the author's community of such people, on whom this message would have had the maximum impact.

There are, moreover, a number of passages in the two volumes which unequivocally point to the presence of the poor among Luke's Christian contemporaries. The clearest of these is the Q Parable of the Great Banquet (Lk 14.15–24; Mt 22.1–10). Luke's version of this parable is distinguished by its specifying two groups of people who are invited to the feast: the first consisting of the beggars,

maimed, blind and lame within the city (14.21), and the second of
guests brought in from the highways and hedges (14.23). T. W. Manson
plausibly interprets the first group as Jews and the second, outside
the city (that is, beyond the boundaries of Israel), as Gentiles.[97] In
any event, the feast is certainly an image for the Kingdom and,
therefore, for the Christian community, and the poor are those who
are first invited to take part. It is surely through no inadvertence on
Luke's part that the types of people specified in Lk 14.21 as replacement guests are virtually identical to the groups promised the good
news in Lk 4.18 and extolled as blessed in the beatitudes in Lk 6.20–1.

The second feature of this kind is the body of material which Luke
offers as a commentary on the Lord's Prayer (11.5–13). A prayer
to 'give us our daily bread' (11.3) would have been uttered very
fervently by the poor in a Hellenistic city. And the story of the man
who asks his friend for bread at midnight (11.5–8) is also set among
the poor, who must often have had no food in their houses for
unexpected guests. But, more importantly, Luke's introduction of
πνεῦμα ἅγιον in 11.13, where Matthew's reading ἀγαθά (Mt 7.11)
is surely original,[98] is plainly meant to remind the poor in his community, who might have been led by the harshness of their existence
to think otherwise, that humanity does not live by bread alone.

Thirdly, it is reasonable to connect Luke's idealization of the social
welfare arrangements in the early Christian community in Jerusalem
with a need in his own congregation for the rich members to help the
poor. The fact that the word πτωχός does not appear in Acts is
definitely not, *pace* E. Bammel,[99] a sign of Luke's lack of interest in
the destitute, but rather indicates that, as a result of the κοινωνία
of the early community, there was no one who was ἐνδεής (Acts 4.34).
In other words, πτωχεία was abolished. Luke presents the early
church as successfully implementing the injunction to give alms which
Jesus had laid upon the rich. This emerges quite unambiguously in
the similarity of language, which has been noticed by S. Brown,[100]
between Lk 18.22 (πάντα ὅσα ἔχεις πώλησον καὶ διάδος πτωχοῖς)
('Sell everything that you own and *distribute* it to the poor') and Acts
4.34–5 (πωλοῦντες ... διεδίδετο δὲ ἑκάστῳ καθότι ἄν τις χρείαν
εἶχεν) ('[those who owned land or houses] sold [them] ... [and the
proceeds] were *distributed* to each according to his need'). In the
Marcan source of Lk 18.22 (Mk 10.21), the phrase used for 'give to
the destitute' is δὸς πτωχοῖς, and Luke's alteration of this seems
clearly designed to bring Jesus' command into line with the language
used of the distribution of alms in Acts 4.35.

Conclusion

This examination of the evidence in the text strongly supports the view that Luke's community contained members from either end of the socio-economic spectrum in the Hellenistic city in which it was located. A similar conclusion has recently been reached by R. J. Karris.[101] Interesting confirmation for this result can be detected in the Parables of the Lost Sheep (Lk 15.4–7) and the Lost Drachma (Lk 15.8–10). These two parables both illustrate the joy in heaven at the repentance of just one sinner. What is striking about them is that the first, which has a parallel in Mt 18.12–14, deals with a man who owns one hundred sheep, which means that he was reasonably well-off,[102] while the second which has no parallel in Matthew, concerns a woman whose total wealth is only ten drachmas, equal to ten *denarii*, or the income from ten days' labour. In other words, Luke is offering the same parable in two versions, to bring home its message to both the rich and the poor in his community.

6. Luke's theology of the poor

Good news for the poor, grim news for the rich

One of the most remarkable aspects of Luke's vision of the Christian community is that, although it contained wealthy and influential members, the privileged places in it were reserved for the very dregs of Hellenistic society, especially the beggars and the physically disabled. For this reason, it is appropriate to speak of a 'theology of the poor' in Luke–Acts. There is abundant evidence in the text of the Lucan emphasis on the priority accorded to the utterly destitute in the scheme of salvation. Jesus' inaugural preaching in Nazareth plays an important role in establishing this priority (4.16–30), but the theme begins even earlier, with the words of Mary in the Magnificat, 'He has exalted the lowly, the hungry he has filled with good things' (1.52–3), and with the humble birth of Jesus in a stable (2.7),[103] to parents who could only afford the offering of the poor when his mother was purified in the Temple afterwards (2.24). After the Nazareth incident, the theme is continued in the beatitudes:

> Blessed are the destitute (οἱ πτωχοί)
> because yours is the Kingdom of Heaven,
> Blessed are you who are hungry now,
> because you will be satisfied (6.20–1).

Luke is here speaking in a literal and physical sense of destitution and hunger and the alleviation of both (contrast Mt 5.3, 6). This literalness and physicality extend to the meaning for Luke of another Q saying: 'The blind see, the lame walk, lepers are cleansed and the deaf hear, the dead are raised, and beggars have good news proclaimed to them' (Lk 7.22; Mt 11.5). In Luke's version of the Parable of the Great Banquet, the first people invited to fill the places of the original guests who have failed to attend are this same group of people: beggars, the crippled, the blind and the lame (14.21); Matthew, on the other hand, in the verse parallel to this, speaks merely of 'the bad and the good' (Mt 22.10). In the story of Zacchaeus, the benefits for the poor which flow from the onset of the Kingdom take the very physical form of Zacchaeus distributing half his property to the beggars (τοῖς πτωχοῖς) and compensating fourfold all those whom he has defrauded (19.8). The story of the rich man and Lazarus, lastly, illustrates the reversal of fortunes which will occur in the next world; but more of that below.

In the light of our previous discussion of the social and economic realities of life in the Roman East, one readily appreciates how novel and appealing a message such as this must have been to the sick and destitute in Luke's city. From passages such as Lk 1.53; 6.21; 14.13 and 14.15–24, it is reasonable to infer that the hunger which we know was often experienced by the poor of Hellenistic society was a grim reality for some of Luke's Christian contemporaries as well. To Christians such as these, the promise held out by the Lucan version of the Gospel must have exercised a potent appeal. Looked at from the other direction, of course, it seems indisputable that the interest which Luke, unique among the evangelists, manifests in the plight of the poor has been motivated by an unusual sensitivity to their hunger and the other forms of physical deprivation to which they are subject.

But where does this leave the rich? The obverse of Luke's good news to the destitute is some very grim news for the rich, threatening them with the total loss of their status, wealth and power. This theme is evident in a number of features unique to Luke, such as, the Magnificat (1.52–3), the woes of the rich in the sermon on the plain (6.24–5), the Parable of the Rich Fool (12.13–21), and the story of the rich man and Lazarus (16.19–31), which exemplifies the reversal of fortune predicted earlier in the Gospel (1.52–3; 6.24–5).

In the urban context of the East, where the ruling elite controlled most of the available resources of wealth, prestige and power, and imposed on the rest of the population a value system which endorsed and extolled this control, the viewpoint espoused by Luke must have seemed threatening indeed. Even granted that the reversal of the socio-economic advantages of the rich might not occur until the next life (on which subject there is more below), the Lucan Gospel questioned the propriety and therefore the legitimacy of the entire system of social stratification in the Hellenistic cities. This was a radical challenge to the prevailing social arrangements. In practical terms, Luke was not advocating the revolutionary overthrow of those arrangements; but he was insisting, as we shall see, that they be eschewed by any of the rich and influential who wished to be members of the Christian community. Luke may not have been entirely successful in this, but that by no means mitigates the radical nature of his case. A little later in this chapter we shall investigate more closely the onus placed upon rich Christians, but in the meantime it will be helpful to consider a Jewish work which also speaks of a reversal of the positions of the rich and poor – 1 Enoch 92–105. A comparison of this text with Luke–Acts will show that Luke appears to have drawn upon Jewish traditions in his treatment of the poor and the rich, yet to have transcended those traditions in response to the particular composition of, and the problems besetting, his own congregation.

The rich and the poor in 1 Enoch 92–105

The attempt to relate Luke's teaching on possessions to the Old Testament and other Jewish writings is hardly novel. In 1930 J.M. Creed, for example, aptly pointed to the existence of some kind of connection between Lk 12.16–21 and Ecclesiasticus 11.18–19.[104] Nevertheless, it is only quite recently that attention has been drawn to the remarkable similarities between 1 Enoch 92–105 and Luke's attitude to the rich and the poor. These similarities seem to have been first noticed by S. Aalen in 1966.[105] In a significant article published in 1979, G.W.E. Nickelsburg has continued Aalen's largely descriptive work and has also ventured an explanation for the resemblances between 1 Enoch and Luke–Acts.[106]

The closest of the similarities exists between Lk 12.16–21 and 1 Enoch 97.8–10. The latter passage runs as follows:

> Woe to you who acquire silver and gold in unrighteousness and say:
> 'We have become rich with riches and have possessions;
> And have acquired everything we have desired.

And now let us do what we purposed:
For we have gathered silver,
And many are the husbandmen in our houses.'
And our granaries are (brim) full as with water, [*sic*]
Yea and like water your lies shall flow away;
For your riches shall not abide
But speedily ascend from you;
For ye have acquired it all in unrighteousness,
And ye shall be given over to a great curse.[107]

As mentioned above, moreover, Lk 12.16–21 also appears to have some connection with Ecclesiasticus 11.18–19. According to Nickelsburg, the explanation for this particular resemblance lies not in a literary dependence by Luke on the Jewish work, but in his general familiarity with the Wisdom tradition from which they both derived.[108]

The broader similarities between Luke's Gospel and 1 Enoch 92–105 emerge from a summary of the portrayal of the rich and the poor in the latter work and the fate in store for both.[109] First of all, in these chapters of 1 Enoch the rich and their riches and possessions are always viewed in a bad light. In some cases the rich have acquired their riches by oppressing the poor and the lowly, and their ostentatious banqueting and luxuriating (cf. 96.5–8; 98.2) underline this oppression. Secondly, the rich trust in their possessions as the sign of a happy life now and as a means of securing their future. Thirdly, the rich will be condemned in the coming judgement of God and will be delivered to eternal punishment, 'into darkness and chains and a burning flame' (1 Enoch 103.8),[110] which will be retribution for their injustice in this life and indicate the futility of their having amassed earthly riches.

For the poor, on the other hand, the situation is entirely different. The author of 1 Enoch promises that their present conditions of misery and oppression will be reversed in the life after death:

> Be hopeful; for aforetime ye were put to shame through ill and affliction; but now ye shall shine as the lights of heaven, ye shall shine and ye shall be seen, and the portals of heaven shall be opened to you ...   (1 Enoch 104.2).[111]

Interestingly enough, the Messianic Banquet is not mentioned as one of the delights the righteous poor will experience in the next world. The poor are not promised relief in this life; it is after death that they will find happiness, while their erstwhile oppressors burn in Sheol.

In 1 Enoch 92–105 there is depicted a bitter conflict between the two groups, the rich and the poor, the sinners and the righteous, and the author sides with the latter without qualification. The message of 1 Enoch, Nickelsburg plausibly suggests, is that God will rectify the grievous injustices in the present age in the coming judgement.[112] He considers that the work was written for a particular oppressed group within Israel, though one perhaps not fully sectarian in the sociological sense of the term.[113]

The area in which Luke–Acts most resembles 1 Enoch 92–105 is in its reiterated prediction of a forthcoming reversal of the conditions of the rich and the poor. To the Hellenistic elite, a message such as that conveyed in these chapters of 1 Enoch would no doubt have appeared novel and surprising. But given its Jewish origins and intended low-status audience, it is unlikely that they would have come to hear of it. This factor clearly distinguishes 1 Enoch from Luke–Acts, which was written for a community which actually contained members who came from the wealthier and more influential strata of Hellenistic society. Furthermore, 1 Enoch 92–105 deals with a purely eschatological punishment of the rich and blessing of the poor. It is written for the victims of injustice and oppression and carries no address to the rich, no admonition to them, for example, to begin acting justly in this life. But where does Luke stand on these last two issues? Is his concept of salvation purely eschatological, or does he see it as beginning in this life? And does he regard the rich as under any responsibility to use their riches to assist the destitute and disabled? Although a great deal of scholarly attention has been devoted to these issues, it is doubtful that the middle-class bias which bedevils Lucan studies has anywhere had a more pernicious influence than here. Luke's unique and radical perspective has been domesticated. His Gospel has not been preached. This judgement must now be justified from the evidence in the text.

Luke's attitude to salvation: its other-worldly dimension

Even if Luke does emphasize the physical aspect of the plight of the poor and the satisfaction of the rich, might it not be the case that he envisages the inevitable reversal of these conditions as an occurrence reserved for the next world? There has never been a shortage of exegetes willing to answer this question in the affirmative. Recent examples include R. Koch ('The great reversal comes with death'),[114]

E. Bammel, who hedges his bets a little ('The hope of the poor was in the world to come, though not entirely')[115] and C.S. Hill, who is representative of a large proportion of the literature, and wider Christian opinion, when he says of the salvation offered by early Christianity that it was '*spiritual* salvation not material; it was *otherworldly* in orientation rather than this-worldly'.[116] Such views do coincide, admittedly, with those of 1 Enoch 92−105, but do they also characterize Luke's attitude or are they merely a bourgeois reading of it?

First of all, it is undeniable that Luke believed in an afterlife where the rich would be punished and deprived of the advantages they possessed on earth, while those who had been destitute would enjoy whatever they had lacked in this world. In other words, the final and complete establishment of justice is reserved for paradise. To this extent, Luke−Acts is similar to 1 Enoch 92−105. The most unambiguous Lucan resemblances to the perspective of 1 Enoch are the story of the rich man and Lazarus (16.19−31) and the account of the criminal crucified next to Jesus to whom Jesus promises 'Today you will be with me in Paradise' (23.43).

The other places in which this belief appears in the Third Gospel differ from 1 Enoch, however, by depicting the afterlife in the imagery of the Messianic Banquet. In the Old Testament the most important source for this eschatological *topos* is Is 25.6, but it also appears in other parts of the Old Testament and in Rabbinic literature. By his additional material and redactional alterations Luke exhibits an interest in the Messianic Banquet which is quite unique in the New Testament. At 13.29, for example, he describes the people who will 'sit-down-at-table' (ἀνακλιθήσονται) in the Kingdom of God as coming from 'the east and the west, and from the north and the south', as opposed to Matthew, probably closer to Q here, who only mentions those from the east and the west (Mt 8.11). Luke's alteration emphasizes the universality of those who will enjoy the Messianic Banquet. Secondly, Luke begins his version of the Q parable of the Great Banquet with the remark of someone dining with Jesus that 'Blessed is he who eats bread in the Kingdom of God' (14.15). Thirdly, whereas all three Synoptists report the saying by Jesus at the Last Supper that he will not drink wine again until he does so in the Kingdom of God (Mk 14.25; Mt 26.29; Lk 22.18), only Luke records a similar saying with respect to eating as well (Lk 22.16). Furthermore, Luke alone includes the promise by Jesus to the disciples at the Supper that they will eat and drink at his table in the Kingdom (Lk 22.30).

Fifthly, the description of Lazarus being carried by angels into the bosom (κόλπος) of Abraham (Lk 16.22) is another reference to the Messianic Banquet. To recline 'on someone's bosom', as R. Meyer has shown, is an image from dining in both classical and Jewish literature.[117] There is an excellent example of this usage at Jn 13.23. Lastly, the promise to the poor in Lk 1.53 and 6.21 that they will have their hunger satisfied certainly has an eschatological element; as we shall soon see, however, it is a very serious misreading of Luke to restrict the ambit of this promise solely to the next life.

We may conclude, therefore, that Luke does direct his readers' attention to a future world in which the sufferings of the poor in this life will be replaced by eternal contentment. That he should fix upon the Messianic Banquet as the appropriate image for this future world, in sharp contrast to 1 Enoch 92–105, is a poignant reminder of the paradigmatic form of deprivation experienced by the urban poor who were members of his community. It must be considered highly likely, in fact, that it was just this appropriateness of the Messianic Banquet as an image of salvation for a significant section of his audience that motivated Luke to give it such a unique emphasis.

Luke's attitude to salvation. Its this-worldly dimension
The time has now come to consider the real cutting-edge of Luke's theology of property – that the elimination of injustice, the alleviation of the sufferings of the poor and the destitute, is not merely an eschatological reality, but is a vital constituent of Christianity in this world, here and now. Looked at in principle, it is evident that the composition of Luke's community, encompassing as it did members from either end of the socio-economic spectrum, must have been a powerful inducement to the evangelist to formulate a theology which specified the correct Christian attitude to riches and poverty. Complicating things for Luke was the fact that it was virtually unknown in Hellenistic cities for representatives from the top and from the bottom of the social hierarchy to gather together in a single association. Even the *collegia*, although they might have an influential patron, almost invariably comprised members from a similar socio-economic level, and while slaves could join the *collegia tenuiorum*, the burial societies, their fellow-members came only from the lower ranks of the urban poor.[118] This culturally derived tension could only have been sharpened by the theology of the Christian community which spoke of unity in Christ, graphically presented in the one loaf and one cup of the eucharist. This latter factor decisively differentiates the

Christian *ekklesiai* from the only other institution where rich and poor normally associated together – the Jewish synagogue, which did not espouse a unity of this kind.

There is one particularly unequivocal example in Luke–Acts of a conflict between the social values of the rich in Greco-Roman society and the new standards which were promulgated in Jesus' name. The passage in question is Lk 14.12–14, the substance of which is unique to Luke. In v. 12 Jesus tells his host that when he holds a feast or a banquet he should not invite his friends, brothers, relatives or rich neighbours, with the hope of receiving return invitations. Although it has rarely been noted, in saying this the Lucan Jesus is rejecting the fundamental rationale of gift-giving in Hellenistic society. As explained by A. R. Hands and others,[119] the whole point of acts of generosity in this culture was to establish reciprocal relations which could be cashed in at a later date. A classic example of this outlook is found in the policy of the dishonest steward in Lk 16.3–7. Of course, it only made sense to be generous to those who were in a position to do you a favour in return, so that the sort of people whom Jesus recommends the host should invite – beggars, the lame, cripples and the blind (Lk 14.13) – are exactly those who would rarely, if ever, be invited. Jesus acknowledges that guests such as these would not be able to repay the host; but he would receive his repayment in the resurrection of the just (14.14). Now there can be little doubt that Luke intends Jesus' views on this subject to apply to the relationships between the rich and the poor *within* the Christian community. The Evangelist, whom we have argued in Chapter 2 to have been addressing a purely Christian audience, wishes his wealthy Christian contemporaries to put the instruction of Jesus into effect within the confines of the *ekklesia*, since the types of people whom Jesus urges them to invite to their banquets are virtually identical to those promised the good news, and therefore included within the community, in Lk 1.52–53; 4.18; 6.20–21; 7.22 and 14.21. Thus, while the complete reversal of the conditions of the rich and the poor will not occur until the next world, the process must begin here on earth. Salvation for Luke is not a purely eschatological reality, for within the Christian community it begins here and now.

We conclude this treatment of Lk 14.12–14 by noting that it is fair to say that in a Hellenistic city the admonition of Jesus contained in these verses could only have been regarded as something akin to a social revolution. Although we have long been accustomed to the idea of giving alms to the destitute, those wealthy Christians who adopted a policy of inviting beggars and the disabled to their homes were repudiating a central aspect of their cultural beliefs and practices.

Having seen the challenge which Luke has Jesus throw down to wealthy Christians to modify quite drastically their customary social values and behaviour, in Lk 14.12–14 at least, the views of R. Koch come as quite a shock:

> ... that Jesus is not against possessions as such. All the same, we should not forget 'that the position of Jesus on possessions is purely religious and does not have an economic or social foundation'.
>
> We can only do justice to the views of Jesus on possessions and wealth if we do not lose sight of the purely religious point of view.[120]

We must now demonstrate that this opinion, a prime example of the widespread spiritualizing of Luke's two volumes, which has emasculated his teaching in this area, is not merely inconsistent with Lk 14.12–14, but also with many other features in the text.

There are a number of passages in Luke–Acts, either peculiar to Luke or marked by his redactional changes, which stress the necessity of giving alms. These are to be taken, in general, as admonitions addressed to wealthy Christians to help the poorer members of the community. The best example is that of the rich ruler in Lk 18.18–23. By two significant modifications to his Marcan source, which have already been noted above, Luke connects the distribution of goods which Jesus urges the man to undertake with the social welfare arrangements in the early Christian community (replacement of δός πτωχοῖς in Mk 10.21 with διάδος πτωχοῖς in Lk 18.22; cf. διεδίδετο in Acts 4.35) and presents the rich ruler as within the community (deletion of ἀπῆλθεν from Mk 10.22; Lk 18.23–4).

In the early chapters of Acts Luke describes how the wealthier Christians, in effect, put into operation Jesus' instruction to the rich ruler by selling their possessions and distributing the proceeds to those in need (2.45) or giving them to the apostles for common use (4.34–7). Thus was κοινωνία established.

This κοινωνία is shaken a little in the story of Ananias and Sapphira (Acts 5.1–11), who pretend to hand over to the apostles the full price of some land they have sold. They are both struck dead as a result. Clearly, there was nothing wrong with their selling the property and giving only a proportion of the apostles. The behaviour of Zacchaeus was similar to this and certainly found favour in the eyes of Jesus (Lk 19.1–10). The sin of Ananias and Sapphira lay in pretending to have given all the price of the land to the apostles, since this constituted an attempt to deceive the Holy Spirit.

One suspects, however, that Luke's picture of early Christianity, apart from the story of Ananias and Sapphira, was an idealization serving to remind his contemporaries of how far they had fallen short of the ideal. Otherwise, it is difficult to explain his concern to sharpen material in his sources or add new sayings and passages which stress the need for almsgiving and the renunciation of possessions. These include the ethical teaching of John the Baptist (Lk 3.11–14), the total renunciation demanded of the first disciples (5.11) and Levi (5.28), the instructions to lend freely (6.34–5) and to sell one's possessions and give alms (12.33) and the direction to use Mammon to win friends for oneself (16.9).

What of the other aspect of Koch's attribution to the Lucan Jesus of a 'purely religious' standpoint on possessions – that Jesus does not condemn riches as such, but, as he further explains, only 'the improper use of riches, the greedy and God-abandoned striving after their increase.'[121] By 'improper use of riches', Koch does not mean failure to help the poor, but merely a preoccupation with them to the exclusion of God *in abstracto*. Thus, he interprets the error of the rich farmer in Lk 12.16–21 not as meanness or miserliness, but as stupidity, as a form of idolatry in making possessions his god to the exclusion of the real God. His interpretation of the parable of the rich man and Lazarus is similar: '... according to the narrative, the rich man does nothing evil. He is not oppressing the poor.'[122] No, he is simply rich and enjoys his wealth and succumbs to Godlessness in doing so.

The logic of Koch's position is that the rich could set themselves right with God by bringing their riches to a bottomless pit and throwing them in, while the starving poor looked helplessly on. This consequence illustrates the inadequacy of Koch's conception of God and his failure to attend to the body of evidence in Luke–Acts dealing with the responsibility of the rich, who have often gained their wealth unjustly, to share what they have with the poor. The saying which Luke preserves from Mark, 'For it is easier for a camel to pass through the eye of a needle than for a rich man to enter the Kingdom of God' (Lk 18.25; Mk 10.25), although made little of by Koch, is taken with deadly seriousness by Luke. The rich stand condemned by their wealth, and the only means they have of avoiding judgement is by helping the poor (Lk 14.12–14; 18.22).

Time and again Luke refers to the fact that riches tend to be acquired unjustly and have to be distributed to the poor as a result. This theme commences as early as Lk 3.11–14, where John the Baptist tells his listeners to share their clothing and food with those in need, and then urges the tax-gatherers to collect no more than their legal limit and soldiers to refrain from extortion and blackmail. A verse unique to Luke (Lk 12.33) encapsulates what is required of the rich, and its lesson is repeated elsewhere in the text. At 14.14, for example, Jesus exhorts his host to expend his wealth on the poor so that he will receive his reward in the resurrection of the just. We are not told if this particular host had obtained his wealth unjustly, but what is virtually a Lucan presumption against the rich on this score surfaces in a verse very similar to 14.14: 16.9, in which Jesus says 'Make friends for yourself out of unjust Mammon (ἐκ τοῦ μαμωνᾶ τῆς ἀδικίας), so that when it fails you, they will receive you into the tents of eternity.' The phrase 'unjust Mammon' picks up traditional Jewish ideas and reveals Luke's presumption that most fortunes are the result of oppression and injustice. In an interesting article on Lk 16.9, R. H. Hiers shows that those who will receive into the eternal tents the rich who have distributed their possessions are the poor.[123] This is in line with Lk 14.14.

7. Conclusion

So far in this chapter we have not sought to introduce the model of legitimation of a sect outlined in Chapter 1 and expanded in Chapter 3 above. Although that model did not deal specifically with the question of tensions which might arise within a new group on account of the different socio-economic levels represented among its members, it is plain that it could be easily modified to do so. The modification of models in the light of further data is a normal procedure of sociological investigation. Although it is not practical to attempt that theoretical exercise here, one observation relating to it does seem to be in order. Luke is addressing both the rich and the poor in his community, but whereas his message for the latter constitutes a form of encouragement which we have seen in earlier chapters of this book to characterize his legitimatory efforts, his line with the rich is rather different. Luke's message for them is parenetic as much as legitimatory. While his exposition of the teaching of Jesus and the practice of the early Jerusalem church in the matter of possessions must have served a legitimatory function for some of his wealthier

Christian contemporaries with clear consciences on this matter, it is highly likely that behind his continual emphasis on the priority of the poor and the duties of the rich lies a failure by some of the latter to live up to their responsibilities. For people such as these, Luke's attitude is homiletic, not legitimatory; he is not encouraging them that all is well, but warning them that all is not.

The content of Luke's teaching on property is based upon a fundamental disparity between the positions of the poor and of the rich. In his scheme the destitute and the physically disabled have priority. The first places in the Kingdom are reserved for them (Lk 14.15–24). This means not only, as in 1 Enoch 92–105, that they will be compensated in the Messianic Banquet of the next world for their plight on earth, but also that within the Christian community a significant start to their redemption has begun, with the provision of money and meals, relief for their physical disabilities, and possibly even manumission or release for slaves and bondsmen.

It is well worth noting that Luke incorporates both features, future bliss and present satisfaction, into his eucharistic theology. In his Passion narrative, Jesus makes two references to the Messianic Banquet in addition to those also in Mark and Matthew (Lk 22.16, 30). This has the effect that the Lucan Jesus ties the Messianic Banquet, that image of the looming establishment of eternal justice, to the eucharist. For Luke's community the weekly eucharist, itself the one meal his poorer Christian contemporaries could be sure of receiving, was a foretaste of the Messianic Banquet. One is reminded of a saying by Fr Pedro Arrupe, SJ that as long as there is anyone in the world who is hungry, our eucharist is incomplete.

The striking novelty of the relationship between the rich and the poor advocated by Luke must not be forgotten. In Hellenistic society the destitute got little if any help from the civic authorities, the *collegia*, or from private benefactors. The scheme of social welfare put forward indirectly in Luke–Acts may, in fact, have been a Christian invention. D. Seccombe has recently published an impressive refutation of the well-known opinion of J. Jeremias that there was an organized system of public relief for the poor operated by the Jewish authorities in Jerusalem in New Testament times.[124]

The rich members of the community were the source of funds and meals for the poor. In Luke's eyes wealth was likely to have been unjustly acquired (Lk 16.9), and if its possessors did not distribute at least some of it to the poor in this world they faced the prospect of eternal punishment in the next. This teaching was a radical challenge to the deeply held beliefs in his Hellenistic milieu, where the ruling elite not only treated the lower orders unjustly and with contempt, but congratulated themselves on doing so. Luke not only attacks the propriety of their attitudes, but also instructs them to modify the very behaviour which expresses their superiority in status, wealth and power (Lk 14.12−14). Let there be no doubt that those people from the upper strata of this society who tried to live a Christian life as Luke defines it were required to abandon some of their most cherished beliefs and practices.

That the Lucan Gospel imposes on the rich an indispensable requirement, quite at odds with the social values of their own society, to provide the destitute with food and the other necessities of life in this world sounds the death-knell over all such interpretations of his theology as, affected by middle-class bias, present salvation as a reality reserved for the individual in the afterlife. But while Luke does stress the physical and this-worldly dimension of salvation, he does not do this to the exclusion of its spiritual dimension. Eternal life is a reality for Luke, and so too is sin; his use of the word ἄφεσις shows that liberation from sin is a central feature of the Christian life. His concern to prevent the poor of his community becoming entirely caught up in the physical aspects of the salvation offered to them emerges most clearly in his substitution of πνεῦμα ἅγιον at Lk 11.13 for the word ἀγαθά, which appeared in Q. Luke's theology, in short, strikes a careful balance between physical and spiritual salvation; he offers hope to men and women at all levels of their troubled existence.

E. Käsemann has described apocalyptic as 'the mother of Christian theology'.[125] But not for Luke's theology of the poor! The author of 1 Enoch, it is true, held out to his poor and oppressed Jewish audience a prospect of purely eschatological salvation. In Luke–Acts, however, this Jewish tradition is fundamentally modified. In addition to eternal bliss, Luke offers the poor this-worldly redemption. A theology of salvation along these lines represents a flight from the eschatological perspective which Käsemann has pointed to in primitive Christian thought. So what has been the mother of this element in Luke's theology? There is only one credible candidate − his unusual compassion for the poorest members of his community and of society generally, together with his passionate belief that the gospel was not gospel unless it offered them immediate relief for their physical miseries and gave them, perhaps for the first time, a sense of their own dignity as human persons. Thus, we may conclude that Luke's understanding of the proper Christian attitudes to poverty and riches is another area of his theology which has been significantly motivated by social and political forces, in this case the realities of life for the urban poor in the Roman East.

8

ROME AND THE ANCESTRAL THEME

1. Politically sensitive material in Luke–Acts

For several generations the extensive material in Luke–Acts bearing upon the relationships between Rome and Christianity has excited much critical attention. Luke's unmistakable sensitivity to the involvement of Jesus and the early Christian missionaries, especially Paul, in the political and judicial realities of the Roman empire is a significant aspect of his theology, given that by 'theology' we mean the unique way in which he has shaped the sources and traditions at his disposal. The aim of this chapter is to describe and explain the political motif in Luke–Acts in order to determine the extent to which Luke's outlook has been shaped by social and political pressures upon the members of his community. During the course of this investigation it will emerge that Luke's political awareness extends to areas of the text with which it has not hitherto been associated, above all, in his appreciation of the political significance of presenting Christianity as an ancestral religion.

The Roman empire in Luke–Acts

Luke presents Christianity and the Roman empire as interacting on a number of distinct, although related, levels. The first level consists of the synchronisms which Luke, alone of the Synoptists, establishes between dates in imperial history and significant events in the beginnings of the Gospel. Thus, the birth of Jesus occurs during the worldwide census ordered by Augustus (Lk 2.1–7),[1] and John the Baptist begins his ministry in the fifteenth year of the reign of Tiberius, while Pontius Pilate was governor of Judaea (Lk 3.1–3). These synchronisms are not merely an aspect of Luke's historiographical technique; they suggest that among his intended audience were readers interested in the position of Christianity in the context of Roman history. To such readers, moreover, that the birth of Jesus in Bethlehem occurs as a direct result of Joseph's unquestioning obedience to an imperial decree must have seemed a revealing example of the possibility that Roman politics were not necessarily inconsistent with the divine purpose.

The second level of interaction is the favourable attitude shown by individual Roman administrative or military personnel to Jesus, or early Christian missionaries, or the gospel itself, outside a judicial context. Not all these Romans were interested in becoming Christians. Such is the case, for example, with the Asiarchs, priests of the imperial cult, in Ephesus, who are described as being Paul's friends (Acts 19.31),[2] with Lysias, the Roman tribune in Jerusalem, who goes to great lengths to protect Paul from the Jews in Acts 21–3, and, lastly, with Julius, the centurion to whom Paul is entrusted for his voyage to Rome, and who allows Paul's friends to visit him (27.3) and later saves him from being thrown overboard by the ship's crew (27.42–3). But many of these Romans do actually express faith in Jesus, and often they become Christians. The first of these is the centurion of Capernaum (Lk 7.1–10). Admittedly, this is a Q passage (cf. Mt 8.5–13), but the additional feature appearing in Luke's version, that the centurion loved the Jewish people and built the syngogue in Capernaum for them (7.5), assimilates the centurion more closely to the experience of the one-time God-fearers who formed an important component of his community. Only Luke describes the centurion who witnesses Jesus' death as having a personal relationship with God; he introduces this aspect by noting that the centurion 'glorified God' (Lk 23.47; cf. Mk 15.39). Next, the conversion which serves to initiate and authorize the inclusion of Gentiles into Christian communities is that of the centurion Cornelius (Acts 10.1–11.18). Lastly, there is the conversion of Sergius Paulus, the proconsul of Cyprus (Acts 13.6–12). Although not falling within the same category as these cases, it is worth remembering that, according to Luke at least, the most eminent early missionary, Paul, was a Roman citizen (Acts 16.37–40; 22.24–9; 25.10–12).[3]

The most important area of interaction between Rome and Christianity, however, is undoubtedly the experience of Jesus and of early Christians, especially Paul, before Roman courts. In the trial of Jesus before Pontius Pilate (Lk 23.1–5, 13–25) Luke presents a version of events very different from that in Mk 15.1–15. For our purposes it is unnecessary to enter into the discussion as to whether Luke has merely modified Mark or also utilized other sources or traditions; the fact remains that his account represents a white-washing of Pilate's role in the condemnation and death of Jesus and a blackening of that of the Jewish leadership.[4] The three accusations against Jesus, that he perverts the nation, prevents the payment of tax to Caesar and claims to be king (23.2), are all political in nature and are also false. That Jesus did not oppose the payment of tax to Caesar has been made clear not long before, by Jesus' response to a question on paying Roman tax, which, unlike the case in Mark, is specifically designed by the Jewish leaders to give them grounds for handing Jesus over to Pilate (Lk 20.20; cf. Mk 12.13). And what is Pilate's response to the Jewish charges? On no fewer than three occasions he specifically affirms the innocence of Jesus (Lk 23.4, 14, 22). That Jesus has done nothing worthy of condemnation in Roman eyes is confirmed a little later by the centurion at the foot of the cross, when he says that Jesus was δίκαιος, a word best translated as 'innocent' (23.47).[5] A good measure of Lucan embarrassment with Pilate's role in Jesus' death is evident in his implication that it was actually the Jews who executed Jesus. Thus, whereas Mark explicitly attributes responsibility for Jesus' death to Pilate when he says καὶ παρέδωκεν τὸν Ἰησοῦν φραγελλώσας ἵνα σταυρωθῇ (Mk 15.15), Luke has at this point: τὸν δὲ Ἰησοῦν παρέδωκεν τῷ θελήματι αὐτῶν (23.25). Luke also omits the Marcan passage which describes the mockery and physical violence to which the Roman soldiers subjected Jesus in the Praetorium (Mk 15.16–20), while introducing a new section in which Jesus receives similar treatment from Herod and his Jewish soldiers (23.6–12). Although Pilate declares Jesus innocent, he does, of course, allow him to be killed. Earlier in the Gospel, moreover, Luke mentions that Pilate had some Galileans slain while they were offering sacrifice (13.1). By combining these aspects, it appears that Luke is differentiating between Pilate's questionable character and his role as arbiter of Roman law, and is thereby establishing a distinction of which he will avail himself again in Acts.

In Thessalonika, a self-governing city which also served as a Roman administrative centre,[6] it is alleged that Paul and Silas have been turning the world upside-down and acting in opposition to the decrees of Caesar by saying that Jesus is king (17.6–7). The city authorities are disturbed by these allegations, but not sufficiently so to do anything more than to take security from Jason and some other Christians, which will apparently be forfeited if Paul and Silas cause any more trouble (17.8–9).

The account of the proceedings brought by the Jews against Paul in Corinth before Gallio, the Roman proconsul of Achaea, exemplifies the proper function of the Roman courts *vis-à-vis* Christians

(18.12–16). Following standard Roman practice,[7] Gallio lets the Jewish plaintiffs present their accusations (18.13), but because these involve matters peculiar to the Jewish religion he declines to exercise his jurisdiction and dismisses the case without needing to hear from Paul in reply (18.14–15). That proceedings against Jesus and the early Christians in Roman courts are the result of the Jews trying to dress up religious disputes as politically relevant is a motif which Luke often takes up in the work.

In Acts 24–6 Paul defends himself on three occasions, the first two in formal proceedings before the Judaean governors Felix and Festus (24.1–23; 25.7–12), and the third in an *ad hoc* defence before Agrippa and others (26.1–32). Paul's innocence of any breach of Roman law is one of the central messages conveyed by Luke in these chapters. Paul himself asserts that he is innocent (25.8), and his view is corroborated by the tribune Lysias (23.29), by Festus (25.18–19, 25) and by Agrippa (26.32). Before Felix and Festus Paul receives the benefit of the Roman rule of law which Festus specifically tells Agrippa he has implemented: namely, that a case must be laid against a defendant in person and he must have the chance to reply (25.16). Unfortunately, in the hands of Felix and Festus the advantages of this excellent system are negated, since they both fail to come to a prompt decision in the case. Put simply, Felix is corrupt; Luke quite openly tells his reader that Felix hoped to receive bribes from Paul (24.26), no doubt in return for ordering his release. At the end of his governorship, moreover, he refuses to release Paul in order to curry favour with the Jews (24.27). Festus also wants to win Jewish approval, by judging Paul in Jerusalem (25.9), although he later lies to Agrippa that his motive in suggesting to Paul that he be tried in the Holy City was his lack of understanding of the matters in issue (25.20). But Paul's appeal to Caesar takes him out of the hands of Festus; Roman judicial procedure prevails over corrupt and lying local governors.[8] Finally, we must note that, although the Jews have made accusations against Paul which include the claim that he has contravened Roman law (Acts 24.5; 25.8), he informs Agrippa that the real basis for their opposition is a religious matter – his belief in the resurrection (26.6–8). In other words, the Jews are concocting breaches of Roman law by Paul to attract Caesar as an ally into their dispute with Christianity.

The general impression communicated by this politically sensitive material is that Jesus and his followers did not contravene Roman law and were therefore not a threat to the empire, even though Jewish authorities repeatedly initiated proceedings designed to prove the opposite and occasionally enjoyed some success before Roman officials whose weakness or self-seeking prevented the judicial system they administered from operating effectively.

2. Apologetic or legitimation?

An historical outline of the apologetic explanation
The usual explanation offered by scholars for this politically sensitive material is that it constitutes some form of apologetic addressed to Roman authorities or Roman citizens generally, with the aim of seeking toleration from them for Christian beliefs and practices. The normal meaning of 'apologetic' is a defence of one's position directed towards outsiders; here the outsiders are seen as Romans, especially those with power and influence, *outside* the Christian community. Recently, P. W. Walaskay has used the word 'apology' in connection with Lucan political teaching directed inwards to the Christian community,[9] but such usage will not be adopted here. We must now delineate the broad features of the development of the apologetic approach as a prelude to rejecting this theory and offering an alternative explanation in the latter sections of this chapter.

The earliest case for Luke–Acts being apologetic in nature appears to have been made by C. A. Heumann in a short article, published in 1720, which dealt with Theophilus, to whom both the Gospel and Acts are dedicated.[10] Heumann argued that Theophilus was a Roman magistrate and that Luke dedicated his work to him as an *apologia* for Christianity against the lies which were being uttered about it.

In 1836 Karl Schrader published a brief commentary on Acts.[11] He used the word *apologetische* with respect to many features which he regarded as non-historical in the work: for example, its alleged anti-gnostic thrust. Without taking up Heumann's suggestion, Schrader did on a few occasions treat some feature of Acts as political apologetic. He considered for example, that the dismissal by Gallio of the charges brought against Paul by the Jews in Corinth was a sign for the authorities (*die Obrigkeit*) of the innocence of the Christians, and a warning for them to stay out of religious matters.[12]

M. Schneckenburger went close to suggesting the possibility of a Rome-directed political apologetic in his *Über den Zweck der Apostelgeschichte*, published in 1841.[13] Schneckenburger thought that Jewish Christians at Rome, and not Roman authorities themselves, were the intended recipients of Luke's deliberate political absolution of Paul.

In his famous commentary on Acts, published in 1854,[14] E. Zeller equivocated a little on the question of political apologetic in Acts. He opined that Schneckenburger's view was certainly not improbable, but he also considered it likely that Luke had intended to refute the accusations of pagan opponents and thought that a presentation along these lines would also assist Christian readers by giving them a ready answer to such accusations.[15]

F. Overbeck's significant work on Acts appeared in 1870.[16] Although Overbeck regarded the primary purpose of Acts as an attempt on the part of Gentile Christianity to clear up its position in regard to the past, he also believed that it had a subordinate political aim, to avert political suspicions from Christianity, and that such an aim could only have been intended for Gentiles outside the church. Overbeck, therefore, advocated a political apologetic in the fullest sense.

In 1897, J. Weiss published a sixty-page treatise on Acts in which he regarded the political apologetic motif as essential to the work; he thought that Acts was written 'as an apology for the Christian religion addressed to the pagans and directed against the accusations of the Jews'.[17]

During the present century the explanation of the political material in Luke–Acts as Rome-directed apologetic has continued to flourish, especially in what has come to be called the *religio licita* theory. Adherents of this theory in its extreme form – and they here included Foakes Jackson and Kirsopp Lake,[18] B.S. Easton[19] and H.J. Cadbury in his earlier days[20] – thought that foreign religions had to be licensed by Rome to be permitted to carry on; Judaism had been so licensed, and Luke was attempting to show that Christianity was a form of Judaism and therefore to bring it under the Jewish umbrella. In its less extreme form – evident, for example, in the commentaries of Haenchen[21] and Fitzmyer[22] – the idea of the licensing of foreign religions by the Romans is dropped, but there is retained the notion that Luke wished to bring Christianity under the privileges which Judaism no doubt enjoyed. Haenchen added the further refinement that Luke also aimed to show a strong connection between Christians and Pharisees, to strengthen the impression of Christianity's being just a part of Judaism.[23]

H. Conzelmann accepted that there was a political apologetic in Luke–Acts. He argued, however, that Luke was not making an appeal for toleration of Christianity under the protective law of *religio licita*, but was appealing to the state to allow Christians to enjoy their rights under Roman law, whatever spurious charges the Jews might bring against them.[24]

Problems with the apologetic approach

Not all Lucan commentators accept that Luke–Acts does attempt to persuade Roman outsiders that Christianity is politically harmless. Before proposing our own view, it will be useful to consider three alternative theories recently published by R. J. Cassidy, by R. Maddox and by P. W. Walaskay.

R. J. Cassidy,[25] who appears to have been inspired by Y. H. Yoder,[26] goes so far as to argue that Luke presented Jesus as posing a threat to Roman authority both by refusing to cooperate with, or actually criticizing, his political rulers, and by consistently contravening social patterns, especially those relating to the distribution of wealth, 'which the Romans were committed to maintain'.[27] Cassidy's work, although an interesting attempt to bring out the social and political implications of the Gospel, suffers from a serious methodological flaw. His claim to be undertaking redaction criticism, to be investigating the attitudes of the Lucan and not the historical Jesus, sits most uneasily with his extensive efforts at relating features of the Third Gospel to the situation in Palestine in the twenties and thirties of the first century CE,[28] these being matched by a total lack of interest in the actual context in which the work was written, in a Hellenistic city in the eighties or nineties.

His interpretation of individual features of Luke's Gospel is also often quite unconvincing. This is particularly so with three items of evidence he regards as especially significant in indicating that Jesus was antipathetic to the existing political order:[29] his reference to Herod as 'that fox' (13.31–3), his warning that the disciples will be brought before kings and governors (21.12), and his remarks on how authority is exercised by Gentile rulers (22.25). Cassidy clearly puts more weight on the first passage than it can bear: when Jesus is brought before Herod in Jerusalem (Lk 23.6–12), there is nothing in his demeanour which induces Herod to regard him as a threat.[30] In any event, since Herod was not strictly speaking a part of the Roman administration, this incident may be disregarded here. Secondly, it is unwise of Cassidy to rely so heavily on Lk 21.12, when the notion of the disciples appearing before kings and governors occurs in the parallel passage in Mark 13.9. Worse than this, however, is Cassidy's interpreting the verse to mean that the disciples will be in conflict with kings and governors.[31] This view ignores a central feature of Roman litigation – and one, moreover, which is continually apparent in Luke–Acts – namely, that prosecutions were almost always conducted by private individuals.[32] To appear before a governor, therefore, did not involve a conflict with him, since the governor's role was to adjudicate, not to prosecute. Thirdly, Cassidy claims that in Lk 22.25 Jesus is criticizing Gentile rulers for dominating their subjects and is using 'benefactors' (εὐεργεταί) sarcastically, to underline the contrast between his own approach and theirs.[33] Both aspects of this interpretation are untenable. P. W. Walaskay convincingly argues that, by his substitution for the verbs κατακυριεύειν and κατεξουσιάζειν, which appear in Mk 10.42, of the verbs κυριεύειν and ἐξουσιάζειν, Luke has actually eliminated the sense of hostility and oppression attributed to the pagan rulers by Mark.[34] Luke is carefully distinguishing the exercise of authority by Gentiles (22.25) from that in the community (22.26), without in any way criticizing the former. Nor is εὐεργεταί meant sarcastically. This word, as F. W. Danker has explained,[35] was regularly used to express the reciprocal relationship which Hellenistic rulers sought to maintain between themselves and their subjects. The rulers made benefactions to the populace and thereby hoped to secure their compliance with official policy. The Lucan Jesus is not espousing the abolition of this political and social pattern in Lk 22.25ff., he is merely denying it any place in the Christian community.

In the last few years R. Maddox[36] and P. W. Walaskay,[37] although working independently, have reached rather similar conclusions to one another on the significance of the political motif in Luke–Acts. Both of them have rejected the notion that it is to be explained as an appeal for toleration to Roman readers outside the Christian community, although Walaskay retains the word 'apology' nevertheless. Both Maddox and Walaskay have also offered similar explanations of their own for Luke's sensitivity to the relationships between Rome and Christianity. Maddox has suggested that, although persecution was probably not a severe problem for Luke's church, it remained a possibility, especially if Christians should be tempted to become provocative towards the authorities, with the aim, for example, of courting martyrdom. Accordingly, Luke holds up the example of their early heroes, especially Jesus and Paul, to encourage his Christian contemporaries to take the best possible view of the regime.[38] Walaskay, secondly, has argued that Luke was offering an *apologia pro imperio* to the church, as a response to the tendency among Christians to deprecate the imperial government in view of the catastrophic end of the empire which was expected soon: 'Luke may have been concerned to counter such anti-Roman sentiment in order to help the church survive in the given political order.'[39]

The principal objection to both these explanations is that there is no evidence in Luke–Acts, apart from the questionable inferences they draw from the political material, that Luke's community, or part of it, was behaving in a provocative way towards Rome or was looking forward hopefully to its apocalyptic demise. The idea that Luke's church was troubled by potential martyrs, as Maddox believed, is difficult to reconcile with the considerable amount of evidence in the text indicating that Luke's fellow-Christians needed encouragement in the face of difficulties, rather than requiring to have their excess enthusiasm curbed. That Luke was concerned to encourage his readers is indicated in particular by two significant modifications by Luke of his Marcan source. In the first (Lk 8.15) he adds that those who hear the Word and keep it will bear fruit 'in steadfast endurance' (ἐν ὑπομονῇ) (cf. Mk 4.20),[40] and in the second (Lk 9.23) he introduces the notion that disciples must take up their cross 'daily' (καθ' ἡμέραν). The need for endurance also forms part of the message of the Parable of the Widow and the Unjust Judge (Lk 18.1–8).

Nor is Walaskay's idea that Luke was countering anti-Roman apocalyptic fervour very plausible. The weakness of his position here is revealed by the evidence he cites in its support – Mk 13, Rev 13, the Sibylline Oracles 4.117–18 and Barnabas 2–3, all of it extra-Lucan![41] Although eschatology does have political implications, as we saw in Chapter 3, Luke's eschatological perspective is better regarded as the result of assisting his community to come to terms with the delay of the *parousia* than as that of quenching apocalyptic excess.[42]

One final objection must be made to Maddox and Walaskay – that their explanations are incompatible with the way Luke actually portrays the relationship between Rome and Christianity. If Luke were desirous of countering Christian resentment and antipathy towards Rome, his strategy would surely have extended to representing the Romans who tried Jesus and Paul as personally attractive, in addition to presenting them as having found Jesus and Paul innocent of offences against Roman law. If Luke wanted to defuse animosity towards Rome, as Maddox and Walaskay suggest, why would he add the detail of Pilate's violence (Lk 13.1) and portray Felix and Festus as self-seeking, deceptive and corrupt? Luke's careful distinction between Roman judicial procedures and the personnel responsible for them seems to require some other explanation.

So what is the explanation? Granted that Luke was writing for an intra-Christian audience, what purpose was served by his inclusion of material which continually asserted that Jesus and Paul had committed no breach of Roman law? Or, to return to the model of legitimation outlined in Chapter 1 above, was there something in the life of his community which necessitated that the Roman treatment of Jesus and Paul be explained and justified to its members? There is only one answer which offers a satisfying explanation for the political theme in Luke–Acts, that among the members of Luke's community were a number of Romans serving the empire in a military or administrative capacity, and that part of Luke's task was to present Christian history in such a way as to demonstrate that faith in Jesus Christ and allegiance to Rome were not mutually inconsistent.

There is quite a body of evidence to suggest that there were Romans in Luke's community. It consists principally of Luke's diverging from his sources and from historical fact to highlight their prominence among early converts to the faith. Examples of this are the centurion of Capernaum (Lk 7.1–10), whom, as mentioned above, Luke assimilates to the experience of the God-fearers in his audience by mentioning his good relationships with the Jews; the centurion at the foot of the cross who glorified God (Lk 23.47); the centurion Cornelius (Acts 10.1ff.), whose conversion did not have the historical significance Luke attaches to it;[43] and the conversion of Sergius Paulus, the proconsul of Cyprus (Acts 13.6–12). To this group may be added Titius Justus, a God-fearer with whom Paul lodged in Corinth (Acts 18.7), and who was possibly a Roman[44] and almost certainly a convert to Christianity. Secondly, Luke's addition of ethical advice from John the Baptist to soldiers and tax-gatherers (Lk 3.12–14), possibly Roman, may point to a Roman element in his audience to whom such advice would have relevance. Lastly, the apparent delight with which Luke plays the trump card of Paul's Roman citizenship (Acts 16.37–40; 22.25–9), especially if this is a non-historical feature, is best explained on the basis of the existence of Roman citizens among his fellow-Christians who could thus identify more closely with the great missionary. The presence of Romans in the Lucan community is indirectly supported by the external evidence for Romans having been members of Paul's communities earlier in the first century.[45]

Before considering how Luke's picture of the interaction between Rome and the early church could have legitimated Christianity to Romans within his own community, it is necessary to analyse more closely the *religio licita* theory. Although the high probability that Luke–Acts was composed for an intra-Christian audience is enough to cast serious doubt on the validity of this theory, its continuing influence among Lucan commentators would justify undertaking a more detailed critique. More importantly, however, in analysing the *religio licita* theory it will become evident that there is another body of evidence in Luke–Acts with direct relevance to the political perspective of its author – the ancestral theme.

An analysis of the religio licita *theory*
We may begin by immediately scotching the idea that Rome had some process for licensing foreign religions. There is no historical support for this whatsoever; it was always the Roman way to treat foreign religions on an *ad hoc* basis, and there never was a juridical category of *religio licita*. This point was made strongly in an article by H. J. Cadbury, published in 1958,[46] although Cadbury did not acknowledge in this article that he himself had been a supporter of the licensing theory in earlier years![47] There is also a careful account of the way in which Rome interfered with foreign religions only in a desultory fashion in an article by A. D. Nock.[48]

However, there is no doubting that Judaism did enjoy a privileged position in the empire, and the question remains whether Luke may not have desired to present Christianity to an outside Roman audience as a form of Judaism and thereby to bring it under the Jewish umbrella. To answer this question the essential first step is to analyse the primary sources dealing with the privileges to Judaism and to determine whether they were of such a nature as to make it likely that Luke would wish, if he were so able, to obtain their benefits for Christianity.

The bulk of the primary sources on Jewish religious liberties occurs in Books 14 and 16 of the *Jewish Antiquities* of Josephus.[49] There are also useful data on the subject in Philo[50] and in some epigraphic remains.[51] In the *Jewish Antiquities* Josephus quotes from nearly thirty decrees by Roman authorities (including Julius Caesar and Augustus) and by Greek cities of the East on the rights of the Jews. Most of these take the form of directions by the Romans to the cities to stop interfering with the Jews in the practice of their religion.

S. G. Wilson has remarked that the authenticity of the Roman decrees on Jewish religious freedom quoted by Josephus is a matter of dispute.[52] On the other hand, E. Mary Smallwood uses them extensively in her discussion of the question.[53] Even if the historicity of these documents could be discounted, however, they would retain their significance for this discussion simply as illustrations of what Josephus thought appropriate as expressions of the Roman attitude to Jewish religious liberty.

It is impracticable to present a complete review of the data in Josephus here. Instead, we shall consider one such decree by way of example and summarize the relevant features of the rest. Our example is a decree by one Julius Gaius, praetor and consul, to the authorities and people of Parium, probably to be dated to 46 BCE.[54] Gaius begins by noting that the Jews of Delos have complained to him of a Parian statute which prevents them from observing their ancestral customs (τὰ πάτρια ἔθη) and sacred rites (ἱερά). He is displeased by such treatment of 'our friends and allies', which is preventing them from living in accordance with their customs (ζῆν κατὰ τὰ αὐτῶν ἔθη) and contributing money to their common meals and sacred rites. Even in Rome, he adds, they are not prevented from doing this. He cites an edict of Julius Caesar forbidding religious societies to assemble in the city, with the specific exception of the Jews; on the strength of this precedent, Gaius has forbidden other religious societies but has allowed the Jews to assemble and feast in accordance with their ancestral customs and ordinances (πάτρια ἔθη καὶ νόμιμα).

It is highly likely that this action by Julius Caesar against religious societies is the same as that recorded by Suetonius, who states that Julius Caesar dissolved all *collegia* except those of ancient foundation (*cuncta collegia praeter antiquitus constituta distraxit*).[55] Julius Caesar set the religious liberty of the Jews upon a firm foundation, and Augustus later confirmed their privileged position,[56] even going further in some respects: for example, by ensuring that the payment of the Temple tax to Jerusalem would not be interrupted.[57]

One striking feature of virtually all the decrees is that they refer to the *ancestral* nature of Jewish religious practices. The word used for 'ancestral' is πάτριος, and there is continual reference to the ancestral customs (πάτρια ἔθη), ancestral law (πάτριος νόμος) ancestral rites (πάτρια ἱερά) and ancestral prayers (πάτριαι εὐχαί) of the Jews. Whatever the broader political reasons for Roman liberality to the Jews, it appears from this repeated emphasis upon the ancestral nature of Jewish religion that it was something which the Romans respected about Judaism. This suggestion can only be confirmed from a broad survey of Roman attitudes to religious tradition, as is attempted below.

It emerges from the decrees that what Rome offered Jews was the freedom to carry on certain practices without interference. They could observe the sabbath, assemble in synagogues, take part in festivals, share common meals, circumcise their children, adhere to the dietary rules of the Torah and send off the Temple tax each year to Jerusalem without let or hindrance from Roman or Greek. The Romans did not interest themselves in what the Jews believed, only in what they actually did. Thus, in determining whether a Jew should be exempted from military service on account of religious scruples (δεισιδαιμονίας ἕνεκα), Roman provincial officials did not look just to the fact of circumcision to establish Jewishness; they ascertained whether the applicant for exemption actually lived the life of a Jew.[58]

What possible benefit under Roman law, then, could a Christian writer, except one whose community was composed entirely of Jewish Christians, as Luke's was not, hope to gain from depicting Christianity as a form of Judaism? Many of his fellow-Christians did not observe the sabbath or the Jewish dietary laws, did not celebrate Jewish festivals, did not circumcise their children, and no longer attended the synagogue. Why would such an author wish to attract Roman protection for a set of practices in which a large part of his community did not engage? But, as well as there being no positive benefits from such a presentation, there would have been one serious negative consequence for a large part of his audience. After the destruction of Jerusalem in 70 CE Vespasian made the Temple tax payable to Jupiter Capitolinus and also extended its incidence to all members of both sexes from the age of three, whereas before it had only been payable by adult males.[59] Payment of the tax was a considerable burden for the poor,[60] and people went to some lengths to avoid paying it – Suetonius remembered seeing an old man of ninety being examined in a crowded court to see if he was circumcised and therefore liable to pay the 'Jewish tax'.[61] Although Jewish members of Christian communities probably remained liable to pay the tax (as is suggested by Mt 17.24–7) on account of their circumcision, it is not difficult to imagine the lack of enthusiasm with which Gentile members would have reacted to the discovery that the efforts of one of their writers had exposed them to an unpleasant fiscal liability.

The *religio licita* argument, even in its moderate form, must therefore be rejected. It is impossible to impute to the author of Luke–Acts a purpose in his work which could have brought no advantages to much of his community and would have increased the tax liability of some of its members.

Roman respect for ancestral tradition

Yet in rejecting the *religio licita* argument we have noticed an apparent Roman respect for ancestral religion. Might it not be the case that the author of Luke–Acts, while not wishing to present Christianity as Judaism, does wish to appropriate to it the Roman fondness for tradition? Might he not be saying: 'Christianity is not Judaism, but you may respect it for much the same reasons as you do Judaism?' To answer this we must first determine whether the attitude to tradition evident in the decrees in Josephus is representative of the broader world of Roman literature and thought. It is impracticable to offer anything more than a sample of the available evidence here.

Marcus Terentius Varro (116–27 BCE)[62] and Marcus Tullius Cicero (106–43 BCE),[63] were close friends and both combined an active and successful public life with a keen interest in philosophy. Varro's main work on religion, *Of Divine and Human Antiquities*, is not extant, but it is summarized and cited in Augustine's *City of God*.[64] Although Varro showed great devotion to restoring Rome's ancient religion, he still had his doubts. Augustine reports his view that if he were founding the city anew, he would name the gods after the principles of nature.[65] Varro favoured adherence to the traditional religion in spite of philosophical problems involved in it for a very practical reason – so that the *vulgus*, the common people, would stick to the old worship. A strong political factor underlay this attitude: a populace devoted to the religious heritage of its fathers was more likely to be politically docile than one given to new rites or no rites at all.

Cicero's attitude was virtually identical, and in one place he explicitly states that traditional religious practices are maintained for reason of their great political expediency.[66] In *de Divinatione* and *de Natura Deorum* he makes it quite clear that, while he has the gravest philosophical reservations about the practices of the Roman cult, yet they must be maintained and respected, both because they are old and in the interests of political stability. In Cicero's writings we observe a profound respect for ancestral tradition and notice time and again the use of such expressions as *instituta maiorum, mos patrius* and *opinio quam a maioribus accepimus*, which are close parallels to phrases such as πάτρια ἔθη, already commented on in the date in Josephus.

Among the documents which the emperor Augustus left behind him on his death in 14 CE was one which was soon entitled *Res Gestae Divi Augusti*[67] – the achievements of the divine Augustus. This is an invaluable source for our present purpose, because in setting out his achievements in the form in which he wanted them to be remembered he reveals what attitudes he regarded as sufficiently typically Roman to be worth playing upon. Chief amongst these is respect for the traditional, both in politics and religion. Thus, in the political area (not that it should be sharply distinguished from the religious) he claims that he restored the Republic to the Senate and the people of Rome.[68] On the religious front, he mentions that he has held all the priestly offices, he has restored eighty-two temples and built many new ones, he has held the secular games and has pushed through legislation to revive Rome's traditional virtues. There is, of course, no hint of philosophic doubt about the traditional religion in the *Res Gestae*. His huge political success shows that the appeal of Augustus to the ancestral in society, politics and religion struck deep chords in the Roman heart.

Our last witness is Lucius Annaeus Seneca, brother of the Gallio mentioned in Acts 18.12–17, who was born around the turn of the century, became a prominent Stoic and adviser to Nero and was forced by that emperor to commit suicide in 65 CE.[69] Although Seneca launched a furious attack on the civil theology of Rome in his now lost work *de Superstitione*, he still, like Cicero and Varro, advocated public adherence to the traditional Roman cult – for reasons of custom if not of truth.[70]

The ancestral theme in Luke–Acts

From this survey of the Roman sources it is apparent that ancestral traditions were respected because of their age and because adherence to them was seen as fostering political stability. Is it possible that Luke wished to make use of this attitude in his Gospel and in Acts? We have already referred to the more blatantly Rome-orientated features scholars have long commented upon in Acts. But we now know that the presentation of a religion as ancestral would also have had a political impact on a Roman; his anxious care that the stability of the state should not be disturbed by new religious forces would be soothed by the assurance that a particular religion was, in fact, not new but traditional. Has Luke utilized this attitude?

We have already seen in Chapter 3 that there is abundant evidence for a Lucan desire to legitimate Christianity *vis-à-vis* Judaism by presenting it as an ancestral religion. But it is now apparent that the ancestral theme would also have served to assuage doubts which Roman members of Luke's community might have entertained as to the political implications of Christianity. There is no need to repeat all the evidence for Luke's interest in presenting Christianity as an ancestral faith, but a few details may profitably be mentioned. First, Luke's desire to disabuse his audience of the notion that Christianity was a new teaching comes out in his deletion of the word καινή from the phrase διδαχὴ καινή in his Marcan source (Lk 4.36; Mk 1.27), his addition of the phrase 'the old is best' (Lk 5.39; cf. Mk 2.22), and the scorn he expresses towards the Athenian love of new teaching (Acts 17.19, 21). Secondly, a recurrent motif in Acts is that Christianity is intrinsically connected with the fathers or ancestors of Israel (3.13; 5.30; 15.10; 22.14; 26.6; 28.25). There are times, indeed, when Paul uses phrases virtually identical to those we have seen in the Josephan documents. Addressing the Jews in Jerusalem, he mentions that he was trained according to 'the ancestral law' (ὁ πατρῷος νόμος) (Acts 22.3), to the Roman governor Felix he proclaims his devotion to the ancestral God (ὁ πατρῷος θεός) (Acts 24.14), and to the Jews in Rome he asserts his adherence to the ancestral customs (τὰ ἔθη πατρῷα) (Acts 28.17). This last phrase is almost identical to τὰ πάτρια ἔθη used in the documents quoted by Josephus. Yet Luke had no wish to maintain that Christianity and Judaism were identical. In Chapter 3 we argued that an institutional estrangement existed between the Lucan congregation and the synagogue, even though there were Jews who had preferred to remain in the congregation. There are many signs of the hostility between the two faiths engendered by this split, and the greater role in the death of Jesus which Luke attributes to the Jewish authorities, as discussed above, is merely one sign of this. Such hostility renders quite implausible the suggested reason which S. G. Wilson floats for the frequent references in Luke—Acts to Jewish ancestral traditions — that Luke might have been inviting 'the reader to view Jewish practices in the same way as those of other peoples and accord them the same respect'.[71] The last thing in Luke's mind was to recommend Jewish customs *per se* to his readers; his energies were devoted to attracting existing Roman respect for Jewish customs to such Christian beliefs and practices as could be shown to possess a lineage deriving from Jewish tradition. Thus, his references in Acts to the Pharisees' belief in the resurrection (23.6, 8; 26.5—6) should not be interpreted, with Haenchen,[72] as an attempt to build a bridge between Pharisees and Christians, but rather as a way of emphasizing that the doctrine of the resurrection, which struck pagans as particularly outlandish (cf. Acts 17.32), was not a novel and therefore politically dangerous belief, but was deeply implanted in Jewish tradition.

Conclusion: political legitimation in Luke–Acts

With respect to the members of his community who had formerly attended synagogue, Luke's legitimatory strategies needed to take into account the residual loyalties felt for the Jewish *ethnos* which they had now largely forsaken. But the position of the Romans who were members of Luke's congregation was very different. They had certainly not broken with Rome as their Jewish fellow-Christians had with the synagogue. Yet how could they remain Christians when Jesus himself had apparently been executed by the Roman governor of Judaea and many of the early Christians, especially Paul, had been brought before Roman courts? Legitimating Christianity to them inevitably involved providing a reassurance that faith in Jesus Christ was not incompatible with allegiance to Rome. This context offers the best explanation for both the explicit and the implicit political motifs in Luke–Acts: that is, for the various levels of interaction between Rome and Christianity in the text, and for the presentation of Christianity as an ancestral religion.

As for the explicitly political material, it was obviously important for the Romans in Luke's audience that Jesus and Paul should have conducted their ministries without contravening Roman law. On the other hand, readers such as these would not have been particularly bothered by the personal failings of Pilate, Felix and Festus. What mattered to them was that the Roman system which they served was not opposed to Christianity *per se*, even if individual Roman officials had occasionally treated Christians unjustly. They needed to feel that, if necessary, they could justify their adherence to Christian beliefs and practices as involving no breach of Roman law. It is somewhat ironic that Luke's use of the word ἀπολογέομαι, which is often thought to corroborate the notion that he was addressing an audience outside the Christian congregation, actually confirms this particular requirement among the Roman members of his church, as well as constituting evidence for his having been engaged in a legitimatory, not an apologetic, task. There are ten instances of ἀπολογέομαι in the New Testament, two in the Third Gospel, two in Paul and six in Acts. Although all the examples of ἀπολογέομαι in Acts concern defences or explanations made to outsiders,[73] we must consider the two occasions in Luke's Gospel in which he uses the verb, to gain an accurate appreciation of its significance. In both cases, at Lk 12.11 and 21.14, Luke has introduced the exact notion, not found in the other Synoptists (cf. Mt 10.19; Mk 13.11), of Christians being assisted in making a defence of their beliefs. The striking feature of ἀπολογέομαι in Lk 12.11 is that it does not have an apocalyptic context, so that it naturally relates to the various defences made by early Christians, such as Paul, before Roman tribunals in Acts. In other words, Luke is reassuring his audience, especially perhaps the Romans among them, that at the appropriate time they will be able to defend themselves against hostile charges. This is legitimation, not apologetic.

Secondly, there is the implicit political motif, the stress on Christianity as an ancestral faith. This emphasis, as we saw in Chapter 3 above, formed part of Luke's strategy for legitimating Christianity *vis-à-vis* Judaism. But it also has a vital political purpose – to attest that Christianity, unlike new and therefore revolutionary religions, was no threat to Rome, nor to the order and stability so prized by the Romans.

There appears to be interesting confirmation that the point of Luke's political interest is to reassure Roman Christians of the possibility of joint allegiance to Rome and to the faith, as seen in the story of Naaman the Syrian, to whom Luke has Jesus refer in his programmatic proclamation in Nazareth (Lk 4.27). Naaman, we recall, was the army commander of the king of Aram (2 Kgs 5.1). Following his purification from leprosy through the agency of Elisha, Naaman decided to become a worshipper of Yahweh. What must have made him a notable precedent for any Roman in Luke's community, especially those holding administrative or military positions, was that his conversion to Yahweh had the potential to bring him into conflict with his master. After Naaman has told Elisha that thenceforth he will sacrifice to no God but Yahweh, he seeks a dispensation:

> Only – and may Yahweh forgive your servant – when my master goes to the temple of Rimmon to worship there, he leans on my arm, and I bow down in the temple of Rimmon when he does; may Yahweh forgive your servant this act! (2 Kgs 5.18; *JB*)

Elisha grants this request by saying 'Go in peace' (2 Kgs 5.19). The story of Naaman offered Romans scriptural authority for the idea that conversion to the faith did not necessitate withdrawal from public life. It suggested that it was permissible for Christians to be present while others carried out sacrifices, so long as they did not actively take part in the process. This assumes that such a passive role was possible for Christians, and some may think this unlikely. However, A. D. Nock has shown that at least in the context of the Roman army, which was continually observing pagan religious festivals of one kind or another, it would have been quite easy for even quite senior officers to avoid any active role in the pagan *cultus*.[74] It must be admitted that neither Lk 4.27 nor 2 Kgs 5.18–19 was interpreted in this way by the early Fathers. This silence is less significant, however, when one considers that around the turn of the first century Rome became hostile to Christianity *per se*, as was explained in Chapter 2 above, so that the type of attitude to the state advocated by Luke became far less relevant to the needs of the times and therefore of less interest to Christian writers. For this reason, although there is no way to prove that the example of Naaman carried the implication we have suggested for Luke's contemporaries, such an interpretation remains an intriguing possibility.

From the discussion in this chapter, one may conclude that the way Luke has handled the relationship between Rome and Christianity has been motivated and influenced by the pressures upon the Roman members of his community generated by their continuing allegiance to the state they served. In responding to these pressures, Luke reshaped Gospel traditions in the service of a particular community at a particular point in its history.

EPILOGUE: COMMUNITY AND GOSPEL

Some time during the late eighties or early nineties of the first century CE, a Christian community in a Hellenistic city of the Roman East was experiencing difficulties from within and opposition from without which threatened its continued existence and unity. Its predicament originated largely in the very mixed nature of the individuals who comprised its membership, the mixture generating tensions within the community and exposing it to the disturbing effects of various influences from the outside world. This mixed composition is illustrated by plotting its members along two fundamental axes. The first is the axis of their religious affiliation prior to becoming Christians, ranging from pagan idolatry on the one hand to conservative Judaism on the other. The second is the socio-economic axis, extending from the maximum possession of wealth, status and power enjoyed by the decurions and senior Roman military and administrative personnel to the total indigence of the city's beggars.

As for the first axis, few of the members of this community had been outright pagans prior to their conversion. The great majority of its Gentile membership had come from the 'God-fearers', those Gentiles who worshipped Yahweh as the one true God and attended synagogue services in furtherance of that worship. The community also contained a significant number of Jews. The Jewish and Gentile members were in the habit of sharing the eucharistic meal, even though such table-fellowship represented a serious assault on the ethnic solidarity of the Jews. Unfortunately for both Jewish and Gentile Christians, their community had become institutionally estranged from the local synagogue and they were no longer welcome at its services. Moreover, pressure was being exerted upon the Jews who were still members of the community to refrain from dining with the Gentiles. This pressure came from the ordinary Jews of the synagogue and also from Jewish Christians, possibly defectors from the community, who accepted Jesus as Messiah but believed, on the

authority of Peter and James, who were now dead but not forgotten, that full adherence to the Mosaic code was also essential for
Christians. Some members of the community were evidently worried
by the force of this argument.

As for the second axis, that of socio-economic position, the community encompassed individuals both from the highest strata in the
city – Roman officers, for example, and possibly even decurions –
and also from the lowest levels, the beggars and the impoverished
day-labourers. The presence within the same group of representatives
from the glittering elite and from the squalid urban poor was very
unusual in this society and created severe internal problems, especially
since some of the traditions of Jesus' sayings known to the community
counselled the rich to a generosity to the destitute quite at odds with
Greco-Roman attitudes to gift-giving.

The members of the community who were Roman soldiers or
officials had to cope with yet another difficulty – the idea that
allegiance to the Christian faith and to Rome were fundamentally
incompatible, since Christianity was a new, and therefore dangerous,
religion, whose founder, Jesus, had been executed by the governor
of Judaea as a revolutionary, and whose leading propagator, Paul,
had also frequently been in trouble before Roman courts.

With the community imperilled by these social and political
problems besetting it from within and without, one of its leaders or
intellectuals, whom tradition calls Luke, decided to compose a work
which would re-interpret existing traditions, both written and oral,
concerning Jesus and the history of the early congregations in such
a way as to reassure his fellow-Christians by answering the various
objections made to their beliefs and practices.

In the critical area of the relationship of his community to Judaism,
which centred upon objections to table-fellowship between Jews and
Gentiles, Luke decided to get the better of his Jewish Christian
opposition by re-writing early Christian history to present the practice
as begun by Peter, with divine authorization (Acts 10.1–48), and
approved by the Jerusalem church on two separate occasions (Acts
11.1–18; 15.6–26). Luke also took great care to ease the pain of
isolation from Judaism felt by the Jews and God-fearers, by maintaining from the beginning of his Gospel to the end of Acts that
Christianity was the genuine fulfilment of Jewish traditions and that
it was Christians, rather than the Jews in the synagogue, who had
remained faithful to the God of Abraham, Isaac and Jacob, of Moses
and David. These themes of table-fellowship and separation from

institutional Judaism find a focus in his treatment of the Temple. Luke was able to trade upon the affectionate memory in which the Temple was still held by many of his Christian contemporaries, and yet also to insinuate into his narrative a recognition that the form of Christianity practised by his community only began with a far-sighted decision by some Greek-speaking Jews in Jerusalem to reject the Temple and the divine election of Israel its architecture so eloquently expressed, by admitting Gentile God-fearers into eucharistic table-fellowship with them.

Luke's response to the wide divergence of socio-economic positions within his community was equally striking. He greatly intensified the preference for the poor which he found in his Marcan source and reassured them of their privileged place in the scheme of salvation inaugurated by Jesus. At the same time he introduced a strong parenetic motif into his treatment of riches and poverty – by forcefully reminding the rich that their chances of salvation depended upon being generous to the poor, even though the practical forms of this generosity violated long-established attitudes and customs of their society.

On the political level, Luke's message for the Romans in his community was that there was no clash between Christianity and Rome. Both Jesus and Paul had been repeatedly adjudged innocent of any breach of Roman law, and Christianity was not a new religion and therefore not liable to contribute to political instability, but was the inevitable development of ancient Jewish tradition.

From the foregoing summary, it is apparent that there is no inconsistency between the findings of this book and Luke's own broad statement of his purpose in Lk 1.1–4. In the emphatically placed last word of Lk 1.4 Luke offers Theophilus ἀσφάλεια, which, translated as 'assurance' or, better, 'reassurance', nicely encapsulates a large proportion of his intentions and strategy.

In relation to the sociological perspectives outlined in Chapters 1 and 3 above, however, Luke's two volumes may be described as an exercise in the legitimation of a sectarian movement, as a sophisticated attempt to explain and justify Christianity to the members of his community at a time when they were exposed to social and political pressures which were making their allegiance waver. Luke re-presents traditions relating how the gospel was initially proclaimed by Jesus and later preached throughout the Roman East in such a way as to erect a symbolic universe, a sacred canopy, beneath which the institutional order of his community is given meaning and justification.

This broad conclusion serves to vindicate our initial proposal that Luke's theology has been largely motivated by the social and political forces operating upon his community. Luke's stimulus to write his Gospel and Acts stemmed from his passionate concern with the troubled situation of his fellow-Christians, not from any interest in theologizing for its own sake.

Finally, the fact that the author of approximately one-quarter of the New Testament has shown such freedom in reshaping the gospel to suit the needs of his local congregation is hardly without significance for contemporary theology. For, although some of the substantive aspects of his theology, such as his attitude to riches and poverty, seem as applicable now as when he was writing, it is not so much the particular details of his interpretation that should inspire modern theologians as his belief that the actual conditions of his community are what govern the theologian's re-interpretation of the Christian tradition. The freedom with which he has moulded the gospel to minister to the needs of his community constitutes a potent authority for all those struggling to realize a Christian vision and a Christian life-style attuned to the social, economic and political realities of our own time.

NOTES

1. The socio-redaction criticism of Luke–Acts

1 Conzelmann, *Luke*, p. 137. The decisive words in the German original are: 'er bestimmt ihre heilsgeschichtliche Stellung und leitet daraus die Regeln des Verhaltens zur Welt ab' — see his *Die Mitte der Zeit. Studien zur Theologie des Lukas* (Tübingen: J. C. B. Mohr (Paul Siebeck), 1954), p. 117.

2 In spite of its frequent use in Mark, the nominal form εὐαγγέλιον does not appear in the Third Gospel and only occurs twice in Acts (15.7; 20.24); Luke may have thought it had acquired the connotation of a literary genre and, if so, that it was less suitable than the word διήγησις, which he uses at Lk 1.1. Nevertheless, Luke's intense interest in the concept of 'gospel', of good news, in connection with the ministry of Jesus and the work of the early church, is evident in his use of the verbal form εὐαγγελίζομαι, which occurs ten times in his Gospel and fifteen times in Acts.

3 P. L. Berger, *The Social Reality of Religion* (London: Faber & Faber, 1969), p. 48. (This work was published in the USA under the title *The Sacred Canopy*.)

4 An approach to the use of Scripture in Christian theology similar to this has recently been advocated by T. W. Ogletree, *The Use of the Bible in Christian Ethics* (Philadelphia: Fortress Press, 1983), pp. 1–14.

5 E. Güttgemanns, *Candid Questions concerning Gospel Form Criticism: A Methodological Sketch of the Fundamental Problematics of Form and Redaction Criticism*, ET of second edition of the German original by W. G. Doty (Pittsburgh: The Pickwick Press, 1979).

6 W. H. Kelber, *The Oral and the Written Gospel: The Hermeneutics of Speaking and Writing in the Synoptic Tradition, Mark, Paul, and Q* (Philadelphia: Fortress Press, 1983).

7 Bultmann, *HST*, p. 4. It should be stressed that *Sitz im Leben* refers to a particular situation *within* the life of a community; it is not an appropriate phrase to describe the entire social setting of a community, although it is often incorrectly used in that sense.

8 M. Dibelius, *From Tradition to Gospel*, ET of second revised edition of the German original by B. L. Woolf (London: Ivor Nicholson and Watson, 1934).

9 Bultmann, *HST*.

10 O. Cullmann, 'Les récentes études sur la formation de la tradition évangélique', *Revue d'histoire et de philosophie religieuses*, 5 (1925), 573.

11 For a detailed treatment of the genesis and characteristics of redaction criticism, see J. Rohde, *Rediscovering the Teaching of the Evangelists* (London: SCM Press, 1968).

12 W. Marxsen, *Mark the Evangelist: Studies on the Redaction History of the Gospel* (New York: Abingdon Press, 1969), p. 24.

13 Peter Burke, *Sociology and History* (London: George Allen & Unwin, 1980), p. 33: 'Sociology is concerned with the establishment of general laws, while history is concerned with the particular, the unrepeatable, the unique ...'

14 There is something of a pre-history to the movement to apply the social sciences to the New Testament. Karl Kautsky's Marxist analysis, *Foundations of Christianity: A Study in Christian Origins* (London: Orbach & Chambers, 1925), first published in German in 1908, is a direct ancestor of more recent efforts at sociological exegesis. For a recent Marxist interpretation, see F. Belo, *A Materialist Reading of the Gospel of Mark*, ET from the French by M. J. O'Connell (New York: Orbis Books, 1981). E. Troeltsch also employed sociological perspectives in his work *The Social Teaching of the Christian Churches* (London: George Allen & Unwin, and New York: The Macmillan Company, 1931), first published in German in 1911. During this period the Chicago school of biblical critics, especially Shirley Jackson Case, were preoccupied with the social aspects of the origins of Christianity, but without investing very seriously in sociological theory – see L. E. Keck, 'On the Ethos of Early Christians', *Journal of the American Academy of Religion*, 42 (1974), 435–52, and R. W. Funk, 'The Watershed of the American Biblical Tradition: The Chicago School, First Phase, 1892–1920', *JBL*, 95 (1976), 4–22.

15 G. Theissen, 'Wanderradikalismus. Literatursoziologische Aspekte der Überlieferung von Worten Jesu im Urchristentum', *Zeitschrift für Theologie und Kirche*, 70 (1973), 245–71. There is an ET of this article, with abbreviated notes, by A. Wire in *Radical Religion*, 2 (1973), 84–93.

16 Most notably, G. Theissen, *The First Followers of Jesus* (London: SCM Press, 1978). This is the ET of his *Soziologie der Jesusbewegung*, published in the USA under the title *Sociology of Early Palestinian Christianity* (Philadelphia: Fortress Press, 1978).

17 G. Theissen, *The Social Setting of Pauline Christianity*, edited and translated with an introduction by J. H. Schütz (Philadelphia: Fortress Press, 1982).

18 G. Theissen, 'Theoretische Probleme religions-soziologischer Forschung und die Analyse des Urchristentums', *NZsTh*, 16 (1974), 35–56.

19 There is a bibliography of the major works of Gerd Theissen in Theissen, *The Social Setting of Pauline Christianity*, pp. 25–6. All

of Theissen's sociological contributions have now been translated into English except for two articles: 'Theoretische Probleme' (see n. 18 above) and 'Die Tempelweissagung Jesu. Prophetie im Spannungsfeld von Stadt und Land', *Theologische Zeitschrift*, 32 (1976), 144–58.

20 W. A. Meeks, 'The Man from Heaven in Johannine Sectarianism', *JBL*, 91 (1972), 44–72.

21 W. A. Meeks, *The First Urban Christians: The Social World of the Apostle Paul* (New Haven and London: Yale University Press, 1983).

22 R. Scroggs, 'The Earliest Christian Communities as Sectarian Movement', in J. Neusner, ed., *Christianity, Judaism and Other Greco-Roman Cults: Studies for Morton Smith at Sixty*, Part II: *Early Christianity* (Leiden: E. J. Brill, 1975), pp. 1–23.

23 J. G. Gager, *Kingdom and Community: The Social World of Early Christianity* (Englewood Cliffs, NJ: Prentice-Hall, 1975). There are reviews of this book by D. L. Bartlett, J. Z. Smith and D. Tracy in *Zygon*, 13 (1978), 109–35.

24 B. Holmberg, *Paul and Power: The Structure of Authority in the Primitive Church as Reflected in the Pauline Epistles* (Lund: Studentlitteratur, 1978).

25 J. H. Elliott, *A Home for the Homeless: A Sociological Exegesis of 1 Peter, its Situation and Strategy* (London: SCM Press, 1982).

26 B. J. Malina, *The New Testament World: Insights from Cultural Anthropology* (London: SCM Press, 1983).

27 There have been a number of articles published which offer a general survey of the renewed interest in the social implications of early Christianity. Examples are W. A. Meeks, 'The Social World of Early Christianity', *Bulletin of the Council on the Study of Religion*, 6 (1975), 1ff.; J. Z. Smith, 'The Social Description of Early Christianity', *Religious Studies Review*, 1 (1975), 19–25; D. J. Harrington, 'Sociological Concepts and the Early Church: A Decade of Research', *TS*, 41 (1980), 181–90, and R. Scroggs, 'The Sociological Interpretation of the New Testament: The Present State of Research', *NTS*, 26 (1980), 164–79.

28 On the question of free will and the formulation of social laws, see F. Kaufmann, *Methodology of the Social Sciences* (New York: The Humanities Press, 1958), pp. 169–81. A. MacIntyre believes that there are a number of sources of systematic unpredictability in human affairs which preclude the possibility of the existence of social laws like those discovered by the natural sciences – see his *After Virtue: A Study in Moral Theory* (London: Duckworth, 1981), pp. 84–102.

29 For an introduction to this debate, see J. Rex, *Key Problems of Sociological Theory* (London: Routledge & Kegan Paul, 1969), pp. 1–26. There is something of a classic attack on the dominance of scientific method in much sociology in C. Wright Mills, *The Sociological Imagination* (Harmondsworth: Pelican Books, 1978), Chapter 3 – 'Abstracted Empiricism', pp. 60–86. A more positive

appreciation of the scientific side of sociology is found in D. Willer, *Scientific Sociology: Theory and Method* (Englewood Cliffs, NJ: Prentice-Hall, 1967), *passim*.

30 M. Duverger, *Introduction to the Social Sciences* (London: George Allen & Unwin, 1964), p. 226.

31 C. Wright Mills, *The Sociological Imagination*, p. 166.

32 M. Duverger, *Introduction*, p. 226.

33 M. Weber, *The Methodology of the Social Sciences* (New York: The Free Press, 1968), p. 90. D. Martindale has written a useful treatment of the background to Weber's use of ideal types and their significance in recent sociology – 'Sociological Theory and the Ideal Type', in L. Gross, ed., *Symposium on Sociological Theory* (Evanston, Ill. and White Plains, NY: Row Peterson & Company, 1959), pp. 57–91.

34 J. C. McKinney, *Constructive Typology and Social Theory* (New York: Meredith Publishing Company, 1966), p. 3.

35 D. Martindale, 'Sociological Theory and the Ideal Type', p. 88.

36 J. C. McKinney, *Constructive Typology and Social Theory*, pp. 61–6.

37 *Ibid.*, p. 17.

38 M. Duverger, *Introduction*, pp. 227–8.

39 D. Willer, *Scientific Sociology*, p. 9.

40 P. Worsley, *Introducing Sociology* (Harmondsworth: Penguin Books, 1970), p. 70.

41 For a detailed account of the process of verification, see H. L. Zetterberg, *On Theory and Verification in Sociology* (New York: The Tressler Press, 1954).

42 There is a revealing schematic representation of the whole process of explanation in P. Worsley, *Introducing Sociology*, p. 70.

43 D. Willer, *Scientific Sociology*, p. 31.

44 *Ibid.*, p. 17.

45 *Ibid.*, pp. 44ff.

46 J. C. McKinney, *Constructive Typology*, p. 41 and *passim*. Don Martindale also rejects McKinney's view that types are explanatory and provides cogent arguments for this not being the case – see his article 'Sociological Theory and Type Construction', p. 58 and *passim*.

47 Confirmation for this view can be found in the remark by M. Weber, in *The Methodology of the Social Sciences*, p. 90: 'The ideal typical concept will help to develop our skill in imputation in *research*: it *is* no "hypothesis" but it offers guidance to the construction of hypotheses.'

48 P. L. Berger and T. Luckmann, *The Social Construction of Reality: A Treatise in the Sociology of Knowledge* (Garden City, NY: Doubleday, 1967).

49 On the whole question of loosening one's imagination, a key text is C. Wright Mills, *The Sociological Imagination*. A statement of his approach occurs in the last chapter of that work: 'Imagination is often successfully invited by putting together hitherto isolated items, by finding unsuspected connexions' (p. 221).

50 A rich collection of essays to do with the comparative method occurs in I. Vallier, ed., *Comparative Methods in Sociology: Essays on Trends and Applications* (Berkeley, Los Angeles and London: University of California Press, 1971).

51 The treatment in M. Duverger, *Introduction*, pp. 261–7, of the comparative method has been used to provide the description here of both close and distant comparisons.

52 M. Duverger, *Introduction*, p. 267.

53 See the essay by N. J. Smelser, 'Alexis de Tocqueville as Comparative Analyst', in I. Vallier, ed., *Comparative Methods*, pp. 19–47.

54 E. Durkheim, *The Elementary Forms of Religious Life*, ET by J. W. Swain (London: George Allen & Unwin, 1964).

55 K. Kautsky, *Foundations of Christianity*.

56 B. J. Malina, 'The Social Sciences and Biblical Interpretation', *Interpretation*, 37 (1982), 229–42 (p. 237).

57 *Ibid.*, p. 238.

58 E. A. Judge, 'The Social Identity of the First Christians: A Question of Method in Religious History', *The Journal of Religious History*, 11 (1980), 201–17. Another article containing a negative attitude to sociological interpretation is that of C. S. Rodd, 'On Applying a Sociological Theory to Biblical Studies', *Journal for the Study of the Old Testament*, 19 (1981), 95–106.

59 See E. A. Judge, *The Social Pattern of Christian Groups in the First Century* (London: The Tyndale Press, 1960).

60 E. A. Judge, 'The Social Identity of the First Christians', p. 210.

61 *Ibid.*, p. 212.

62 B. R. Wilson, *Magic and the Millennium: A Sociological Study of Religious Movements of Protest Among Tribal and Third-World Peoples* (London: Heinemann, 1973), pp. 9–30.

63 T. F. Carney, *The Shape of the Past: Models and Antiquity* (Lawrence, Kan.: Coronado Press, 1975), p. xiv.

64 P. Brown, *Religion and Society in the Age of Saint Augustine* (London: Faber & Faber, 1972), pp. 18–20.

65 See n. 48 above.

66 B. C. Thomason, *Making Sense of Reification: Alfred Schutz and Constructionist Theory* (London: The Macmillan Company, 1982), *passim*, and R. Gill, *Theology and Social Structure* (London and Oxford: Mowbrays, 1977), pp. 18–20. Neither the criticism of Thomason nor that of Gill, which essentially relates to epistemological aspects of *The Social Construction of Reality*, affects the use of the ideas in that work for instituting comparisons with the data in Luke–Acts carried out in this book.

67 P. L. Berger, *The Social Reality of Religion* (London: Faber & Faber, 1969), p. 48.

68 A. F. C. Wallace, 'Revitalization Movements', *American Anthropologist*, 58 (1956), 264–81.

69 J. Baechler, *Revolution* (Oxford: Basil Blackwell, 1975), p. 106.

70 N. Cohn, *The Pursuit of the Millennium: Revolutionary Millenarians and Mystical Anarchists of the Middle Ages* (London:

TempleSmith, 1970). See, for example, the pamphlets *Restitution* and *Announcement of Vengeance* written by one of the Anabaptists while they were besieged in Münster – N. Cohn, *The Pursuit of the Millenium*, p. 274. Another document, the *Reformation of Sigismund*, which advocated radical improvements in the plight of the urban poor, first appeared in 1439 CE, but became widely used as a programme for oppressed groups from 1480 onwards – *ibid.*, pp. 118, 233.
71 C. K. Barrett, *Luke the Historian in Recent Study* (London: Epworth Press, 1961), p. 57.
72 Conzelmann, *Luke*, pp. 95–136.
73 P. L. Berger, *The Social Reality of Religion*, p. 33.
74 C. Johnson, *Revolutionary Change* (London: University of London Press, 1968), p. 137.
75 *Ibid.*, p. 138.
76 W. A. Meeks, *The First Urban Christians*, pp. 172–6.
77 Peter Richardson, *Israel in the Apostolic Church* (Cambridge: Cambridge University Press, 1969), p. 46.
78 N. Cohn, *The Pursuit of the Millennium*, pp. 241, 248.
79 David B. Barrett, *Schism and Renewal in Africa: An Analysis of Six Thousand Contemporary Religious Movements* (Nairobi: Oxford University Press, 1968), p. 220.
80 For Diaspora *politeumata*, see E. Mary Smallwood, *The Jews under Roman Rule* (Leiden: E. J. Brill, 1976), pp. 139, 141, 247, 285, 359–61, 369–70.

2. The community

1 Two examples are C. A. Heumann, 'Dissertatio de Theophilo cui Lucas Historiam Sacram Inscripsit', *Bibliotheca Historico–Philologico–Theologica*, Classis IV (Bremen, 1720), pp. 483–505, and Maddox, *Purpose*, p. 12.
2 Cadbury, *Making*, pp. 194–209.
3 G. Klein, 'Lukas 1,1–4 als theologisches Programm', in E. Dinkler, ed., *Zeit und Geschichte. Dankesgabe an Rudolf Bultmann zum 80. Geburtstag* (Tübingen: Mohr (Siebeck), 1964), pp. 193–216.
4 See Fitzmyer, *Commentary*, pp. 290–301.
5 See I. I. Du Plessis, 'Once More: The Purpose of Luke's Prologue (Lk 1.1–4)', *NovT*, 16 (1974), 259–71.
6 Maddox, *Purpose*, p. 14.
7 A. D. Nock, *Conversion: The Old and the New in Religion from Alexander the Great to Augustine of Hippo* (Oxford: The Clarendon Press, 1933), p. 79.
8 Maddox, *Purpose*, p. 15.
9 E. A. LaVerdiere and W. G. Thompson, 'New Testament Communities in Transition: A Study in Matthew and Luke', *TS*, 37 (1976), 567–97.
10 R. F. O'Toole, 'Luke's Position on Politics and Society in Luke–Acts', in R. J. Cassidy and P. J. Scharper, eds., *Political Issues in Luke–Acts* (Maryknoll, NY: Orbis Books, 1983), pp. 1–17 (p. 2).

11 Supporters of the early date in the last few decades include F. F. Bruce, R. Koh, B. Gärtner, A. Hastings, O. Michel, B. Reicke, D. Guthrie, R. E. Cottle and J. Munck – see the list in Gasque, *History*, p. 264.

12 J. A. T. Robinson, *Redating the New Testament* (London: SCM Press, 1976), pp. 86–117.

13 J. C. O'Neill, *The Theology of Acts in its Historical Setting*, second edition (London: SPCK, 1970), *passim*; J. T. Townsend, 'The Date of Luke–Acts', in C. H. Talbert, ed., *Luke–Acts: New Perspectives from the Society of Biblical Literature Seminar* (New York: The Crossroads Publishing Company, 1984), pp. 47–62.

14 The members of the Tübingen school thought that Acts was written in the second century. Harnack was an eminent defender of the early date and eventually reached the conclusion that Acts was published around 62 CE – see Gasque, *History*, p. 155.

15 See Acts 20.22–4, 36–8; 21.11–14. E. J. Goodspeed, in an excellent treatment of this subject in *New Solutions of New Testament Problems* (Chicago: Chicago University Press, 1927), pp. 94–100, notes that the foreboding in verses such as these would have been quite pointless if Paul was not already dead at the time the work was written.

16 M. Krenkel, *Josephus und Lukas* (Leipzig, 1894). I. I. Du Plessis accurately states the modern consensus on Krenkel's thesis when he says that it 'cannot be seriously debated any longer' – see Du Plessis' article 'Once More: The Purpose of Luke's Prologue', p. 260. Also see *Beginnings*, Vol. II, pp. 355–8.

17 C. H. Dodd, 'The Fall of Jerusalem and the Abomination of Desolation', *JRS*, 37 (1947), 47–54.

18 Josephus, *BJ*, 5.491–501.

19 Josephus, *BJ*, 7.1–4.

20 Josephus, *BJ*, 6.418.

21 For details on the date of the collection of Paul's letters, see J. Finegan, 'The Original Form of the Pauline Collection', *HTR*, 49 (1956), 85–103 (especially pp. 85–6), and Kümmel, *Introduction*, pp. 480–1. There is very little to recommend the view of J. Knox, in *Studies in Luke–Acts*, pp. 279–87, that Luke knew Paul's letters but chose not to use them; E. Haenchen shows throughout his *Commentary* that Luke suffered from a dearth of sources, not a surfeit. Far more plausible than Knox is the suggestion of E. J. Goodspeed, *New Solutions*, pp. 1–10, that it was the appearance of Acts that stimulated the collection and publication of the Pauline corpus.

22 Pliny, *Epistulae*, X.96.

23 For this date, see A. N. Sherwin-White, *The Letters of Pliny: A Historical and Social Commentary* (Oxford: The Clarendon Press, 1966), pp. 80–1 and 693.

24 A. N. Sherwin-White, *Roman Society and Roman Law in the New Testament* (Oxford: The Clarendon Press, 1963), p. 4.

25 Pliny, *Epistulae*, X.96.1.

26 The earliest evidence for some kind of persecution or harassment of Christians under Domitian occurs in the letter of Clement of Rome to the Corinthian church (Chapter 7), on which see J. B. Lightfoot, *The Apostolic Fathers*, Part I: *S. Clement of Rome*, Vol. I (London and New York: Macmillan & Co., 1890), pp. 350–2. Lightfoot also notes that virtually all the early church writers speak of an initial persecution under Nero and a second under Domitian – *ibid.*, p. 350.

27 J. B. Lightfoot, *The Apostolic Fathers*, Part II: *S. Ignatius and S. Polycarp*, Vol. I (London: Macmillan & Co., 1885), p. 30.

28 *Ibid.*, p. 32.

29 E. M. Smallwood, *The Jews under Roman Rule* (Leiden: E. J. Brill, 1976), pp. 381ff., regards Pliny's letter as evidence that Christians were under pressure in the early nineties, but thinks that Domitilla, Clemens and Glabrio, who were persecuted by Domitian (see Cassius Dio, *Historiae*, 67.14), and have long been regarded as Christians, were actually Jews.

30 R. Travers Herford, *Christianity in Talmud and Midrash* (London: Williams & Norgate, 1903), pp. 127–35.

31 Cadbury, *Making*, pp. 245–9.

32 The only time there is missionary teaching in the countryside in Acts is in the area around Lystra and Derbe (Acts 14.6–7).

33 Cf. Lk 8.27, 39; 9.10.

34 Examples include Lk 18.2, 3; 19.17; 23.19.

35 See the descriptions of Philippi and Tarsus (Acts 16.12; 21.39).

36 The present writer believes that Antioch-on-the-Orontes was the place of composition of Luke–Acts and has prepared an essay on the subject which he hopes will appear elsewhere.

37 See pp. 171–9 below, for a survey of the political, economic and social realities of Greco-Roman cities.

38 This position appears to be taken by M. A. Moscato, 'Current Theories Regarding the Audience of Luke–Acts', *Currents in Theology and Mission*, 3 (1976), 355–61; this article is abstracted in *NTA*, XXI, 136.

39 J. Jervell, *Luke and the People of God* (Minneapolis: Augsburg Publishing House, 1979), pp. 68, 146–7, 174–5.

40 F. Overbeck, *Kurze Erklärung der Apostelgeschichte, von W. M. L. de Wette, Vierte Auflage bearbeitet und stark erweitert von Franz Overbeck* (Leipzig, 1870). Note the ET of the introduction to this work in J. Dare's translation of Zeller's book on *Acts*, referred to in Chapter 8, n. 14 below. See the discussion in Gasque, *History*, pp. 80–6.

41 ET by Gasque, in Gasque, *History*, p. 331.

42 Gasque, *History*, p. 83.

43 Even in a work such as S. G. Wilson's *The Gentiles and the Gentile Mission in Luke–Acts* (Cambridge: Cambridge University Press, 1973), the existence of a Gentile community behind Luke is asserted rather than proved.

44 Fitzmyer, *Commentary*, p. 58.

45 G. D. Kilpatrick, 'The Gentiles and the Strata of Luke', in O. Böcher and K. Haacker, eds., *Verborum Veritas: Festschrift für G. Stählin* (Wuppertal: Theologischer Verlag Rolf Brockhaus, 1970), pp. 83–8; 'Λαοί at Luke II.31 and Acts IV.25, 27', *JTS*, n.s. 16 (1965), 127; and 'Luke – Not a Gentile Gospel', address delivered to the Origen Society in the Oxford Faculty of Theology on 14 February 1984.

46 G. D. Kilpatrick believes ('Luke – Not a Gentile Gospel') that the Gentiles see the light but are not necessarily illuminated by it; but this interesting view appears to be precluded by Acts 13.47 and 26.23.

47 S. G. Wilson, *The Gentiles*, pp. 39–40.

48 T. W. Manson, *The Sayings of Jesus* (London: SCM Press, 1977), p. 130.

49 See B. Violet, 'Zum rechten Verständnis der Nazareth-perikope Lc 4: 16–30', *ZNW*, 37 (1938), 251–71; and H. Schürmann, 'Zur Traditionsgeschichte der Nazareth-Perikope Lk 4,16–30', in A. Descamps and A. de Halleux, eds., *Mélanges bibliques en hommage au R. P. Béda Rigaux* (Gembloux: Duculot, 1970), pp. 187–205.

50 U. Busse, *Das Nazareth-Manifest. Eine Einführung in das lukanische Jesusbild nach Lk 4,16–30* (Stuttgart: Katholisches Bibelwerk, 1978), pp. 21–67; Fitzmyer, *Commentary*, p. 527.

51 L. C. Crockett, 'Luke 4:25–27 and Jewish–Gentile Relations in Luke–Acts', *JBL*, 88 (1969), 177–83.

52 See G. F. Moore, *Judaism in the First Centuries of the Christian Era*, Vol. I (Cambridge, Mass.: Harvard University Press, 1932), pp. 323–7; and K. Lake, 'Proselytes and God-Fearers', *Beginnings*, Vol. V, pp. 74–96.

53 A. T. Kraabel, 'The Disappearance of the "God-Fearers"', *Numen*, 28 (1981), 113–26. The present writer hopes to publish an extended reply to this article elsewhere in the near future.

54 For two examples among many, see the quotation from Epictetus in Stern, Vol. I, p. 543, and Juvenal, *Saturae*, XIV.96–101.

55 Josephus, *Contra Apionem*, II.282; *BJ*, 7.45 (Antioch); *BJ*, 2.461–3 and *AJ*, 14.110.

56 B. Lifshitz, *Donateurs et fondateurs dans les synagogues juives* (Paris: Gabalda, 1967), No. 33 (pp. 34–6).

57 Cited by B. Lifshitz, *Donateurs*, p. 35.

58 Josephus, *AJ*, 14.110. I accept the interpretation of R. Marcus, 'The Sebomenoi in Josephus', *Jewish Social Studies*, 14 (1952), 247–50.

59 See the discussion in H. Schürmann, *Das Lukasevangelium. Erster Teil: Kommentar zu Kap. 1, 1–9, 50* (Freiburg: Herder, 1969), pp. 395–7.

60 My case for the non-historicity of the incident is given at pp. 95–6.

61 Cf. the reaction of the Jerusalem church in Acts 11.3. This matter is discussed at pp. 93–7 below.

62 K. Romaniuk, 'Die "Gottesfürchtigen" im Neuen Testament', *Aegyptus*, 44 (1964), 66–91 (p. 88).

63 In Acts 11.20 Ἕλληνας is a better reading than Ἑλληνιστάς – so C. D. F. Moule, 'Once More, Who Were the Hellenists?', *ExpT*, 70 (1958–9), 100–2.

64 The translation of καθαρός as 'unpolluted' is justified at p. 100 below.
65 W. A. Meeks, *The First Urban Christians*, p. 29.
66 *Ibid.*, pp. 26–8.
67 J. H. Elliott, *A Home for the Homeless*, pp. 45–6, p. 56, n. 80.
68 S. G. Wilson, *The Gentiles*, p. 232.
69 See W. K. L. Clarke, 'The Use of the Septuagint in Acts', in *Beginnings*, Vol. II, pp. 66–105; and H. F. D. Sparks, 'The Semitisms of St. Luke's Gospel', *JTS*, 44 (1943), 129–38.
70 F. L. Horton, 'Reflections on the Semitisms of Luke–Acts', in Talbert, *Perspectives*, pp. 1–23.

3. Sectarian strategies

1 Robin Scroggs, 'The Earliest Christian Communities as Sectarian Movement', in J. Neusner, ed., *Christianity, Judaism and Other Greco-Roman Cults*, Part II, pp. 1–23.
2 See especially, J. H. Elliott, *A Home for the Homeless*, and W. A. Meeks, *The First Urban Christians*.
3 T. L. Donaldson, 'Moses Typology and the Sectarian Nature of Early Christian Anti-Judaism: A Study in Acts 7', *JSNT*, 12 (1981), 27–52.
4 This essay, the introduction to a series of articles entitled 'Die Wirtschaftsethik der Weltreligionen', is translated in H. H. Gerth and C. Wright Mills, eds., *From Max Weber: Essays in Sociology* (London: Routledge & Kegan Paul, 1970), pp. 267–301. For its date of publication, see *ibid.*, p. 267.
5 *Ibid.*, pp. 287–8.
6 *Ibid.*, p. 288.
7 See Chapter 1, n. 80 above.
8 E. Troeltsch, *The Social Teaching of the Christian Churches*, Volume I, pp. 331–43.
9 Bryan Wilson, *Religion in Sociological Perspective* (Oxford and New York: Oxford University Press, 1982), p. 91. Wilson notes, however, that multiple allegiance is not uncommon outside Western (Christian) society – see pp. 101–2.
10 *Ibid.*, pp. 90–1.
11 *Ibid.*, p. 92.
12 Bryan R. Wilson, *Magic and the Millennium*, p. 19.
13 The summary given in the text is taken from Wilson's most recent version of his sectarian typology, in *Magic and the Millennium*, pp. 18–26.
14 *Ibid.*, p. 26.
15 See n. 2 above.
16 H. Richard Niebuhr, *The Social Sources of Denominationalism* (1929; New York: World Publishing, 1972), p. 19.
17 B. R. Wilson, 'An Analysis of Sect Development', *American Sociological Review*, 24 (1959), 3–15 (p. 3 and *passim*).
18 For a good introduction to Weber's notion of charismatic authority,

see the selections from his *Wirtschaft und Gesellschaft*, ET in H.H. Gerth and C. Wright Mills, eds., *From Max Weber*, pp. 245–52.

19 D.B. Barrett, *Schism and Renewal in Africa: An Analysis of Six Thousand Contemporary Religious Movements* (Nairobi: Oxford University Press, 1968).

20 See n.18 above.

21 See n.1 above.

22 Bryan R. Wilson, *Religion in Sociological Perspective*, p.105.

23 The allusion, to Ps 73.1–2 (LXX), has been noted by W. Schrage, article on συναγωγή and its derivatives – *TDNT*, Vol. VII, pp. 798–852 (p. 829); and K.L. Schmidt, article on ἐκκλησία – *TDNT*, Vol. III, pp. 502–36 (p. 504).

24 Haenchen, *Commentary*, pp. 436, 592; Fitzmyer, *Commentary*, p. 253.

25 Hans von Campenhausen, *Ecclesiastical Authority and Spiritual Power in the Church of the First Three Centuries*, ET by J.A. Baker (London: Adam & Charles Black, 1969), p. 94.

26 The fact that elders have a position of authority in the community does not mean that its organization is 'hierarchical'. Hans von Campenhausen has explained that in the early stages of the development of the presbyterate, to which period Luke–Acts is assigned, the position of the elders was as much patriarchal and moral as official and authoritarian – *Ecclesiastical Authority*, pp. 76, 84. This is a far cry from the truly hierarchical system evident in the Epistles of Ignatius, where virtually all power has been vested in the bishop, around whom stands a council of elders, with the deacons under them – *Ecclesiastical Authority*, p. 97.

27 W. Schrage, article on συναγωγή, *TDNT*, Vol. VII, p. 849.

28 R.T. Herford, *Christianity in Talmud and Midrash*, pp. 127–35.

29 Quoted in Emil Schürer, *The History of the Jewish People in the Age of Jesus Christ (175 B.C. – A.D. 135)*, revised edition by Geza Vermes, Fergus Millar and Matthew Black, Vol. II (Edinburgh: T.&T. Clark, 1979), p. 461.

30 W. Schrage, article on συναγωγή, *TDNT*, Vol. VII, pp. 848–9; J. Louis Martyn, *History and Theology in the Fourth Gospel*, first edition (New York and Evanston, Ill.: Harper & Row, 1968), pp. 31–41.

31 W. Horbury, 'The Benediction of the *Minim* and Early Jewish–Christian Controversy', *JTS*, 33 (1982), 19–61.

32 Horbury's argument is more convincing on this point than that of R. Kimelman, '*Birkat Ha-Minim* and the Lack of Evidence for an Anti-Christian Jewish Prayer in Late Antiquity', in E.P. Sanders, ed., *Jewish and Christian Self-Definition*, Vol. II (London: SCM Press, 1981), pp. 226–44.

33 W. Horbury, 'The Benediction of the *Minim*', p. 51.

34 J.L. Martyn, *History and Theology*, pp. 29–31.

35 The *Mishnah* was later to prescribe that judicial stoning began with the condemned person being hurled from a height twice that of a man, and only if this initial fall did not kill him or her were stones

then thrown by the onlookers – see M. *Sanhedrin* 6.4, for example, in the edition of H. Danby, *The Mishnah* (Oxford: Clarendon Press, 1933), p. 390.
36 R. C. Tannehill, 'The Mission of Jesus according to Luke iv 16–30', in W. Eltester, ed., *Jesus in Nazareth* (Berlin: de Gruyter, 1972), pp. 51–75 (p. 61).
37 D. L. Tiede, *Prophecy and History in Luke–Acts* (Philadelphia: Fortress Press, 1980), p. 43.
38 Paul went off into Arabia immediately after his conversion (Gal 1.16–17) and his colourful escape from Damascus, to avoid Aretas, not the Jews, must have occurred at a later date (2 Cor 11.32–3).
39 The similarities between Lk 4.16–30 and Acts 9.20–5 are: 1. both Jesus and Paul enter a synagogue as the first public step in their ministry and deliver a message of salvation; 2. their respective audiences are astonished and also confused by the change of roles they observe in Jesus and Paul, with the Jews in Nazareth asking if this is not the son of Joseph and those in Damascus asking if this is not the man who has hitherto opposed Christianity; 3. there is an attempt to kill Jesus and a plot to kill Paul; 4. both Jesus and Paul escape.
40 For example, Haenchen, *Commentary*, p. 729; and S. G. Wilson, *Luke and the Law* (Cambridge: Cambridge University Press, 1983), p. 115.
41 J. L. Houlden, 'The Purpose of Luke', *JSNT*, 21 (1984), 53–65.
42 See Eckhardt Plümacher, *Lukas als hellenistischer Schriftsteller. Studien zur Apostelgeschichte* (Göttingen: Vandenhoeck & Ruprecht, 1972); and Charles H. Talbert, *Literary Patterns, Theological Themes, and the Genre of Luke–Acts* (Missoula, Mont.: Society of Biblical Literature and Scholars Press, 1974).
43 For succinct summaries of the treatment of repentance, conversion and baptism in Luke–Acts, see Fitzmyer, *Commentary*, pp. 237–41.
44 G. Theissen, *The First Followers of Jesus*, pp. 39–46.
45 Conzelmann, *Luke*, p. 120.
46 *Ibid.*, p. 96.
47 Kümmel, *Introduction*, pp. 466–9, argues for a date towards the end of the reign of Domitian, *c.* 90–5 CE.
48 The latter alterantive is the more likely – see pp. 209–10 below.
49 R. E. Brown, *The Birth of the Messiah: A Commentary on the Infancy Narratives in Matthew and Luke* (London: Geoffrey Chapman, 1977), pp. 346–55.
50 Such as Haenchen, *Commentary*; E. Grässer, *Das Problem der Parusieverzögerung in den synoptischen Evangelien und in der Apostelgeschichte*, second edition (Berlin: Töpelmann, 1960); and G. Schneider, *Parusiegleichnisse im Lukas-Evangelium* (Stuttgart: Katholisches Bibelwerk, 1975).
51 E. Franklin, *Christ the Lord: A Study in the Purpose and Theology of Luke–Acts* (London: SPCK, 1975); R. H. Hiers, 'The Problem of the Delay of the Parousia in Luke–Acts', *NTS*, 20 (1973–4),

145–55; A. J. Mattill, Jr, 'Naherwartung, Fernerwartung, and the Purpose of Luke–Acts: Weymouth Reconsidered', *CBQ*, 34 (1972), 276–93; C. H Talbert, 'Shifting Sands: The Recent Study of the Gospel of Luke', *Interpretation*, 30 (1976), 381–95; and S. G. Wilson, 'Lukan Eschatology', *NTS*, 16 (1969–70), 330–47.

52 R. H. Hiers, 'The Problem of the Delay'.

53 S. G. Wilson, 'Lukan Eschatology'.

54 Josef Ernst, *Herr der Geschichte. Perspektiven der lukanischen Eschatologie* (Stuttgart: Katholisches Bibelwerk, 1978), pp. 28, 46.

55 For example, S. G. Wilson, 'Lukan Eschatology', p. 340; and R. H. Hiers, 'The Problem of the Delay', p. 153.

56 This is so despite the fact that Luke's three other examples of ἐν τάχει all mean 'quickly' or 'soon' (Acts 12.7; 22.18; 25.4).

57 Conzelmann, *Luke*, p. 105.

58 G. Schneider, *Parusiegleichnisse* (Stuttgart: Katholisches Bibelwerk, 1975), p. 60.

59 For an analysis of the original Jesus movement in Galilee having been characterized, at least in part, by the age-old antipathy of country folk for the city, see G. Theissen, 'Die Tempelweissagung Jesu. Prophetie im Spannungsfeld von Stadt und Land', *ThZ*, 32 (1976), 144–58.

60 J. Neusner, *From Politics to Piety: The Emergence of Pharisaic Judaism* (Englewood Cliffs, NJ: Prentice-Hall, 1973), *passim*.

61 For L. T. Johnson, for example, Luke's problem is one of 'theodicy', to show that God has not been untrue to his word to Israel and that the Gentiles may therefore be confident in their faith – see his *The Literary Function of Possessions in Luke–Acts* (Missoula, Mont.: Scholars Press, 1977), p. 122.

62 See p. 203 and p. 255, n. 4.

63 Conzelmann, *Luke*, pp. 95–6.

64 H. J. Cadbury's essay, 'Names for Christians and Christianity in Acts', *Beginnings*, Vol. V, pp. 375–92, remains the best treatment of this subject.

65 On 'believers', see *ibid.*, p. 382.

66 *Ibid.*, pp. 387–8.

67 *Ibid.*, pp. 379–80.

68 H. B. Mattingly, 'The Origin of the Name "Christiani"', *JTS*, n.s. 9 (1958), 26–37.

69 H. J. Cadbury, 'Names', p. 386, notes that the word is absent from all the Apostolic Fathers except Ignatius. Its only other occurrence in the New Testament outside Acts is at 1 Peter 4.16.

70 H. J. Cadbury, 'Names', p. 390.

71 Josephus, *BJ*, 2.119–166.

72 Haenchen, *Commentary*, p. 643, and elsewhere.

73 For example, N. A. Dahl, 'The Story of Abraham in Luke–Acts', *Studies in Luke–Acts*, pp. 139–58; and L. T. Johnson, *The Literary Function of Possessions*, pp. 17–18.

4. Table-fellowship

1 G. Theissen, *The Social Setting of Pauline Christianity*, p. 121.
2 *Ibid.*, Chapters 1, 2, 3 and 4.
3 Mary Douglas, *Purity and Danger: An Analysis of Concepts of Pollution and Taboo* (London: Routledge & Kegan Paul, 1966), pp. 114–15.
4 Louis Dumont, *Homo Hierarchicus: The Caste System and its Implications* (London: Paladin, 1970), pp. 80–1.
5 *Ibid.*, pp. 123–9, 180–7.
6 Edmund Leach, 'The Legitimacy of Solomon', in his *Genesis as Myth and Other Essays* (London: Jonathan Cape, 1969), pp. 25–83 (p. 39).
7 Mary Douglas, 'Deciphering a Meal', in her *Implicit Meanings: Essays in Anthropology* (London and Boston: Routledge and Kegan Paul, 1975), pp. 249–75.
8 *Ibid.*, p. 272.
9 J. Jeremias, *Jerusalem in the Time of Jesus: An Investigation into Economic and Social Conditions during the New Testament Period* (London: SCM Press, 1969), p. 246.
10 G. Vermes, *The Dead Sea Scrolls in English* (Harmondsworth: Penguin Books, 1980), p. 78.
11 *Ibid.*, p. 36.
12 J. Neusner, *Fellowship in Judaism: The First Century and Today* (London: Valentine Mitchell, 1963), pp. 22–3.
13 K. G. Kuhn, 'The Lord's Supper and the Communal Meal at Qumran', in K. Stendahl, ed., *The Scrolls and the New Testament* (London: SCM Press, 1958), pp. 65–93 (p. 68); M. Black, *The Scrolls and Christian Origins* (London: Thomas Nelson and Sons, 1961), pp. 108–11.
14 J. D. G. Dunn, 'The Incident at Antioch (Gal. 2:11–18)', *JSNT*, 18 (1983), 3–75 (p. 23).
15 S. G. Wilson, *Luke and the Law* (Cambridge: Cambridge University Press, 1983), p. 70.
16 Dunn, 'The Incident at Antioch', pp. 7–11, for criticism of which see Rabbi Dan Cohn-Sherbok, 'Some Reflections on James Dunn's: "The Incident at Antioch (Gal. 2.11–18)"', *JSNT*, 18 (1983), 68–74.
17 Dunn, 'The Incident at Antioch', pp. 35–6.
18 *Ibid.*, p. 21, citing *Mishnah Berakhot* 7:1 and *Abodah Zarah* 5:5, and the Babylonian Talmud, b. *Abodah Zarah* 8a–b. This evidence is discussed below.
19 Wilson, *Luke and the Law*, p. 70, together with n. 19 on p. 124, citing G. Alon, 'The Levitical Uncleanness of Gentiles', in *Jews, Judaism and the Classical World* (Jerusalem: The Magnes Press, 1977), pp. 146–89. Alon never suggests in this essay that Jews ate with Gentiles, and the whole point of his argument, that Gentiles had been regarded as ritually impure through their association with idolatry from early in Israel's history, is quite antipathetic to the notion of Jews dining with them. Alon's essay is considered in more detail later in this chapter.

20 J. Neusner, *From Politics to Piety*, pp. 146ff.
21 Cf. Stern. This work replaces T. Reinach, *Textes d'auteurs grecs et latins relatifs au Juifs et Judaisme* (Paris: Ernest Leroux, 1895).
22 John G. Gager, *The Origins of Anti-Semitism: Attitudes Toward Judaism in Pagan and Christian Antiquity* (New York and Oxford: Oxford University Press, 1983).
23 *Ibid.*, p. 31, in reply to J. N. Sevenster, *The Roots of Pagan Anti-Semitism in the Ancient World* (Leiden: E. J. Brill, 1975), especially Chapter 3, pp. 89–144, in which Sevenster attempts to show that 'the most fundamental reason for pagan anti-Semitism almost always proves to lie in the strangeness of the Jews midst ancient society' (p. 89).
24 A failure to appreciate the significance of the table-fellowship question also characterizes Sevenster's *The Roots of Pagan Anti-Semitism*, which devotes three sentences (p. 139) out of 235 pages to the question, and other writings on ancient anti-Semitism, such as Jerry L. Daniel, 'Anti-Semitism in the Hellenistic–Roman Period', *JBL*, 98 (1979), 45–65.
25 Stern I, p. 20.
26 John Bright, *A History of Israel*, second edition (London: SCM Press, 1976), pp. 416–17.
27 Stern I, p. 24, in reference to the views of Theophrastus, Megasthenes, Clemens Alexandrinus and Clearchus. Also see J. G. Gager, *The Origins of Anti-Semitism*, p. 39.
28 J. G. Gager, *The Origins of Anti-Semitism*, p. 40.
29 Stern I, p. 26 (Greek text) and p. 28 (English translation).
30 *Ibid.*, p. 148.
31 *Ibid.*, p. 149.
32 *Ibid.*, p. 155.
33 *Ibid.*, p. 156.
34 *OCD*, p. 347.
35 J. G. Gager, *The Origins of Anti-Semitism*, p. 68.
36 Stern I, p. 182 (Greek text) and p. 183 (English translation).
37 *Ibid.*, p. 332.
38 *Ibid.*, pp. 335–6 (Latin text).
39 C. T. Lewis and C. Short, *A Latin Dictionary* (Oxford: The Clarendon Press, 1969), s.vv. *convivo* and *convivor* (pp. 465 and 466).
40 Stern II, p. 1.
41 *Ibid.*, p. 19, for the excerpt from Tacitus, *Historiae*, V.5.2. The English translation is mine.
42 Stern II, p. 339.
43 *Ibid.*, p. 341 (text and translation).
44 See J. Bright, *A History of Israel*, pp. 420–5.
45 Otto Eissfeldt, *The Old Testament: An Introduction*, ET by Peter R. Ackroyd (Oxford: Basil Blackwell, 1966), pp. 520–2.
46 *Ibid.*, p. 587.
47 G. Alon, 'The Levitical Uncleanness of Gentiles', p. 154.

48 M. Hengel, *Judaism and Hellenism: Studies in their Encounter in Palestine during the Early Hellenistic Period*, Vol. I (London: SCM Press, 1974), p. 77.

49 Eissfeldt, *Introduction*, p. 510.

50 *Ibid.*, p. 585.

51 It is, for example, omitted from the lists of passages pertinent to Jewish attitudes to table-fellowship given in Marc Philonenko, ed., *Joseph et Aséneth* (Leiden: E. J. Brill, 1968), p. 49, and by S. G. Wilson, *Luke and the Law*, p. 69.

52 James H. Charlesworth, *The Pseudepigrapha and Modern Research*, reprint with supplement of the 1976 edition (Chicago: Scholars Press, 1981), p. 78, and Sidney Jellicoe, *The Septuagint and Modern Study* (Oxford: The Clarendon Press, 1968), pp. 47–52.

53 For a possible connection between the seventy (-two) Septuagint translators and the despatch by the Lucan Jesus of the seventy (-two) disciples in Lk 10.1, see Sidney Jellicoe, 'St Luke and the "Seventy (-Two)"', *NTS*, 6 (1959–60), 319–21.

54 Sidney Jellicoe, *The Septuagint and Modern Study*, pp. 49–50. George Howard has forcefully argued that the Letter was written in response to unjustified criticism of Diaspora Judaism by Palestinian Judaism – 'The Letter of Aristeas and Diaspora Judaism', *JTS*, 22 (1971), 337–48.

55 *Letter of Aristeas*, 139; the Greek text is taken from André Pelletier, ed., *Lettre d'Aristée à Philocrate* (Paris: Les Éditions du Cerf, 1962), p. 170, and the ET from Charles, Vol. II, p. 108.

56 *Letter of Aristeas*, 151 – Pelletier, ed., *Lettre*, p. 174 (Greek text); ET in Charles, Vol. II, p. 109.

57 *Letter of Aristeas*, 187–294.

58 *Letter of Aristeas*, 182–3 – Pelletier, ed., *Lettre*, p. 188 (Greek text); ETT by the author.

59 *Letter of Aristeas*, 183.

60 J. H. Charlesworth, *The Pseudepigrapha and Modern Research*, p. 143.

61 *Jubilees*, 22.16 – Charles, Vol. II, p. 46 (ET).

62 J. H. Charlesworth, *The Pseudepigrapha and Modern Research*, p. 143.

63 J. Neusner, *The Idea of Purity in Ancient Judaism* (Leiden: E. J. Brill, 1973), p. 58.

64 Marc Philonenko, ed., *Joseph et Aséneth*, pp. 99–109. There is an ET by E. W. Brooks, *Joseph and Asenath* (London: SPCK, 1918).

65 *Joseph and Asenath*, 7.

66 *Ibid.*; for the Greek text, see M. Philonenko, ed., *Joseph et Aséneth*, p. 150.

67 J. D. G. Dunn, 'The Incident at Antioch', pp. 20–1.

68 H. Danby, *The Mishnah*, p. 444.

69 *M. Berakhot* 4.8.–5.12.

70 See M. L. Rodkinson, *The Babylonian Talmud*, Vol. X (Boston: New Talmud Publishing Company, 1903), pp. 146–52.

71 *Ibid.*, p. 148.
72 *M. Abodah Zarah*, 5.12.
73 G. Alon, 'The Levitical Uncleanness of Gentiles'.
74 Z. W. Falk, *Introduction to the Jewish Law of the Second Common-wealth*, Part I (Leiden: E. J. Brill, 1972), pp. 5–8.
75 G. Alon, 'The Levitical Uncleanness of Gentiles', pp. 153–4.
76 Josephus, *BJ*, 2.150.
77 Josephus, *AJ*, 14.285.
78 *Ibid.*, 18.94.
79 J. D. G. Dunn, 'The Incident at Antioch', p. 14.
80 Cited by J. N. Sevenster, *The Roots of Pagan Anti-Semitism in the Ancient World*, p. 112.
81 Galatians should probably be dated to between 50 and 55 CE – see H. D. Betz, *Galatians: A Commentary on Paul's Letter to the Churches in Galatia* (Philadelphia: Fortress Press, 1979), pp. 9–12.
82 For other interpretations of οἱ ἐκ περιτομῆς, see Betz, *Galatians*, p. 109, n. 467.
83 On the location and characteristics of Paul's addressees, see Betz, *Galatians*, pp. 1–4.
84 J. D. G. Dunn, 'The Incident at Antioch', pp. 35–6.
85 For example, by S. G. Wilson, *Luke and the Law*, p. 52. If Wilson were correct in thinking that this verse constituted a 'profound and radical criticism of the law', why would Matthew have retained it (Mt 15.11)?
86 Ecclesiasticus 35.5: 'All these things must be sacrificed because of the commandment' (χάριν ἐντολῆς). And see T. A. Burkill, *New Light on the Earliest Gospel* (Ithaca and London: Cornell University Press, 1972), p. 81.
87 V. Taylor, *The Gospel According to St. Mark*, second edition (London: Macmillan & Co. 1966), p. 343.
88 T. A. Burkill, *New Light*, p. 82.
89 *Ibid.*, pp. 71–2.
90 V. Taylor, *St. Mark*, p. 350; for a discussion of bread and leaven motifs in Mk 6.30 – 8.21, see V. K. Robbins, 'Last Meal: Preparation, Betrayal, and Absence', in W. H. Kelber, ed., *The Passion in Mark: Studies on Mark 14–16*, (Philadelphia: The Fortress Press, 1976), pp. 21–40 (pp. 25–8).
91 F. W. Beare, *The Gospel According to Matthew: A Commentary* (Oxford: Basil Blackwell, 1981), p. 341.
92 For a recent discussion, see G. Stanton, ed., *The Interpretation of Matthew* (Philadelphia and London: Fortress Press and SPCK, 1983), pp. 12–18, from the editor's Introduction.
93 Such as the Ebionites and Cerinthus – see J. Daniélou, *The Theology of Jewish Christianity*, ET by J. A. Baker (London: Darton, Longman & Todd, 1964), pp. 58 and 68.
94 D. R. A. Hare, *The Theme of Jewish Persecution of Christians in the Gospel According to St Matthew* (Cambridge: Cambridge University Press, 1967), *passim*.
95 F. Hauck, 'Clean and Unclean in the NT', part of an article on

καθαρός, *TDNT*, Vol. III, pp. 423–6 (p. 424); S. G. Wilson, *Luke and the Law*, p. 68.

96 See the excellent discussion in Haenchen, *Commentary*, pp. 355–63.
97 I. Howard Marshall, *The Acts of the Apostles: An Introduction and Commentary* (London: Inter-Varsity Press, 1980), p. 182.
98 Haenchen, *Commentary*, p. 362.
99 Martin Dibelius, 'The Conversion of Cornelius', in Dibelius, *Studies*, pp. 109–22 (especially p. 122).
100 I. Howard Marshall, *The Acts of the Apostles*, p. 181.
101 R. R. Williams, *The Acts of the Apostles* (London: SCM Press, 1969), p. 94.
102 Cited by Haenchen, *Commentary*, p. 356.
103 Martin Dibelius, 'The Apostolic Council', in Dibelius, *Studies*, pp. 93–101 (pp. 95–7).
104 *Ibid.*, p. 96.
105 Haenchen, *Commentary*, p. 463.
106 *Ibid.*, pp. 447–8.
107 R. P. C. Hanson, *Acts* (Oxford: The Clarendon Press, 1978), pp. 155–6.
108 Contact with idols appears to be proscribed by Lev 17.8–9, which does not just regulate the location of sacrifices (so S. G. Wilson, *Luke and the Law*, p. 87), but effectively prevents sacrifice to any God but Yahweh. The consumption of blood is prohibited by Lev 17.10–14 and of animals that have been strangled, that is, not ritually slaughtered, by Lev 17.15–16. Incest is banned by Lev 18.6ff., which apply to resident foreigners by virtue of Lev 18.26.
109 S. G. Wilson, *Luke and the Law*, p. 70.
110 As supposed by the editor of Acts in *JB*; see the footnote to 16.15, p. 229.
111 Haenchen, *Commentary*, p. 495, considers that prior to moving in with Lydia they had probably lived in an inn at their own expense. But while the Lucan Paul refuses to take money or clothes from anyone (Acts 20.33–5), he has no objection to staying in disciples' houses (Acts 18.3, 7). In both respects he parallels the attitudes of the historical Paul.
112 R. P. C. Hanson, *Acts*, p. 243.
113 So Zahn, Ramsay and E. Meyer – cited Haenchen, *Commentary*, p. 709.
114 V. K. Robbins, 'By Land and by Sea: The We-Passages and Ancient Sea Voyages', in Talbert, *Perspectives*, pp. 215–42.
115 R. P. C. Hanson, *Acts*, p. 243, denies this with respect to the Sidon to Malta section of the voyage at least. But even in this section Paul is presented as a visionary in touch with God's purpose – Acts 27.10 (θεωρέω being used of a vision as at 7.56 and 10.11), 23–5 and 34.
116 Haenchen, *Commentary*, p. 711. Haenchen adopts the position that Luke did, indeed, possess a journal of this voyage but that he has heightened Paul's role in the proceedings – *ibid.*, p. 709.
117 *Beginnings*, Vol. IV, p. 336.
118 Haenchen, *Commentary*, p. 707.

119 G. W. H. Lampe, Commentary on Acts, in *Peake's Commentary on the Bible*, edited by Matthew Black and H. H. Rowley (London: Thomas Nelson & Sons, 1963), pp. 882–926 (p. 925).

120 So Belser, Blass, Olshausen, Ewald, Reicke and Menoud – cited Haenchen, *Commentary*, p. 707.

121 P. W. Walaskay, *'And So We Came to Rome': The Political Perspective of St Luke* (Cambridge: Cambridge University Press, 1983), pp. 60–2.

122 Bo Reicke, 'Die Mahlzeit mit Paulus auf den Wellen des Mittelmeers Act. 27, 33–38', *ThZ*, 4 (1948), 401–10 (pp. 402–4).

123 *Ibid.*, pp. 404–6.

124 *Ibid.*, pp. 406–8.

125 *Ibid.*, pp. 408–9.

126 G. Bornkamm, 'The Stilling of the Storm in Matthew', in G. Bornkamm, G. Barth and H. H. Held, *Tradition and Interpretation in Matthew* (London: SCM Press, 1982), pp. 52–7.

127 J. B. Lightfoot, *The Apostolic Fathers*, Part II, Vol. I (London: Macmillan & Co., 1885), p. 30.

128 *Philadelphians*, 6.1; *Magnesians*, 8.2, 10.

129 *Philadelphians*, 4 and 8.

130 See J. Daniélou, *The Theology of Jewish Christianity*, pp. 55–64, on the Ebionites.

131 Relevant extracts from these two works are conveniently provided by H. D. Betz, *Galatians*, pp. 331–3. For the possible connection between the *Epistula Petri* and the *Pseudo-Clementine Homilies* and the Ebionites, see J. Daniélou, *The Theology of Jewish Christianity*, pp. 59–64.

5. The law

1 J. Jervell, 'The Law in Luke–Acts', in *Luke and the People of God*, pp. 133–51.

2 S. G. Wilson, *Luke and the Law*.

3 C. L. Blomberg, 'The Law in Luke–Acts', *JSNT*, 22 (1984), 53–80.

4 Cited by Jervell in 'The Law in Luke–Acts', p. 133.

5 Haenchen, *Commentary*, p. 223.

6 H. Schürmann, *Traditionsgeschichtliche Untersuchungen zu den synoptischen Evangelien* (Düsseldorf: Patmos–Verlag, 1968), pp. 126–36.

7 R. Banks, *Jesus and the Law in the Synoptic Tradition* (Cambridge: Cambridge University Press, 1975), pp. 172, 247 and *passim*.

8 B. H. Branscomb, *Jesus and the Law of Moses* (London: Hodder & Stoughton, 1930), pp. 100–1.

9 S. G. Wilson, *Luke and the Law*, p. 57.

10 J. Jervell, 'The Law in Luke–Acts', p. 141.

11 S. G. Wilson, *Luke and the Law*, pp. 111–12.

12 P. S. Minear, 'Luke's Use of the Birth Stories', in *Studies in Luke–Acts*, pp. 111–30.

13 G. Schrenk, article on ἐντολή, *TDNT*, Vol. II, pp. 545–56 (p. 546).

14 G. Shrenk, article on δικαίωμα, *TDNT*, Vol. II, pp. 219–23 (p. 220).
15 Fitzmyer, *Commentary*, p. 425.
16 The word ἐυλαβής also occurs in Acts 2.5; 8.2 and 22.12 to express pious dedication to God's law. S. G. Wilson, inexplicably, thinks that its occurrence at Lk 2.25 is unique in the New Testament – *Luke and the Law*, p. 22.
17 For G. D. Kilpatrick's view on 'the light of the Gentiles', see Chapter 2, no. 46.
18 Fitzmyer, *Commentary*, p. 9 and *passim*.
19 S. G. Wilson, *Luke and the Law*, p. 56.
20 R. Banks, *Jesus and the Law*, pp. 247–8.
21 S. G. Wilson, *Luke and the Law*, p. 39.
22 G. Theissen, *The First Followers of Jesus*.
23 B. J. Malina, *The New Testament World*, especially pp. 94–121.
24 S. G. Wilson, *Luke and the Law*, p. 40.
25 J. A. Ziesler, 'Luke and the Pharisees', *NTS*, 25 (1979), 146–57, has argued that Luke aimed to soften the opposition evident in Mark between Jesus and the Pharisees and to present the Pharisees favourably in Acts, although Ziesler does not venture an explanation as to why the evangelist should have adopted such a policy. This view is, however, difficult to reconcile with the many features unique to Luke which are antipathetic to the Pharisees: for example, Lk 7.30; 11.53; 12.1 (Luke specifies the 'yeast' as hypocrisy); 16.14–15 and 18.10–14. The alleged friendliness of the Pharisees in Acts founders on the anti-Christian campaign waged by that eminent Pharisee, Paul.
26 Similarly, R. E. Brown argues that John's uniformly hostile references to the chief priests and scribes express antipathy towards the synagogue authorities of his own time – see his *The Community of the Beloved Disciple* (London: Geoffrey Chapman, 1979), p. 66.
27 R. Banks, *Jesus and the Law*, p. 170.
28 Bultmann, *HST*, p. 196.
29 Conzelmann, *Luke*, p. 23.
30 For an interesting treatment of Lk 16.18, see J. L. Houlden, *Ethics and the New Testament* (London and Oxford: Mowbrays, 1979), pp. 79–80.
31 So S. G. Wilson, *Luke and the Law*, p. 53.
32 H. Schürmann, *Traditionsgeschichtliche Untersuchungen*, pp. 280, 281 and 287.
33 H. Schürmann, *ibid.*, proposes the joint operation of a number of factors to explain Luke's omission of Mk 6.45–8.26. Certainly, there are difficulties with this approach. One of his factors, for example, is the desire to avoid doublets. Yet, as H. Hübner has noted, there is no shortage of doublets in Luke's work – see his *Das Gesetz in der synoptischen Tradition* (Witten: Luther Verlag, 1973), p. 183. For detailed statistics on Lucan doublets, see R. Morgenthaler, *Die lukanische Geschichtsschreibung als Zeugnis*, two volumes (Zürich: Zwingli Verlag, 1949), Vol. I. Nevertheless,

it is better to explain the omission of Mk 6.45–8.26 as due to Lucan redactional habits than as a vast omission in the text, which rests upon the sheer hypothesis of mutilated copies of Mark. *Contra*, S.G. Wilson, *Luke and the Law*, pp. 52–3.

34 H. Hübner, *Das Gesetz in der synoptischen Tradition*, pp. 182–91.
35 In Mk 10.1–12 Jesus interprets Gen 1.27 and 2.24 as flatly contradicting Dt 24.1–4. No rabbi would have engaged in such interpretation – D.E. Nineham, *The Gospel of St Mark* (Harmondsworth: Penguin Books, 1979), p. 261. Matthew was obviously embarrassed by Jesus' attack on the law and has toned down the pericope to bring it within the bounds of rabbinical discussion (Mt 19.1–12).
36 Haenchen, *Commentary*, p. 286.
37 As to a defence 'on the law', it is clear that the wide powers of discretion vested in provincial governors by virtue of their *imperium* meant that there could be no rigid rule of *nullum crimen sine lege, nulla poena sine lege* – so F. Schulz, *Principles of Roman Law*, ET by M. Wolff (Oxford: The Clarendon Press, 1936), pp. 173–4. Nevertheless, defendants still occasionally claimed that their actions were not in breach of Roman law, just as Paul does at Acts 25.8. Secondly, Paul's 'appeal' to Caesar (Acts 25.11) is not an appeal in the strict sense of the term, since Festus had not yet delivered judgement in the case, but is actually a defence 'as to jurisdiction', an assertion that Caesar and not Festus is the proper judge. On this right of provincial citizens to take their case to Rome (*reiectio Romam*), see P. Garnsey, *Social Status and Legal Privilege in the Roman Empire* (Oxford: The Clarendon Press, 1970), pp. 14, 263–4.
38 Cited by Haenchen, *Commentary*, p. 286.
39 *Ibid.*, p. 286.
40 K. Schrader, *Der Apostel Paulus* (Leipzig, 1836), Theil V, p. 524.
41 Dibelius, *Studies*, p. 167.
42 In its context, the word νόμος in Acts 18.13 refers to the Jewish law not the Roman.
43 The law which the High Priest appears to have breached is found in Lev 19.15: 'You shall do no injustice in judgement.'
44 Haenchen, *Commentary*, p. 446.
45 J. Nolland, 'A Fresh Look at Acts 15.10', *NTS*, 27 (1980), 105–15.
46 E.P. Sanders, *Paul, the Law and the Jewish People* (Philadelphia: Fortress Press, 1983), *passim*.
47 The attempt by Blomberg (see no. 3 above) to argue the contrary is not convincing.
48 S.G. Wilson, *Luke and the Law*, pp. 54–8, 105.

6. The Temple

1 Fitzmyer, *Commentary*, p. 164.
2 For example, M. Bachmann, *Jerusalem und der Tempel. Die geographisch-theologischen Elemente in der lukanischen Sicht des jüdischen Kultzentrums*, (Stuttgart, Berlin, Cologne and Mainz:

Kohlhammer, 1980), which has an excellent bibliography; P. Simson, 'The Drama of the City of God: Jerusalem in St Luke's Gospel', *Scripture*, 15 (1963), 65–80; K. Baltzer, 'The Meaning of the Temple in the Lukan Writings', *HTR*, 58 (1965), 263–77; F. D. Weinert, 'The Meaning of the Temple in Luke–Acts', *Biblical Theology Bulletin*, 11 (1981), 85–9; J. Knox, *Chapters in a Life of Paul* (London: Adam & Charles Black, 1954), pp. 25–7.

3 T. W. Manson, *The Sayings of Jesus* (London: SCM Press, 1977), pp. 42–3.

4 For the view that this central travel narrative in Luke is dependent upon the literary refashioning of Mark's account and not on some special historical or geographical knowledge, see C. C. McCown, 'The Geography of Luke's Central Section', *JBL*, 57 (1938), 51–66.

5 Acts 2.46; 3.1ff.; 5.21, 42.

6 So Bachmann, Simson and Weinert, as cited in n. 2 above.

7 F. D. Weinert, 'The Meaning of the Temple', p. 89.

8 M. Bachmann, *Jerusalem und der Tempel, passim*.

9 The symbolism discussed by B. Gärtner, *The Temple and the Community in Qumran and the New Testament: A Comparative Study in the Temple Symbolism of the Qumran Texts and the New Testament* (Cambridge: Cambridge University Press, 1965), is very different from that suggested here. The primary focus of the symbolism proposed by Gärtner is of the Temple as an image of the people of God, among whom God's presence abode, in the writings of Qumran and the New Testament.

10 Hatch and Redpath, *Concordance*, Vol. I, p. 1467, cite fourteen instances of χειροποίητος in the Septuagint, all of them used of idols.

11 Acts 7.41: 'καὶ ἐμοσχοποίησαν ... καὶ εὐφραίνοντο ἐν τοῖς ἔργοις τῶν χειρῶν αὐτῶν.'

12 C. H. H. Scobie, 'The Origins and Development of Samaritan Christianity', *NTS*, 19 (1972–3), 390–414, (p. 396); M. Simon, *St Stephen and the Hellenists in the Primitive Church* (London: New York and Toronto: Longmans, Green and Co., 1958), pp. 25 and 43.

13 Cited from F. C. Baur, *Paulus*, Vol. I, p. 48, in M. Hengel, *Between Jesus and Paul: Studies in the Earliest History of Christianity* (London: SCM Press, 1983), p. 1.

14 F. F. Bruce, *The Acts of the Apostles* (London: The Tyndale Press, 1962), pp. 150–1.

15 Gasque, *History, passim*, but especially Chapters 6 and 7.

16 H. J. Cadbury, 'The Hellenists', in *Beginnings*, Vol. V, pp. 59–74.

17 See the argument for this on p. 141 below.

18 W. G. Braude, *Jewish Proselytising in the First Five Centuries of the Common Era: The Age of the Tannaim and Amoraim* (Providence, RI: Brown University, 1940), Chapters 2, 4 and 8.

19 C. D. F. Moule, 'Once More, Who Were the Hellenists?', *The Expository Times*, 70 (1958–9), 100–2.

20 E. C. Blackman, 'The Hellenists of Acts vi.1', *The Expository Times*, 48 (1936–7), 524–5 (p. 524); C. D. F. Moule, 'Once More', p. 101.

21 A. Spiro, 'Stephen's Samaritan Background', Appendix V in J. Munck, *The Acts of the Apostles*, The Anchor Bible (Garden City, NY: Doubleday, 1967), pp. 285–300. In addition to Spiro's work, see M. H. Scharlemann, *Stephen: A Singular Saint* (Rome: Biblical Institute Press, 1968), and the critical review of the case for a Samaritan influence in Acts by R. J. Coggins, 'The Samaritans and Acts', *NTS*, 28 (1982), 423–34.

22 O. Cullmann, *The Johannine Circle: Its Place in Judaism, among the Disciples of Jesus and in Early Christianity* (London: SCM Press, 1976), pp. 41–3.

23 M. Simon, *St Stephen and the Hellenists in the Primitive Church*, *passim*.

24 *Ibid.*, p. 84; and see Simon's earlier essay, 'Saint Stephen and the Jerusalem Temple', *The Journal of Ecclesiastical History*, 2 (1951), 127–141 (pp. 132–3).

25 M. Hengel, *Between Jesus and Paul*, pp. 1ff.

26 *Ibid.*, p. 6.

27 *Ibid.*, pp. 8–9.

28 *Ibid.*, p. 8; and C. D. F. Moule, 'Once More', p. 100, who notes it is most unlikely that the first wave of evangelists at Antioch would not have preached to *Hellenistae*.

29 So E. Haenchen, *Commentary*, p. 297.

30 M. Simon, *St Stephen and the Hellenists in the Primitive Church*, p. 27.

31 For a recent discussion of this debate, see T. L. Donaldson, 'Moses Typology and the Sectarian Nature of Early Christian Anti-Judaism: A Study in Acts 7', *JSNT*, 12 (1981), 27–52 (pp. 29–33).

32 So also W. Manson, *The Epistle to the Hebrews: An Historical and Theological Reconsideration* (London: Hodder & Stoughton, 1957), p. 29.

33 This view is explained later in this chapter (p. 151 below).

34 Final authority at Qumran lay in the hands of the priests, the sons of Zadok – see G. Vermes, *The Dead Sea Scrolls in English*, p. 18; cf. the Community Rule (1QS), viii, 1. This has prompted the suggestion that there were priests from Qumran among the priests mentioned in Acts 6.7 – so, for example, S. E. Johnson, 'The Dead Sea Manual of Discipline and the Jerusalem Church of Acts', in K. Stendahl, ed., *The Scrolls and the New Testament* (London: SCM Press, 1958), pp. 129–42 (pp. 134–5). Although J. A. Fitzmyer has lent his support to this notion ('Jewish Christianity in Acts in Light of the Qumran Scrolls', in *Studies in Luke–Acts*, pp. 233–57 (pp. 239 and 249)), it has little to recommend it. The only natural way of interpreting the phrase πολύς τε ὄχλος τῶν ἱερέων in Acts 6.7 is as a reference to the priests who took part in the Temple worship in Jerusalem; if Zechariah (Lk 1.5ff.) had still been alive, for example, he would undoubtedly have joined the community. But the sectarians at Qumran had rejected the current form of the Temple cult as corrupt, and the priests amongst them were specifically forbidden from taking part in the worship

there – see the Damascus Rule, vi, ET in G. Vermes, *The Dead Sea Scrolls in English*, p. 103.

35 Stephen because he had been engaged in discussion with the members of the undoubtedly Greek-speaking synagogue(s) mentioned in Acts 6.9, Nicholaus because he would have spoken Greek in Antioch, and Philip because we are probably to imagine the conversation he had with the Ethiopian eunuch as having taken place in Greek (see Acts 8.26ff).

36 C. D. F. Moule, 'Once More', p. 101.

37 B. Hartmann and J. Boyce, *A Quiet Violence: View from a Bangladesh Village* (London: Zed Press, 1983), pp. 62–3.

38 M. Hengel, *Between Jesus and Paul*, pp. 14, 25–9.

39 E. Käsemann, *Commentary on Romans*, ET by G. W. Bromiley (London: SCM Press, 1980), p. 401.

40 J. Munck, *Paul and the Salvation of Mankind*, ET by F. Clarke (London: SCM Press, 1959), pp. 303–4.

41 K. F. Nickle, *The Collection: A Study in Paul's Strategy* (London: SCM Press, 1966), pp. 129–42.

42 G. Bornkamm, *Paul*, ET by D. M. G. Stalker, (London: Hodder & Stoughton, 1971), p. 41.

43 M. Simon, *St Stephen and the Hellenists, passim*; Haenchen, *Commentary*, p. 268.

44 For this range of possibilities, see J. T. Borhek, 'Ethnic-Group Cohesion', in A. M. Rose and C. B. Rose, eds., *Minority Problems*, second edition (New York, Evanston, San Francisco and London: Harper & Row, 1965), pp. 332–41, with an extensive bibliography on the subject at pp. 340–41.

45 S. Safrai, 'Relations between the Diaspora and the Land of Israel', in Safrai and Stern, *The Jewish People*, Vol. I, pp. 184–215 (pp. 184–6).

46 M. Weber, *Ancient Judaism*, translated and edited by H. H. Gerth and D. Martindale (New York and London: The Free Press and Collier-Macmillan, 1967), p. 3.

47 See H. J. Schoeps, *Paul: The Theology of the Apostle in the Light of Jewish Religious History*, ET by H. Knight (London: Lutterworth Press, 1961), pp. 27–32.

48 See J. L. Daniel, 'Anti-Semitism in the Hellenistic–Roman Period', p. 55, for classical reactions to the sabbath.

49 Josephus, *AJ*, 14. 185–267 and 16. 160–173.

50 J. Jeremias, *Jerusalem in the Time of Jesus*, pp. 62–71; S. Safrai, 'Relations', pp. 191–9.

51 J. Jeremias, *Jerusalem in the Time of Jesus*, pp. 77–84.

52 Philo, *de Providentia*, 2.64.

53 A number of tombs, datable to the first century CE and belonging to Jews from Cyrene who had returned to the city, have been discovered around Jerusalem – see S. Applebaum, *Jews and Greeks in Ancient Cyrene* (Leiden: E. J. Brill, 1979), p. 216.

54 K. F. Nickle, *The Collection*, pp. 74–86, has a detailed discussion of the Temple tax.

55 Josephus, *AJ*, 16.167–8 and 172–3 (Ephesus); *AJ* 16.169–70 (Cyrene); and *AJ*, 16.171 (Sardis).
56 S. Safrai, 'Relations', p. 192, notes that synagogues of Jews from Alexandria and Tarsus in Jerusalem are mentioned in Talmudic literature (*T. Megillah* 3.6; *T. B. Megillah* 26a).
57 For the Greek text, see B. Lifshitz, *Donateurs*, pp. 70–1.
58 S. Safrai, 'Relations', pp. 192–3, argues against identifying the synagogue of Theodotus with that mentioned in Acts 6.9.
59 A. F. J. Klijn, 'Stephen's Speech – Acts vii 2–53', *NTS*, 4 (1957–8), 25–31 (especially pp. 28–31).
60 For an example of the usefulness of factor and function analysis in understanding the rise of Palestinian Christianity, see G. Theissen, *The First Followers of Jesus: A Sociological Analysis of Earliest Christianity* (London: SCM Press, 1978), *passim*.
61 Josephus, *BJ*, 5.223.
62 Josephus, *AJ*, 15.380.
63 Josephus, *AJ*, 20.219.
64 The primary sources are the Mishnah, especially the tractate *Middoth*, and Josephus. These are sensibly treated by F. J. Hollis, in the light of archaeological findings and of his own careful inspection and measurements of the site, in his work *The Archaeology of Herod's Temple* (London: J. M. Dent & Sons, 1934). There is also an excellent article on the Temple in *EJ*, Vol. XV, cols. 942–94.
65 Josephus, *BJ*, 5.184–9.
66 F. J. Hollis, *Herod's Temple*, p. 106.
67 Josephus, *BJ*, 5.190–2.
68 Josephus, *AJ*, 20.220–2.
69 Josephus, *AJ*, 15.417; and *BJ*, 5.194.
70 The translation is from the Loeb edition of Josephus, Vol. VIII, pp. 202–3 (*AJ* XV–XVII).
71 J. Jeremias, *Jerusalem*, p. 356.
72 Cf. Acts 21.28–9; and G. Alon, *Jews, Judaism and the Classical World: Studies in Jewish History in the Times of the Second Temple and Talmud* (Jerusalem: The Magnes Press, 1977), p. 167 and 187.
73 Josephus, *BJ*, 5.204.
74 Josephus, *BJ*, 5.209–12.
75 Josephus, *BJ*, 5.209.
76 Josephus, *BJ*, 5.216–18.
77 Josephus, *BJ*, 5.219.
78 Heb. 9.6–7.
79 F. J. Hollis, *Herod's Temple*, pp. 104, 123, 131, and 174ff.
80 R. de Vaux, *Ancient Israel: Its Life and Institutions* (London: Darton, Longman & Todd, 1961), p. 319.
81 *Ibid.*, p. 328.
82 The details are taken from *EJ*, Vol. XV, cols. 974–6.
83 All private sacrifices stopped at the eighth and a half hour – *EJ*, Vol. XV, cols. 976ff., so that the *tamid* could occur at the ninth hour.

84 The details of the three broad types of sacrifice offered in the Temple are taken from R. de Vaux, *Israel*, pp. 415–21.

85 R. de Vaux, *Israel*, p. 453.

86 This restriction, which is plainly based upon the words of Lev 22.18–25, is specifically enunciated in the mishnaic tractate *Shekalim*, 1:5.

87 Josephus, *AJ*, 3.318–19.

88 An example is the sacrifice by Vitellius, Roman governor of Syria, noted by Josephus, *AJ*, 18.122.

89 M. Eliade, *The Sacred and the Profane: The Nature of Religion* (New York and London: Harcourt Brace Jovanovich, 1959), p. 20.

90 *Ibid.*, p. 26.

91 *Ibid.*, p. 63.

92 *Ibid.*, pp. 38–40.

93 R. de Vaux, *Israel*, pp. 325–7.

94 On this subject, see G. Vermes, *The Dead Sea Scrolls in English*, pp. 42–7.

95 M. Eliade, *The Sacred and the Profane*, p. 65.

96 J. Jeremias, *Jerusalem in the Time of Jesus*, pp. 35–8.

97 Josephus, *AJ*, 14.149ff.

98 E. Schürer, *The History of the Jewish People in the Age of Jesus Christ (175 B.C. – A.D. 135)*, second edition by G. Vermes, F. Millar and M. Black, Vol. II (Edinburgh: T. & T. Clark, 1979), pp. 309–13 (p. 309).

99 Josephus, *BJ*, 6.427–8.

100 Josephus, *BJ*, 5.17.

101 E. Schürer, *The History of the Jewish People*, p. 309.

102 So also S. Safrai, 'Relations', pp. 199–200.

103 H. Mol, *Identity and the Sacred: A Sketch for a New Social-scientific Theory of Religion* (Oxford: Basil Blackwell, 1976), p. 31.

104 See the discussion on the readiness with which Catholic Puerto Rican immigrants to New York attached themselves to small Pentecostal sects in H. Carrier, *The Sociology of Religious Belonging* (London: Darton, Longman & Todd, 1965), pp. 88–90.

105 See G. Theissen, 'Die Tempelweissagung Jesu', *ThZ*, 32 (1976), pp. 144–58.

106 Mk 14.24; 1 Cor 15.3.

107 G. Klein, in reviewing E. Haenchen's *Commentary on Acts*, in *Zeitschrift für Kirchengeschichte*, 68 (1957), 368, very briefly suggested the possibility of the Hellenists having begun baptising uncircumcised Gentiles in Jerusalem, but he appears never to have developed this idea.

108 W. Manson, in *The Epistle to the Hebrews* (London: Hodder & Stoughton, 1951; third impression 1957), pp. 25–41, raised the possibility of a connection between Stephen's theology and that expressed in Hebrews. The connection is probably more likely if Hebrews should be dated to before 70 CE, as recently argued by J. A. T. Robinson, *Redating the New Testament* (London: SCM Press, 1976), pp. 200–20.

109 Dt 23.1 (eunuchs). For the ban on Samaritans, see p. 149 below.
110 Lev 2.2,9; 6.15. Also cf. Ecclesiasticus 45.16.

7. The poor and the rich

1 My translation. This passage may be punctuated differently, by inserting a full stop after 'anointed me' and continuing 'He has sent me to proclaim ...'.
2 See pp. 34–5 above.
3 A. Plummer, *A Critical and Exegetical Commentary on the Gospel according to St Luke* (Edinburgh: T. & T. Clark, 1896), pp. xxv–xxvi.
4 Conzelmann, *Luke*, p. 233.
5 D. L. Mealand, *Poverty and Expectation in the Gospels* (London: SPCK, 1981), pp. 16–20.
6 *Ibid.*, p. 17.
7 Fitzmyer, *Commentary*, p. 527; and U. Busse, *Das Nazareth-Manifest*, pp. 21–67.
8 H. Schürmann, 'Zur Traditionsgeschichte der Nazareth-Perikope Lk 4,16–30'.
9 D. L. Mealand, *Poverty*, p. 17.
10 T. W. Manson, *The Sayings of Jesus*, p. 51.
11 *Ibid.*, p. 43, for the argument that Matthew's version of this saying cannot have stood in Q, since it is a quotation from the Septuagint.
12 *Ibid.*, p. 129.
13 Examples are H.-J. Degenhardt, *Lukas Evangelist der Armen. Besitz und Besitzverzicht in den lukanischen Schriften. Eine traditions- und redaktionsgeschichtliche Untersuchung* (Stuttgart: Katholisches Bibelwerk, 1965), who refers to the classic German work by H. Bolkestein, *Wohltätigkeit und Armenpflege im vorchristlichen Altertum* (Utrecht: A. Oosthoeck, 1939); G. E. M. de Ste Croix, *The Class Struggle in the Ancient Greek World from the Archaic Age to the Arab Conquests* (London: Duckworth, 1981), pp. 425–33; and R. J. Karris, 'Poor and Rich: The Lukan *Sitz im Leben*', in Talbert, *Perspectives*, pp. 112–25.
14 L. T. Johnson, *The Literary Function of Possessions in Luke–Acts* (Missoula, Mont.: Scholars Press, 1977).
15 H.-J. Degenhardt, *Lukas Evangelist der Armen*, pp. 180–1, cited by R. J. Karris, 'Poor and Rich', p. 117.
16 J. A. Sanders, 'From Isaiah 61 to Luke 4', in J. Neusner, ed., *Christianity, Judaism and Other Greco-Roman Cults*, Part I (Leiden: E. J. Brill, 1975), pp. 75–106, and 'Isaiah in Luke', *Interpretation*, 36 (1982), 144–55.
17 A. S. Herbert, *The Book of the Prophet Isaiah: Chapters 40–66* (Cambridge: Cambridge University Press, 1975), p. 2, argues that Third Isaiah (i.e. Is 55–66) was written in Palestine around 500 BCE, after Zechariah and before Nehemiah.
18 H. Richard Niebuhr, *The Social Sources of Denominationalism*, p. 82.
19 *Ibid.*, p. 85.

20 *Ibid.*, p. 82.
21 A. H. M. Jones, *The Roman Economy: Studies in Ancient Economic and Administrative History*, edited by P. A. Brunt (Oxford: Basil Blackwell, 1974), pp. 1–9.
22 P. Garnsey, *Social Status and Legal Privilege in the Roman Empire* (Oxford: The Clarendon Press, 1970), pp. 251–6.
23 J. Gagé, *Les Classes sociales dans l'empire romain* (Paris: Payot, 1971), p. 40.
24 R. MacMullen, *Roman Social Relations: 50 B.C. to A.D. 284* (New Haven and London: Yale University Press, 1974), pp. 88–9.
25 *Ibid.*, p. 89.
26 J. Gagé, *Les Classes sociales*, p. 163.
27 W. G. Runciman, 'Class, Status and Power', in J. A. Jackson, ed., *Social Stratification* (Cambridge: Cambridge University Press, 1968), pp. 25–61.
28 For the position in pre-industrial societies generally, see G. Sjoberg, *The Preindustrial City* (Glencoe, Ill.: The Free Press, 1960), p. 112. For Greece and Rome, see G. E. M. de Ste. Croix, *The Class Struggle*, p. 40.
29 'In the average city then the governing aristocracy was a group of local landowners, resident in the town' – A. H. M. Jones, *The Roman Economy*, p. 42.
30 R. MacMullen, *Roman Social Relations*, p. 108.
31 P. Garnsey, *Social Status*, p. 244. For the honorific use of epithets in the late empire, see H.-G. Pflaum, 'Titulature et rang social sous le haut-Empire', in C. Nicolet and C. Leroy, eds., *Recherches sur les structures sociales dans l'antiquité classique* (Paris: Éditions du Centre National de la Recherche Scientifique, 1970), pp. 159–85.
32 P. Garnsey, *Social Status*, pp. 221–3.
33 R. MacMullen, *Roman Social Relations*, pp. 110–11.
34 P. Garnsey, *Social Status*, pp. 242–3.
35 Cicero, *Ad Atticum*, I.xvi.11, cited by G. E. M. de Ste Croix, *Class Struggle*, p. 355.
36 A. H. M. Jones, *The Roman Economy*, p. 41.
37 R. MacMullen, *Roman Social Relations*, p. 75. The standard work on the Roman *collegia* is J.-P. Waltzing, *Étude historique sur les corporations professionelles chez les Romains*, 4 volumes (Louvain: Charles Peeters, 1895–1900).
38 S. Dill, *Roman Society from Nero to Marcus Aurelius* (London: Macmillan & Co., 1904), pp. 272–3.
39 *Ibid.*, pp. 269–70.
40 W. A. Meeks, *The First Urban Christians*, p. 31.
41 See G. E. M. de Ste Croix, *Class Struggle*, pp. 186–9 and p. 577 n. 21.
42 *Ibid.*, p. 190.
43 G. Sjoberg, *The Preindustrial City*, p. 122.
44 For street-sellers thronging the streets of Antioch in the fourth century CE, see J. H. W. G. Liebeschütz, *Antioch: City and Imperial Administration in the Later Roman Empire* (Oxford: Clarendon Press, 1972), p. 74.

45 G.E.M. de Ste Croix, *Class Struggle*, pp. 136–7.
46 *Ibid.*, p. 168.
47 *Ibid.*, pp. 165–70.
48 Varro, *Res Rusticae*, I.17.2.
49 C. Sallustius Crispus, *de Catilinae Coniuratione*, 37.2–3.
50 S. Dill, *Roman Society*, pp. 258–9, has a useful discussion of the Roman horror of the loneliness of death.
51 *Ibid.*, p. 261.
52 *Ibid.*, p. 259, for the Latin text of the *senatusconsultum* authorizing meetings at monthly intervals. F. de Robertis, *Il fenomeno associativo nel mondo romano* (Naples: Libreria Scientifica Editrice, 1955), p. 37, dates this *senatusconsultum* to the period 41–69 CE.
53 J.-P. Waltzing, *Corporations professionelles*, Vol. I, p. 149.
54 G. Rickman, *The Corn Supply of Ancient Rome* (Oxford: The Clarendon Press, 1980), pp. 5–7.
55 D. van Berchem, *Les Distributions de blé et d'argent à la plèbe romaine sous l'empire* (Geneva: George & Co., 1939).
56 G. Rickman, *The Corn Supply of Ancient Rome*.
57 D. van Berchem, *Les Distributions*, pp. 32–54.
58 H.J. Leon, *The Jews of Ancient Rome* (Philadelphia: The Jewish Publication Society of America, 1960).
59 G. Cardinali, 'Frumentatio', in E. de Ruggiero, ed., *Dizionario epigrafico di antichità romane*, Vol. III (1922), pp. 225–315 (pp. 312–15).
60 J.R. Rea, ed., *The Oxyrhynchus Papyri*, Vol. XL (London: The British Academy, 1972), pp. 1–116.
61 See J.-M. Carrié, 'Les Distributions alimentaires dans les cités de l'Empire romain tardif', *Mélanges de l'École française de Rome*, 87 (1975), 995–1101 (pp. 1070–84).
62 A.R. Hands, *Charities and Social Aid in Greece and Rome* (London: Thames & Hudson, 1968), provides translations of a number of inscriptional and literary sources relevant to his subject – see pp. 175–209. For examples of benefactions covering peregrines as well as citizens, see documents nos. 5, 10, 13 and 55.
63 *Ibid.*, pp. 34–5.
64 *Ibid.*, p. 43.
65 Plutarch, *Moralia*, 822 A.
66 A.H.M. Jones, *The Greek City from Alexander to Justinian* (Oxford: Clarendon Press, 1940), pp. 217–18.
67 J.-P. Waltzing, *Corporations professionelles*, Vol. I, pp. 300–6.
68 R. MacMullen, *Enemies of the Roman Order: Treason, Unrest, and Alienation in the Empire* (Cambridge, Mass.: Harvard University Press, 1967), Appendix A, 'Famines' (pp. 249–54), p. 249.
69 *Ibid.*, Appendix A; P. Garnsey and C.R. Whittaker, eds., *Trade and Famine in Classical Antiquity*, Supplementary Volume No. VIII of the Cambridge Philological Society (Cambridge: Cambridge University Press, 1983); and G.E.M. de Ste Croix, *Class Struggle*, pp. 219–21 and p. 583, nn. 23–31.

70 D. Magie, *Roman Rule in Asia Minor* (Princeton, NJ: Princeton University Press, 1950), p. 580; G. E. M. de Ste Croix, *Class Struggle*, p. 11.
71 See G. E. M. de Ste Croix, *Class Struggle*, pp. 9–19.
72 G. Rickman, *The Corn Supply*, pp. 96–9.
73 See the discussion of Jones' calculation in G. Rickman, *The Corn Supply*, p. 14.
74 A. H. M. Jones, *The Greek City*, p. 218.
75 G. Rickman, *The Corn Supply*, p. 14.
76 Tacitus, *Annales*, XV. 18.3.
77 A. H. M. Jones, *The Greek City*, p. 218.
78 See the references to the relevant passages in John Chrysostom (especially Hom. de Lazar, I.8) in J. H. W. G. Liebeschütz, *Antioch*, pp. 97–8.
79 Gregory of Nyssa, *De pauper. amand.*, I, translated by R. MacMullen, *Roman Social Relations*, p. 87.
80 G. Sjoberg, *The Preindustrial City*, pp. 97–8.
81 For the residential buildings in Ostia, see R. Meiggs, *Roman Ostia* (Oxford: The Clarendon Press, 1960), pp. 235–62.
82 L. Homo, *Rome impériale et l'urbanisme dans l'antiquité* (Paris: Albin Michel, 1951), pp. 567–74.
83 *Ibid.*, p. 571.
84 T. F. Carney, *The Shape of the Past: Models and Antiquity* (Lawrence, Kan.: Coronado Press, 1975), p. 87.
85 E. Bammel, article on πτωχός, *TDNT*, Vol. VI, pp. 886–912 (p. 888).
86 A. R. Hands, *Charities*, p. 62.
87 So A. S. Herbert, *Isaiah*, p. 162, and R. N. Whybray, *Isaiah 40–66* (London: Oliphants, 1975), p. 241. Also see D. W. Blosser, 'Jesus and the Jubilee: Luke 4.16–30: The Year of Jubilee and its significance in the Gospel of Luke', unpublished Ph.D. dissertation, University of St Andrews, 1979; and R. Sloan, *The Favourable Year of the Lord* (Austin, Tex.: Schola Press, 1977).
88 R. Bultmann, article on ἀφίημι, ἄφεσις, *TDNT*, Vol. I, pp. 509–12, at p. 511.
89 S. Applebaum, 'The Social and Economic Status of the Jews in the Diaspora', in Safrai and Stern, *The Jewish People*, Vol. II, pp. 701–27, at p. 701.
90 R. Bultmann, article on ἀφίημι, *TDNT*, Vol. I, p. 510.
91 See W. A. Meeks, *The First Urban Christians*, pp. 51–73.
92 G. Theissen, *The Social Setting of Pauline Christianity*, pp. 70–3.
93 A. H. M. Jones, *The Greek City*, p. 285.
94 For the historical improbability of the Asiarchs, who were priests of the imperial cult in Asia, having been personally well disposed towards Paul, see Haenchen, *Commentary*, p. 574.
95 S. Legasse, cited by R. J. Karris, 'Poor and Rich', p. 123.
96 E. Bammel, article on πτωχός, p. 907. Also see Cadbury, *Making*, pp. 262–3.
97 T. W. Manson, *The Sayings of Jesus*, p. 130.

98   *Ibid.*, p. 81.
99   E. Bammel, article on πτωχός, *TDNT*, Vol. VI, p. 907.
100 S. Brown, *Apostasy and Perseverance in the Theology of Luke* (Rome: Pontifical Biblical Institute, 1969), p. 102.
101 R. J. Karris, 'Poor and Rich'.
102 One sheep was worth two to four *denarii* – see F. M. Heichelheim, 'Roman Syria', in T. Frank, ed., *An Economic Survey of Ancient Rome*, Vol. IV (Baltimore, Md: The Johns Hopkins Press, 1938), pp. 121–257 (p. 155).
103 So H. Greeven, *Das Hauptproblem der Sozialethik in der neueren Stoa und im Urchristentum* (Gütersloh: Bertelman, 1939), p. 78.
104 J. M. Creed, *The Gospel According to St. Luke* (London: Macmillan & Co., 1930), p. 173.
105 S. Aalen, 'St Luke's Gospel and the Last Chapters of 1 Enoch', *NTS*, 13 (1966), 1–13.
106 G. W. E. Nickelsburg, 'Riches, the Rich, and God's Judgement in 1 Enoch 92–105 and the Gospel according to Luke', *NTS*, 25 (1979), 324–44.
107 ET in Charles, Vol. II, p. 268.
108 G. W. E. Nickelsburg, 'Riches, the Rich', p. 335.
109 *Ibid.*, p. 332, for a summary of 1 Enoch 92–105.
110 ET in Charles, Vol. II, p. 275.
111 ET in Charles, Vol. II, p. 276.
112 G. W. E. Nickelsburg, 'Riches, the Rich', p. 327.
113 G. W. E. Nickelsburg, during a 1977 Seminar of the *Studiorum Novi Testamenti Societas*, as reported in *NTS*, 25 (1979), 320.
114 R. Koch, 'Die Wertung des Besitzes im Lukasevangelium', *Biblica*, 38 (1957), 151–69 (p. 161).
115 E. Bammel, article on πτωχός, p. 906.
116 C. S. Hill, 'The Sociology of the New Testament Church to A.D. 62: An Examination of the Early New Testament Church in relation to its Contemporary Social Setting', unpublished Ph.D. dissertation, University of Nottingham, 1972, p. 145.
117 R. Meyer, article on κόλπος, in *TDNT*, Vol. III, pp. 824–6 (p. 825).
118 Both free and slave members were, however, admitted to a Dionysian cult group known from an important inscription from Philadelphia – see S. G. Barton and G. H. R. Horsley, 'A Hellenistic Cult Group and the New Testament Churches', *Jahrbuch für Antike und Christentum*, 24 (1981), 7–41 (pp. 33–4).
119 A. R. Hands, *Charities and Social Aid in Greece and Rome*; H. Bolkestein, *Wohltätigkeit und Armenpflege im vorchristlichen Altertum*.
120 R. Koch, 'Die Wertung des Besitzes', p. 154. The quotation in the first sentence is from J. Schmid, *Das Evangelium nach Markus*, pp. 156–7.
121 R. Koch, 'Die Wertung', p. 154.
122 *Ibid.*, p. 163.
123 R. H. Hiers, 'Friends by Unrighteous Mammon: The Eschatological Proletariat (Luke 16:9)', *JAAR*, 38 (1970), 30–6.

124 D. Seccombe, 'Was there Organized Charity in Jerusalem before the Christians?', *JTS*, 29 (1978), 140–3.

125 E. Käsemann, 'On the Subject of Primitive Christian Apocalyptic', in *New Testament Questions of Today*, ET by W. J. Montague (London: SCM Press, 1969), pp. 108–37 (p. 137). In this essay Käsemann uses 'apocalyptic' as a virtual synonym of 'eschatology', 'to denote the expectation of an imminent Parousia' – p. 109.

8. Rome and the ancestral theme

1 For a judicious discussion of the extent to which Luke has got his history right on this census, see Fitzmyer, *Commentary*, pp. 399–406.

2 It does not appear very likely that the historical Paul was actually a friend of the Asiarchs – so Haenchen, *Commentary*, p. 574.

3 Although Paul does not mention in his letters that he was a Roman citizen, it is historically possible that he was – see *Beginnings*, Vol. IV, pp. 284–5. For a case against Paul's Roman citizenship, see E. R. Goodenough, 'The Perspective of Acts', in *Studies in Luke–Acts*, pp. 51–9 (pp. 55–6).

4 Corresponding to Luke's attributing to the Jewish leadership a greater responsibility for, and satisfaction with, Jesus' death than in Mark (see discussion in the text) is his desire to minimize the role of the Jewish people. Thus, although the Jewish crowd does ask for the death of Jesus in Luke's Gospel as well as in Mark's (Lk 23.1, 18), only Luke relates that a crowd of weeping women, who were obviously opposed to his condemnation, followed Jesus to Golgotha (23.27). Moreover, whereas in Mark passers-by blaspheme against Jesus (Mk 15.29), while the high priests and the scribes jeer at him (Mk 15.31), Luke omits the first detail and actually records that when Jesus died the crowds passing by beat their beasts (in repentance) (Lk 23.48). This wedge which Luke drives between the attitudes of the Jewish authorities and the ordinary Jews is readily explained on the basis of the relationship between Luke's community and the synagogue which we proposed in Chapters 2 and 3 above – that an institutional estrangement existed between the two, although there were individual Jews in the Lucan congregation.

5 So G. D. Kilpatrick, 'A Theme of the Lucan Passion Story and Luke xxiii.47', *JTS*, 43 (1942), 34–6.

6 Haenchen, *Commentary*, p. 506.

7 An essential aspect of the *cognitio* system of jurisdiction exercised by Roman provincial governors was that prosecutions were normally instigated by independent third parties, not the court – see A. N. Sherwin-White, *Roman Society and Roman Law in the New Testament* (Oxford: Clarendon Press, 1963), pp. 13–23.

8 Conzelmann, *Luke*, p. 144.

9 P. W. Walaskay, *'And So We Came to Rome'*, p. 1.

10 C. A. Heumann, 'Dissertatio de Theophilo cui Lucas Historiam Sacram Inscripsit', *Bibliotheca Historico-Philologico-Theologica*, Classis IV (Bremen, 1720), pp. 483–505.

11 In K. Schrader, *Der Apostel Paulus*, Theil V (Leipzig, 1836), pp. 508–74.

12 *Ibid.*, p. 552.

13 M. Schneckenburger, *Über den Zweck der Apostelgeschichte* (Berne, 1841).

14 E. Zeller, *Die Apostelgeschichte nach Ihrem Inhalt und Ursprung kritisch untersucht* (Stuttgart, 1854). There is an English translation of this by J. Dare, *The Contents and Origin of the Acts of the Apostles Critically Investigated by Dr. Edward Zeller, to which is affixed Dr. F. Overbeck's Introduction to the Acts from De Wette's Handbook*, two volumes (London: Williams & Norgate, 1876).

15 J. Dare, trans., *The Contents and Origin of the Acts of the Apostles*, Vol. II, p. 164.

16 F. Overbeck, *Kurze Erklärung der Apostelgeschichte, Von W. M. L. de Wette, Vierte Auflage bearbeitet und stark erweitert von Franz Overbeck* (Leipzig, 1870).

17 J. Weiss, *Über die Absicht und den literarischen Charakter der Apostelgeschichte* (Marburg and Göttingen, 1897).

18 *Beginnings*, Vol. II, pp. 177–87.

19 B. S. Easton, *Early Christianity, The Purpose of Acts and Other Papers* (London: SPCK, 1955), pp. 41–57.

20 Cadbury, *Making*, pp. 308ff.

21 Haenchen, *Commentary*, pp. 630–1, 691–4.

22 Fitzmyer, *Commentary*, p. 10.

23 Haenchen, *Commentary*, p. 223.

24 Conzelmann, *Luke*, pp. 142–4.

25 R. J. Cassidy, *Jesus, Politics and Society: A Study of Luke's Gospel* (Maryknoll, NY: Obis, 1978; fourth printing 1983).

26 Y. H. Yoder, *The Politics of Jesus: Vicit Agnus Noster* (Grand Rapids, Mich.: William B. Eerdmans Publishing Co., 1972; third printing 1975).

27 R. J. Cassidy, *Jesus*, p. 130.

28 Cassidy devotes 40 pages out of 130 pages of text, for example, to four appendices dealing with Palestinian background – R. J. Cassidy, *Jesus*, pp. 87–127.

29 *Ibid.*, p. 51 (13.31–3), p. 61 (21.12) and p. 39 (22.25).

30 On Lk 13.31–3, see the sensible remarks by P. W. Walaskay, *'And So We Came to Rome'*, pp. 12–13.

31 Cassidy, *Jesus*, p. 61.

32 See n. 7 above.

33 Cassidy, *Jesus*, p. 39.

34 P. W. Walaskay, *'And So We Came to Rome'*, p. 36.

35 F. W. Danker, 'Reciprocity in the Ancient World and in Acts 15:23–29', in R. J. Cassidy and P. J. Scharper, eds., *Political Issues in Luke–Acts* (Maryknoll, NY: Orbis, 1983), pp. 49–58 (especially pp. 53–5); 'On Stones and Benefactors', *Currents in Theology and Mission*, 8 (1981), 351–6 (abstracted in *NTA*, 26 (1982), entry 755); and his extended study *Benefactor: Epigraphic Study of a Graeco-Roman and New Testament Semantic Field* (St Louis, Miss.: Clayton, 1982).

36 Maddox, *Purpose*, pp. 91–9.
37 P. W. Walaskay, *'And So We Came to Rome'*, pp. 64–7.
38 Maddox, *Purpose*, pp. 96–7.
39 P. W. Walaskay, *'And So We Came to Rome'*, p. 65.
40 Also note Luke's insertion of ὑπομονή at Lk 21.19 (cf. Mk 13.13).
41 P. W. Walaskay, *'And So We Came to Rome'*, p. 102, n. 6.
42 One or two features in Luke's Gospel, such as the addition of ὁ καιρὸς ἤγγικεν at Lk 21.8 (cf. Mk 13.6), taken in isolation, appear to support Walaskay's view. But when these are set in the total context of the Third Gospel, Conzelmann's approach remains the most convincing one.
43 On the non-historicity of Luke's account of the conversion of Cornelius, see pp. 95–6 above.
44 W. A. Meeks, *The First Urban Christians*, p. 63.
45 *Ibid.*, pp. 57ff.
46 H. J. Cadbury, 'Some Foibles of New Testament Scholarship', *Journal of Bible and Religion*, 26 (1958), 215–16.
47 Cadbury, *Making*, pp. 308ff.
48 A. D. Nock, 'The Roman Army and the Roman Religious Year', *HTR*, 45 (1952), 187–252 (especially pp. 211–23), and in the collection of his works edited by Z. Stewart, *Arthur Danby Nock: Essays on Religion and the Ancient World* (Oxford: The Clarendon Press, 1972), pp. 757–63. Also see Peter Garnsey, 'Religious Toleration in Classical Antiquity', in W. J. Sheils, ed., *Persecution and Toleration* (Oxford: published for The Ecclesiastical Society by Basil Blackwell, 1984), pp. 1–27 (pp. 6–12).
49 Josephus, *AJ*, 14.186–265 and 16.160–74.
50 Philo, *Legatio ad Gaium*, 156–7.
51 See the letter by the Emperor Claudius to the Alexandrians, in E. Mary Smallwood, ed., *Documents Illustrating the Principates of Gaius Claudius and Nero* (Cambridge: Cambridge University Press, 1967), pp. 99–101.
52 S. G. Wilson, *Luke and the Law*, p. 11.
53 E. Mary Smallwood, *The Jews Under Roman Rule*, pp. 120–43.
54 Loeb edition of Josephus, Vol. VII, p. 561 (*AJ*, 14.213–16).
55 Suetonius, *Divus Iulius*, 42.3.
56 See the important decree by Augustus on Jewish privileges of 2/3 CE, quoted in Josephus, *AJ*, 16.162–5.
57 *Ibid.*, 16.163 in particular.
58 *Ibid.*, 14.228–30, 231–2, 234, 236–7, 237–40.
59 E. Mary Smallwood, *The Jews under Roman Rule*, p. 345.
60 A half-shekel was equivalent to two Attic drachmas – see K. F. Nickle, *The Collection* (London: SCM Press, 1966), pp. 76–8. Two drachmas were roughly equivalent to two *denarii*, the amount a man earned for two days' labour, when work was available.
61 Suetonius, *Domitian*, XII.2.
62 For Varro's biography, see *OCD*, pp. 1107–8.
63 For Cicero's biography, see *ibid.*, pp. 234–8.
64 Augustine, *The City of God*, 6.3ff.

65 *Ibid.*, 6.4.
66 Cicero, *de Divinatione*, II.75.
67 P.A. Brunt and J.M. Moore, eds., *Res Gestae Divi Augusti* (London: Oxford University Press, 1973), p.1.
68 *Ibid.*, p.35.
69 For Seneca's biography, see *OCD*, pp.967–77.
70 As referred to in Augustine, *City of God*, 6.10.
71 S.G. Wilson, *Luke and the Law*, p.10.
72 Haenchen, *Commentary*, p.643.
73 Acts 19.33; 24.10; 25.8; 26.1, 2, 24.
74 A.D. Nock, 'The Roman Army'.

INDEX OF BIBLICAL REFERENCES

INDEX OF SECONDARY AUTHORS

Printed in the United Kingdom
by Lightning Source UK Ltd.
129256UK00001B/208-210/A